Orchestrating Symphony

THE WAITE GROUP
DAN SHAFER WITH MARY JOHNSON

Orchestrating Symphony

BANTAM BOOKS
TORONTO • NEW YORK • LONDON • SYDNEY • AUCKLAND

To the memory of my grandfather

GORDON LEGRET

who always believed I'd succeed
but didn't live to see it happen.

ORCHESTRATING SYMPHONY
A Bantam Book/ November 1985

ISBN 0-553-34200-2

Published simultaneously in the United States and Canada

Bantam Books are published by Bantam Books, Inc. Its trademark, consisting of the words "Bantam Books" and the portrayal of a rooster, is registered in the U.S. Patent and Trademark Office and in other countries. Marca Registrada. Bantam Books, 666 Fifth Avenue, New York, NY 10103.

PRINTED IN THE UNITED STATES OF AMERICA

HL 0 9 8 7 6 5 4 3 2 1

ACKNOWLEDGMENTS

Undoubtedly the biggest vote of thanks for the completion of this book — and a large dose of credit for whatever success it enjoys — goes to my editor at The Waite Group, Mary Johnson. Not only did she fight to get me the assignment, sometimes over my own interference, but she nursed the project along, over rough spots in design and disappointments caused by contributors whose plans changed.

Finally, when push came to shove and the manuscript had to be finished, she brought her considerable experience and her Lotus 1-2-3™ library of applications to bear. The fact that she is responsible for over half of the full-blown applications that make up the Fourth Movement of this book attests to the degree of her contribution. She went well beyond her assignment as my editor and became, in a very real sense, a co-author.

The people at Lotus Product Support and the members of the World of Lotus forum on-line at CompuServe™ came to my rescue more times than I'm comfortable admitting. Thanks to one and all for the good advice and helpful hints . . . some of it offered at ungodly hours of the night and early morning.

Don Huntington's blue pencil gets credit for many of the improvements in readability that took place between draft versions of the manuscript. In addition, he assembled the alphabetical command listing in Coda A virtually single-handedly.

I know, from my days as a newspaper reporter-editor and publisher, that there is a vast army of production people out there somewhere whom I'll never meet: copy editors and typesetters and artists and paste-up experts and proofreaders and printing gurus. Each of them makes an invaluable contribution to the quality of the finished product. I thank them here.

My wife, Carolyn, put up with more than the usual dose of long hours, intemperate relations with computers, and the other forms of alienation that are part and parcel of the life of the writer. I appreciate her more than she'll ever know.

CONTENTS

OVERTURE

I did not think of the title for this book. But I loved it from the first moment I heard it. I have tried, in every possible way, to be true to its meaning as I have written the words that appear in its pages. That is why I have titled this section Overture...to be consistent with the rest of the book.

What's Here?

This book takes a different approach to the powerful integrated software package known as Symphony™ from any other book I saw or heard about as I worked on it. Rather than focusing on how to use the package's major functions, our purpose here was to enable the more sophisticated user to take full advantage of the incredible power available in Symphony's programmability. The idea of incorporating programming languages into applications packages can probably be traced, on micros at least, to Lotus' arch-rival, Ashton-Tate™, makers of dBASE II™, dBASE III™ and Symphony's nearest competitor, Framework™. The dBASE II language permitted those of us (who found the functions furnished with the database manager itself somewhat limiting) to expand well beyond those horizons with our own packages. In so doing, Ashton-Tate launched a whole sub-industry. Companies making "templates" and "overlays" to be used *with* such packages as dBASE II sprung up overnight. Many have done very well.

Symphony Command Language (SCL) takes a giant step in the direction of permitting untrained users to take advantage of the built-in power of an applications package while allowing more sophisticated users to get maximum power from it. SCL is a powerful programming language incorporating many features traditionally found only in full-scale languages. The purpose of this book is to unveil its power to those interested in going a step beyond Symphony's already considerable sophistication.

Who's It For?

The material in this book is aimed at the Symphony user who wants to develop stand-alone, semi-automatic solutions that take advantage of Symphony's power and yet are easy for unsophisticated operators to use. Using SCL, it is possible to guide an operator, step by step, through an intricate series of processes that would be difficult to describe in a manual. Repetitive steps that involve a high demand for accuracy can also be subjected to SCL programming strategies.

It will be helpful if you have some programming background, but you need not consider yourself a programmer. The basic ideas in programming with which you must be familiar are outlined early.

If you are thinking of starting a new software company to produce and market Symphony applications, this book is for you. By careful instruction, detailed explanation, and full-scale example, we will teach you to use the power of SCL as easily as you now move from one type of window to another.

How Does it Relate to 1-2-3?

One of the questions most often asked during the time that this book was being written was, "Isn't Symphony just like 1-2-3, but with a few more features?" The question isn't easy to answer, so we haven't attempted to do so here. What we *have* done is avoid the temptation of making comparisons between the two products. If you *are* an experienced user of 1-2-3, you don't need us to point out the similarities. If you're not such a person, the fact that such similarities are pointed out certainly isn't very helpful to you. We have even avoided mentioning in the text that the SCL command statement {Menu}, which we almost always abbreviate to {M}, is equivalent to the 1-2-3 slash (/). In fact, it is perfectly legal, as it turns out, to substitute the slash anywhere in an SCL program that the {M} appears.

How is it Organized?

The book is organized into four movements, like a good symphony. We start with the Prelude, in which we explore some basic ideas that will be helpful as you begin your experience with the programming side of Symphony. The First Movement offers an introductory look at SCL, what it is, how it it structured, how a command is programmed, and other basic skills you'll need.

In the Second Movement, you'll be given detailed descriptions of each SCL command. The commands are grouped functionally, but Appendix ("Coda") A provides a quick alphabetical reference to them. You'll find that helpful as you become more and more comfortable with the commands. The Third Movement takes a look at the issue of integration: how do we implement several different aspects of an application? The judicious use of windows forms the heart of the integration issue, as you will see.

Finally, the Fourth Movement pulls it all together by providing four full-scale applications that are presented and explained, both in terms of what they do and how they work and in terms of how they were designed and programmed.

With any good software product, change is inevitable. As we were completing the manuscript for this book, Lotus made version 1.1 of Symphony available. We have taken the changes and enhancements that 1.1 brings to SCL and its use in macros, and incorporated information you will need. In Coda C, at the end of the book, we give you a concise guide to the advantages of Symphony 1.1. In particular, we show you how the Macro Library Manager add-in application can give your macro applications levels of sophistication difficult to achieve before.

What's the Point?

We hope that when you finish this book you will feel at home with SCL as a programming language and with the hidden power of Symphony it represents. If you find yourself only understanding better how to take full advantage of Symphony without ever programming an application for anyone else to use, the book will have served its purpose.

Now, let the music begin!

PRELUDE

Tuning Up

This section of the book presents essential background information that will help you learn to program in Symphony Command Language (SCL) using "macro" definitions. (We'll tell you what a "macro" is in just a few moments.)

The section will cover the mechanics of SCL programming and review some useful Symphony commands that make programming easier. It will also look at essential programming techniques that are applicable regardless of the language being used. Finally, the section will expand your understanding of Symphony macros to encompass some more advanced concepts.

Why Program Symphony at All?

Before beginning this discussion, it seems fitting to ask why we should bother programming an application in Symphony in the first place. After all, Symphony is one of the most powerful, integrated, and flexible programs on the market. Why in the world would it be necessary to do something as complex as write a *program* to use Symphony?

There are a number of possible answers to this question. The primary reason is to enable ourselves and others to carry out identical or similar operations in Symphony repeatedly and in different environments with a minimum amount of knowledge about how Symphony works.

For example, we could create a checkbook-balancing and budget-tracking routine using the SHEET, FORM, and DOC window types, shifting data among multiple windows, incorporating complex formulas and the like. When completed, our SCL program will "walk" us — and others who may wish to use the program — through the steps, pausing to ask for data when necessary, adjusting Settings Sheets automatically to generate the kinds of reports we'll find useful, and even saving our data automatically so that we don't end up with problems down the road.

Obviously, it would also be useful to learn to program Symphony applications if we could *sell* SCL solutions to people who are using Symphony to deal with commonly encountered business or personal data management problems.

What Can a Symphony Program Do?

What can we create as a Symphony application that we couldn't do just as easily by simply *using* Symphony and the features with which it is equipped?

A Symphony program coded in SCL can automatically do such things as

Create, resize, reposition, and hide windows

Set up, store, and modify FORM windows

Use predefined selection and sorting criteria to create a customized report in the FORM environment

Establish single-keystroke equivalents of long phrases or even paragraphs in the DOC world

Guide a user through a complex spreadsheet in the SHEET environment, prompt the user to enter data at appropriate points, and then carry out complex calculations with the data provided

In short, Symphony programs can do anything we can do inside Symphony with commands, plus some things we can't do very easily, if at all, without using SCL programming techniques. For example, with SCL we can cause the computer to "beep" if a user of one of our macros puts in an incorrect bit of information or tries to move outside what the program is designed to accomplish.

We can change the contents of the small Indicator window in the upper right corner of the screen that usually tells us what kind of environment — SHEET, DOC, FORM, GRAPH, or COMM — we are using.

We can, in fact, control the use of Symphony for specific applications by any user in almost any way desired.

You will see as you progress through this book that programming in SCL opens up possibilities for new uses of the program and the computer system. Some of these may be ideas that had not occurred to you, primarily because it was not immediately apparent how to carry them out.

Mechanics of SCL Programming

Strictly speaking, SCL "programming" is the process of *defining macros* that you can later call into action by simply ordering the Symphony program to carry them out. These macros *look* like highly structured documents in the DOC environment. They are typed into a window just like any other document; then they are passed through a built-in processing step so that they create a program useful for solving specific kinds of problems.

There are two ways to "teach" the computer and Symphony about the applications we wish to program: the first is an explicit definition of macros, and the second uses the program's built-in Learn mode to create macros indirectly. The following pages will examine each of these approaches briefly and, in the process, provide a bird's-eye view of SCL programming.

Don't worry if much of the material isn't entirely clear; for now you should simply get a "feel" for the process of creating and using Symphony macros.

Macro Definition

The first method by which an SCL macro can be defined is explicitly — that is, by typing the macro into Symphony, saving it, and then recalling it later for use. This is the more exacting method of macro creation but is the more efficient in all but fairly simple applications.

What's a Macro?

Before proceeding further, let's define "macro". "Macro" means "big"; it is therefore the opposite of "micro" (as in "microcomputer"), which means "small". In computerese, "macro" means something large that gets turned on by something smaller. As one writer has put it, "In its simplest form, a [macro] is a single computer instruction that stands for a given sequence of instructions."

In Symphony, a macro becomes a collection of keystrokes stored in conjunction with a label in a worksheet. When we run the macro, Symphony reads these keystrokes as if they had been typed in at the moment instead of having been typed in some time before and stored for later use. By prestoring keystroke sequences, we can cause Symphony to do some very sophisticated things indeed.

Structure of a Macro

A macro consists of a series of cell entries arranged as a single column in the SHEET environment. Every entry in a macro will be one of two things, a command or a string-valued formula.

The sequence of cells must be continuous; when Symphony encounters a cell that is either numeric or blank, it assumes that it has reached the end of the macro and quits.

Each macro is given a name. We give it a name by defining the range of cells containing the macro and then using the Range Name Create or Range Name Labels command, depending on how we've set up the macro and its associated labels during the process of entering it.

The content of each cell in an SCL macro is called a statement. Statements typically begin and end with a brace (also called "a curly bracket"). On the IBM PC™ keyboard, braces are shifted square brackets. One or more "keywords" or SCL "commands" are placed inside these braces. Many commands must also include some information called an "argument" — a term that will be explained below in detail.

Arguments are "passed" to the statement. When present, arguments must be separated from the command by at least one space (SCL ignores extra spaces here). Multiple arguments are separated from one another by commas. Figure 1 shows the proper structure for an SCL command line.

Creating a Macro

Creating a macro by explicit definition is fairly straightforward. We simply position the cell pointer to the location in the SHEET where we

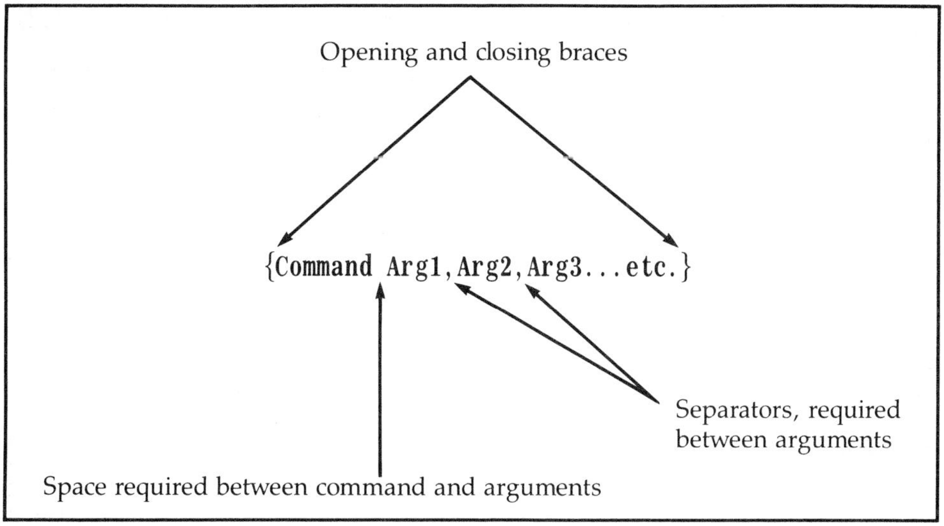

Figure 1
SCL Command Structure

would like to store the macro. Then we type in a single column of SCL commands (which we will discuss in detail in the Second Movement of *Orchestrating Symphony*) or string-valued formulas, until the entire process the program is to carry out has been described.

As far as Symphony is concerned, command entries are indistinguishable from other keywords, labels, or alphanumeric data being entered into a worksheet.

Naming a Macro

Once we've typed in our one-column sequence of SCL commands and formulas, we must name the macro. To do this, we define the macro as a range of cells and then name the range using the Range Name (RN) command's Create or Labels option. As with any range name, a Symphony macro can have a name up to 15 characters long.

If we use the Create option of the RN command, we will be shown up to five existing range names that have been defined on the sheet in use. Then we will be asked to either select one of the existing names or enter a new name up to 15 characters long. Having done that, we will have to

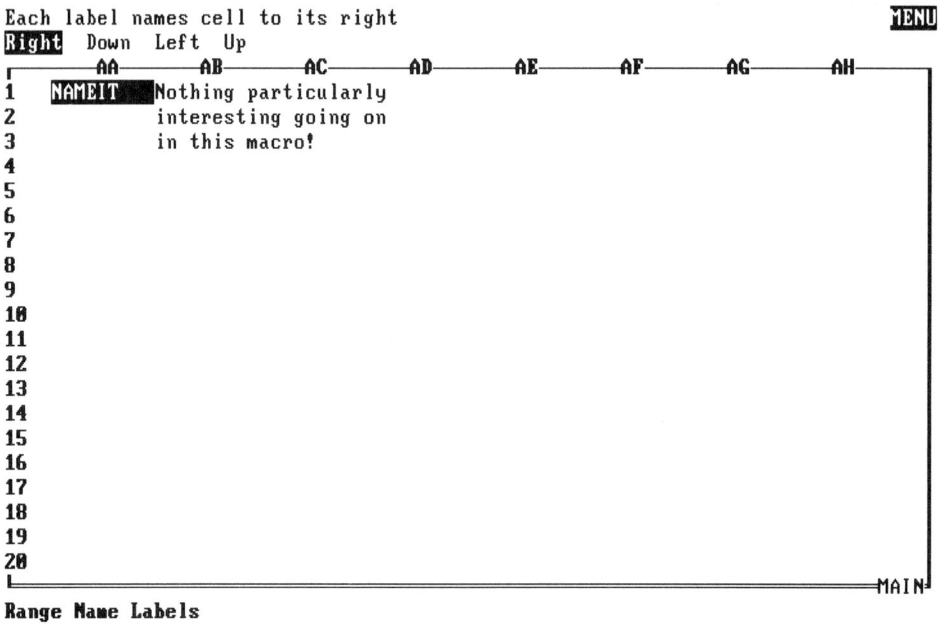

Figure 2
Using a Label to Name a Macro

describe (by pointing or other Symphony techniques) the range of cells to which the range name is to be applied.

Using the Labels option of the RN command requires us to tell Symphony whether the label to be associated with the range as a name is found to the left, right, above, or below the range itself. For example, if we define a macro as shown in Figure 2, we could use the RN Labels option and choose the Right selection from the menu presented. Note that the macro in Figure 2 is pure nonsense and is there only for the purpose of this discussion. This is *our* personal favorite among the ways to name a macro because it has a major advantage over the RN Create option: the name of the macro is saved along with the macro so that there is never any confusion later about what the macro is called.

Two macro names, or types of names, have special significance to Symphony. If we name a macro by using a two-character sequence combining a backslash (\) with either a letter (as in \z) or a number (\5), they can then be invoked by simpler keystroke combinations than can those macros with more descriptive (and of necessity *longer*) names. Details of invoking a macro are found in the section "Using a Macro", below.

Saving a Macro

Symphony saves macros along with all the other information contained in a work environment. Even though the windows and menus we create to guide us through the worksheet make it appear that there are several different sheets, there is only one. When we save the worksheet, the macros we create are saved with it. No explicit command sequence is needed to save a macro with a worksheet. If you have attached the Macro Library Manager add-in, you can store your macro in a library as well.

Using a Macro

When calling a macro into use in Symphony, we are "invoking" it. With the SHEET containing the macro(s) to be used retrieved and in the computer system's memory, we simply press the User key [F7], followed by the macro's range name.

There are two exceptions to this method of invoking a macro, both of which are a function of the alternate ways of naming macros, described above. If the macro has been named with a two-character sequence consisting of a backslash and a letter (as in "\Q", for example), we can invoke it by merely holding down the [Alt] and Q keys together. If a number is substituted for the letter in such a macro name, we can invoke it by pressing the [F7] key followed by the function key number that corresponds to the macro's definition. In other words, a macro named "\3" is invoked by typing [F7] and then [F3].

Once we have invoked a macro, the only way to get out of it cleanly is to take whatever steps the programmer who designed it decided we should take to stop the processing.

A more drastic method of escaping from a macro is to press the [Break] key on the keyboard.

Learn Mode

The second major way to create a macro is by using Symphony's very handy, built-in Learn mode method of defining a macro. When we place Symphony into Learn mode, we are essentially asking the program to "remember" every keystroke we carry out from the keyboard until we tell it to stop remembering. As we enter Learn mode (see next section), we will tell Symphony where to store our keystrokes. Once those keystrokes have been captured and saved into a range of cells, we can name, save, and invoke this macro exactly as described in the preceding pages.

Initiating Learn Mode

To place Symphony into Learn mode so that it will record the keystrokes we enter and create a macro from them, we should first identify the area of the SHEET environment where we want the macro stored. (Remember that macros must be created and stored in a SHEET window.) Lotus recommends that we store macros *above* the data area of the worksheet, a recommendation we should take to heart.

Because of the way macros handle relative addressing within themselves, inserting rows below where the macro ends is much safer than moving the whole macro down on the worksheet, a step that can have unfortunate results.

Having decided where in the SHEET we want to place the macro we are creating from the keyboard, we next give that range a name. We do this by using the Settings Learn Range option from the Services menu. Remember that macro instructions are stored in a one-column format, so define the range to be only a single column.

The number of rows we assign to the range is a function of how many keystroke instructions we plan to use to carry out the procedure. It is important to allow plenty of room. We can always redefine the range later if we have worksheet capacity problems, but getting an error "Learn Range Is Full" in the middle of entering a long macro can be very frustrating.

Figure 3 shows the screen as it looks when we are defining a Learn range. It is similar to other Settings screens in Symphony and is used in the same way. We can define the range to be associated with a macro either by pointing or by typing in the starting and ending cell addresses.

After defining the range, we are ready to return to our worksheet to capture the keystrokes in our macro. As we do so, we want to be sure to avoid one fairly common error.

> Choose the Quit option rather than the Yes option from the control panel after you've identified the Learn range. The Yes option will result in Symphony beginning to record your keystrokes as soon as you leave this step, which is almost never what you want.

```
Specify range to store keystrokes                                    MENU
Range  Erase  Cancel  No  Yes  Quit

 Memory Available    218309 of 219120 Bytes (99%)
 Learn:              No
   Range:
 Security:           Unlocked
 Global-Protection:  No
 Auto-Execute:
 Communications:
                                                      Global Settings

Settings Learn
```

Figure 3
Learn Mode Settings

Using Learn Mode

After defining the *range* of cells into which we wish to store the keystrokes that will make up our macro, we should name the range. We could, of course, name the range of cells in advance and then use the name to tell Symphony what the Learn range is. The order in which we do these two steps is arbitrary.

We use the menu's Range Name Create option to give the macro a name. Remember, we can use special two-character naming conventions to make it easier to invoke the macro later, though we do this at the expense of giving the macro a meaningful name.

Now we position the cell pointer at the location where it should be when we (or anyone else) start the procedure. We are now ready to place Symphony into Learn mode.

Press the Learn key (using the [Alt][F5] combination held down together) to begin Learn mode. The key is a "toggle" that turns the Learn mode on and off. When in Learn mode, Symphony reminds us of that fact by displaying the word *Learn* at the bottom of the screen on which we are working.

To define the desired macro, we merely carry out the procedures we wish the macro to duplicate when it is invoked. Any key on the keyboard will generate a step in the macro except for the [Scroll/Lock] and [Num/Lock] keys. By the way, this includes the [Bksp] key, so we can't simply use this key to correct a mistake without having the error, the [Bksp] key, and the corrected key show up in the macro definition.

We can toggle into and out of Learn mode at any time during our procedure. We should consider, for example, that if we turn off Learn mode, reposition the cell pointer, and turn Learn mode back on, the macro will not include the commands to relocate the pointer to the new cell location. That could have unexpected and undesirable consequences the next time someone uses our macro.

A common use of the Learn mode toggle, however, is to define two or more short macros. We type the keystrokes for the first macro, relocate the pointer with Learn mode off, turn Learn mode back on, and enter the next set of keystrokes. We will later edit the Learn range to insert blank lines at the end of each macro and give each new short range its own name to invoke each macro separately.

That brings up a good point to recall as we work with macros. The macro range is no different from the rest of the SHEET from Symphony's perspective. So the fact that we have captured keystrokes in a range rather than entering labels, data, or formulas doesn't mean we can't edit the range's contents in the same way we edit any other cell in the worksheet. If we make a mistake in typing, we can correct it later by deleting portions of the macro range.

A caution bears repeating at this point. When you edit the macro range, don't leave any blank rows. Doing so will cause the macro to stop processing at the blank row. Use the Move command to close up any unwanted spaces created by deleting unwanted macro statements.

Once the worksheet containing the newly created macro is saved, we can use the macro exactly as if we had created it by explicit program definition, as described above under "Using a Macro". Symphony, of course, has no way of knowing whether we created the macro at the keyboard in Learn mode or by using SCL programming techniques.

Advantages of Learn Mode Versus Macro Coding

The major reason we might use Learn mode rather than macro coding to create a macro is that it is much easier to use. There are no commands to learn; everything is driven from Symphony's control panel, just as we are accustomed to using all of Symphony's other features and commands.

Particularly if we are going to define relatively short and simple macros, using Learn mode is a convenient and fast way to get Symphony to set up a list of instructions we may want to carry out many times.

Disadvantages of Learn Mode Versus Macro Coding

Learn mode has two significant disadvantages in macro creation when compared to doing the same thing in SCL programming.

First, a number of SCL commands have no keyboard equivalents, which means that a great deal of programming power available in Symphony simply cannot be used in Learn mode. Much of this book concerns these SCL commands. Some of the more powerful ones include:

Conditional processing (which permits us to cause the program to choose among two or more courses of action depending on some condition)

Display control (turning windows and control panels on and off, for example)

Use of subroutines (which we can think of as macros within macros) to carry out repetitive steps inside the macro itself

In addition, it is impossible in Learn mode to cause the system to pause, ask the user to enter some information, and then proceed with the processing of the macro. In a macro, we can not only wait for users to enter information into the window in which they are working, we can direct that output to the right place in the window and even prompt the user for appropriate information.

This ability to get data "on the fly" from the user of our macros is one of the great sources of power of SCL programming.

The second disadvantage of using Learn mode for SCL programming is that typing errors tend to clutter up the macro definition, slow down its processing, and defeat the purpose of having defined a macro in the first place. Removing such errors requires that we edit the macro, which can turn out to take as long as capturing the keystrokes in the first place.

```
AA1: 'TEST1                                                              SHEET

        AA      AB       AC       AD       AE       AF       AG       AH
1    TEST1    {Services}wcMY_WINDOW~s                        Create new window
2             {Tab 2}{Down 7}{Tab}{Bigleft 2}~q
3             This is my first SCL Macro                     Enter text
4             {Down}
5             23.45                                          Enter number
6             {Down}
7             {Getnumber "Number, please.",D10}              Ask user for entry
8             {Services}fsPRELUDE1~                          Save as PRELUDE1
9             {S}wd~                                         Delete new window
10            {wait @NOW+@TIME(0,0,1)}                       Pause 10 seconds
11            {S}ny                                          Start new sheet
12
13
14
15
16
17
18
19
20
                                                                          MAIN
03-Jul-85   12:48 PM
```

Figure 4
First Sample Macro Listing

There are, however, situations where Learn mode should be used to create a macro. For example, if we wanted to define a macro that simply typed a string of characters for which we have frequent need (for example, the name of the company for which we are preparing the Symphony application), we could easily choose the Learn mode, carefully type the name in once, and then have the ability to use a very small number of keystrokes to type the long name of the company!

A Simple Macro

You now have enough background to take a look at a working macro to get further insight into what macros are and how they might be useful.

Figure 4 shows the macro we will work with for the rest of this section. You don't need to understand the commands it contains right now. We will explain them in due course. For now, let's concentrate on the structure of the macro and the methods of entering, naming, storing, and invoking it.

Let's walk a step at a time through the process of entering this macro. While doing so, you will learn a number of things about creating and using macros that will be useful as you move through this book.

Positioning the Macro

We have previously indicated that Lotus recommends placing macros above the data area on which they will be working. Generally speaking, that is good advice. However, for now we'll ignore it and place this first macro in an area of our worksheet that will not be disturbed by the macro's actions. This enables us to simplify the macro somewhat.

To begin entering this macro, move to cell AA1 on the worksheet, then type the macro's name, TEST1, into that cell and press the Right Arrow key.

Placement of Commands and Comments

Your cell pointer is now in cell AB1. We will place all our SCL commands in this column. The Symphony commands we wish to associate with a particular label name — if we want to use labels as names — must always appear in the column immediately adjacent to the macro label.

Arbitrarily, we've chosen column AG of the worksheet to contain the comments we will add to our program as we enter it. These comments will remind us and inform others what the program statements are doing. They could legally go into any column; normally, we might put them into column AC, but since we are going to have macro entries longer than one column wide, the use of a column more removed from the macro itself seems appropriate. Of course, we can simply resize the column into which we type the SCL command lines and then put the comments in the adjacent column.

Where you position the comments is not material to Symphony, *provided* that you don't put them into the column where you store the macro labels and then use the Range Name Create rather than Range Name Labels command. Doing this could cause your macro not to execute correctly, displaying your comment lines in the worksheet where you intended something else entirely to happen.

Typing a Macro Command Line

With the cell pointer in cell AB1, type the first command line shown, which reads:

```
{Services}wcMY_WINDOW~s
```

This line adopts two conventions that we will follow throughout the book, so let's stop for a moment and discuss them.

First, notice that a series of characters that are run together follow the {Services} command. Some of them are in lowercase and some in uppercase letters. Symphony command abbreviations are the single letters you would use if you were running Symphony manually a step at a time. We will always print these in lowercase letters.

We have brought up the Services menu with the {Services} command and wish to choose the Windows option. This would require us to type a "w" from the Symphony worksheet if we were carrying out this process manually, so the same command is used here.

Next, we create a new window, so we choose "c" to call for the Create option from the Windows menu.

All this will become clearer in a few moments when we discuss this sample macro in greater detail.

The second convention shown in this sample command line is that when responding to Symphony prompts requiring us to type more than one character — in this case, the name of the window we wish to create — we will print those answers in uppercase letters.

Don't forget to type the tilde (~) after the name of the window you are supplying to Symphony. This character is used in SCL command lines to signify a carriage return. Omitting it when it is needed can result in the macro stopping at some point, with results that may be incomprehensible.

Typing the First Comment

After typing the first SCL command line into the worksheet, move the cell pointer to AG1 and type the comment "Create new window". Then press the carriage return key and use the Left arrow to move the cell pointer to AB2.

Comments are very important in programming, and, because Symphony makes supplying them so easy, we highly recommend their liberal use. Some languages require that comment lines be differentiated from the rest of the program, usually with a special symbol or indicator. Because

Symphony is a blank worksheet into which we put our programs as if they were ordinary data to be manipulated in the worksheet environment, we can put comments almost anywhere we want. Of course, we will want them in close proximity to the statements they are clarifying.

A Macro Line That Types!

Enter the next macro command line exactly as shown in Figure 4. Note that it does not have a comment. Comments are always entirely optional. The line continues the window creation process we've already identified in the program.

The next line doesn't look like a program command line. It says simply:

```
This is my first SCL Macro
```

This macro statement simply enters the text it contains into the worksheet at the current cell pointer location, as the comment would lead us to conclude.

Line 4 of the macro called TEST1 contains the single SCL command {Down}. This command could have been placed at the end of the preceding line with the same result, but we find that placing such commands on separate lines helps show where things are happening in the program. Any command that moves the cursor can be placed on the line below the one that placed the data into a particular cell location. This produces more readable programs.

Displaying a Number

The next two lines place the value 23.45 into a cell location and then move the cell pointer down again. When you *enter* the value 23.45, though, precede it with a single quotation mark so that it is entered as a string value rather than a numeric one. A numeric entry, formula, or blank cell will terminate the execution of a macro.

To cause Symphony to place a number in a worksheet so that the value can be used in a calculation, use the {Let} command, described elsewhere in this book. Normally, though, we will confine ourselves to entering labels and string-valued expressions (also called formulas) in macro command lines. A macro is, after all, a "standard" way of dealing with variable information, so it is unlikely that we will want to enter specific values via the macro. That will usually be left up to the user.

Entering a Formula

Go ahead and type the next four lines and their associated comments into cells AB6 through AB9. The tenth line of the program in Figure 4 bears a bit of explanation.

The "@" function here indicates that a Symphony function is being called. It is perfectly legal to use functions in a macro.

The line shows two functions being used in a formula that calculates what the time serial number will be ten seconds from the time the line is encountered and waits until that time arrives before proceeding.

Here, we are not storing the formula itself into a cell location. We are, rather, ordering the program to pause in its execution until some event — namely, the arrival of the current time plus ten seconds — occurs and then to proceed with the execution of the macro.

Abbreviations for Keys

You may have noticed a new command, {S}, on line 9 of our macro. A brief inspection will reveal that we are calling the Services menu, choosing the Window Delete function, and pressing the [↵] key. Four keys have abbreviated forms of entry in SCL. These keys are Services, Menu, Backspace, and Escape.

To call the Services Key [F9], we simply code {S}. To call the Menu key [F10], we code {M}. The [Bksp] key is abbreviated as {BS} and the [Esc] key as {ESC}.

Naming the Macro

The macro is named as a range of cells. There are, as we have indicated, two ways of providing this name: creating a range name or using the label by which we have identified the macro in our worksheet. We choose the latter method exclusively.

To name this macro TEST1 and save it on the disk, follow these steps:

1. Position the cell pointer in AA1.
2. Select the Menu Range Name Labels Right sequence.
3. Press the [↵] key.
4. Select the Services File Save sequence and give the file a name. We suggest TEST1 as the name.

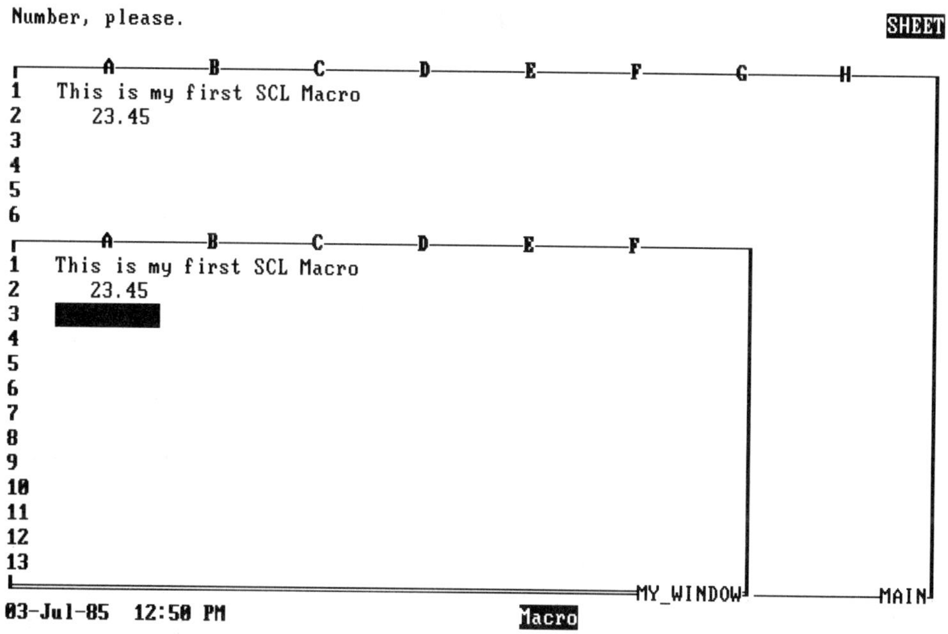

Figure 5
Macro TEST1 Waits for Input

Running the Macro TEST1

By now, you're probably anxious to try your first SCL macro. Let's not keep you in suspense! Use the [Home] key to position the cell pointer back in cell A1. (You can actually position your cell pointer anywhere you like; here, it is not going to interfere with the values stored in the macro range itself.)

Press the User key, [F7], and then type TEST1 and press the [↵] key. Within a few seconds, your screen should look like Figure 5. The program is waiting for you to enter a number. Do so and press the [↵] key again. In a few more seconds, the screen will "freeze" with the window MAIN displaying the data you entered in the macro and at the keyboard; then Symphony will clear that window and return to its initial operating condition.

Congratulations! You've just successfully carried out your first SCL macro!

What TEST1 Does

Let's take a brief look at TEST1 to analyze what it is doing. Again, don't be concerned if you don't understand the commands or precisely how they work. That will come in due time.

The first line of the macro has the macro label TEST1 in the first column. As we've seen, this is the method by which we name the macro.

The rest of the first line and all of the second line create a new window called MY_WINDOW, which is slightly smaller than the window called MAIN and positioned in its lower left corner. It does this by commanding Symphony to carry out the same sequence of steps we would follow if we typed it at the keyboard. To verify that fact, try typing the first two lines of the macro into a new worksheet, not as commands but as keystrokes. Start with [F9] to invoke the Services menu; then type "w", "c", and then MY_WINDOW, followed by the [↵] key. At that point, the Symphony program is asking you what kind of window you wish to create. We've coded — and you should type — an "s" here so that Symphony will create a worksheet.

Typing the next line requires you to understand that when we use some SCL commands, we can tell Symphony how many times to execute them. Here, for example, we tell Symphony to act as if the [⇆] key had been pressed twice. If you try this after typing the "s" in the previous step, the blinking cursor will appear in the upper left corner of the window. Then press the Down arrow (signified by the {Down} command) seven times.

Follow the procedure just outlined for the rest of these two lines of SCL macro commands. When done, your screen should look like Figure 6, which ought to be quite familiar since it's precisely the way our macro-created window looked.

Now that we've demonstrated that SCL macro command lines have direct typing equivalents (in most cases, that is), don't type in the rest of the lines from the keyboard. Just follow the discussion of those lines in the rest of this section.

Displaying Information in the Windows

To instruct Symphony to display information in one of the windows on the screen, simply type in that information as a macro line. That is essentially what the next four lines do. Each set of two lines instructs Symphony to type the information provided into the current cell in the worksheet and then to move the cell pointer down to the next position.

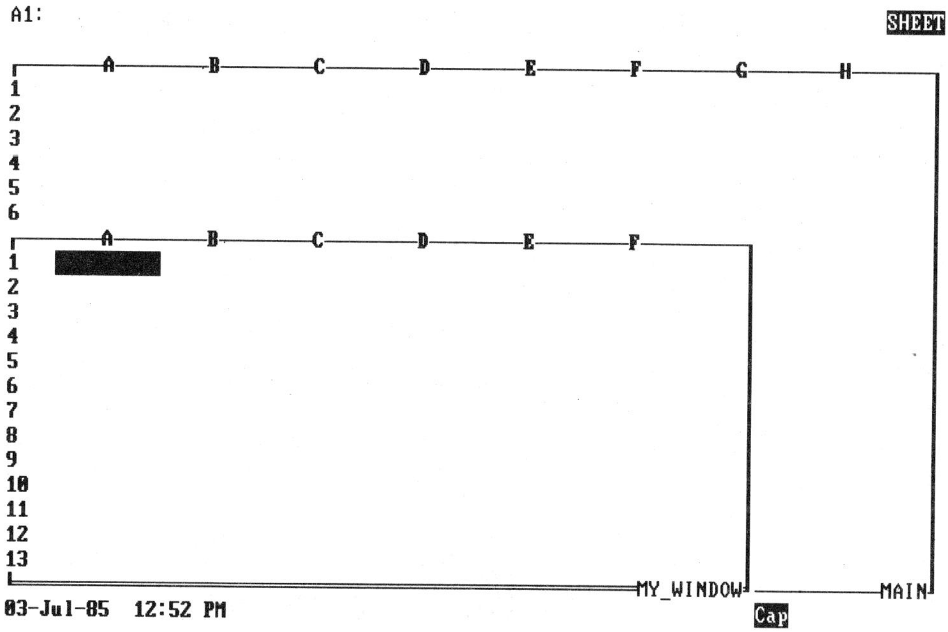

Figure 6
Manually Created Window

As it turns out, we could have omitted the second {Down} command since the next line doesn't use the current window. However, good programming practice dictates that we normally remove the cursor from the cell in which we've been working so that we don't inadvertently write over the cell's contents with the next command.

Save the File

Line 7 of the TEST1 macro calls the Services menu (the equivalent of pressing the F9 key) and then invokes the File Save operation by typing "f" and "s". It then types in the name of the file (which we know Symphony will ask for) and acts as if the ↵ key had been pressed (remember the tilde).

Return to Starting Point

The last three lines of the macro restore the original Symphony work environment as it existed before we created the new window or entered any data. They do so by invoking the Services menu and then choosing the Window Delete function. The ↵ key must then be pressed in response to Symphony's query as to whether we really *want* to delete the window. After the ten-second wait discussed above, the Services New sequence is called for, and the "y" response is given to Symphony's inquiry to be sure it's what we really want to do.

That's all there is to SCL macro programming. Well, practically all. There are still a number of powerful commands to learn, and we want to explore more complex sample macros to give you a better idea of what's involved. But before doing that, we should pause for a few moments to review Symphony commands that you may not remember or may have never met before. We're not going to attempt a refresher course in Symphony. We will, however, provide reminders about those Symphony sequences that are particularly valuable when you are learning to program in SCL.

Some Useful Symphony Commands and Techniques

This section will discuss several Symphony commands and techniques that will be particularly useful as we design and use SCL macros. Some of these commands will be familiar, but they will find frequent application to SCL programming. A brief refresher may save time and prevent confusion when the commands are needed later.

Special Function Keys

We'll find frequent use for three different function keys while programming in SCL: the Draw, Step, and Learn keys.

To call the Draw key's function into operation, we simply code the SCL command {Draw}. This command will force Symphony to update information in a window, even though one or more windows may have the Auto Update attribute set to No.

Coding {Draw} in a macro produces the same results as holding down the Alt and F8 keys simultaneously. You've almost certainly never before encountered the Step function, since its use is restricted to macro execution. From the keyboard, hold down the Alt key at the same time as you hold down the [F7] key. This key cannot be coded into a macro, since its use is limited to a macro execution.

We have already discussed the Learn function. It is turned on and off by pressing the [Alt] and [F5] keys at the same time. For obvious reasons, it cannot be coded in an SCL macro.

Menu Options

A number of options from the menu command set will prove useful as we program macros in SCL. The two most useful are the ones used to name a range of cells: Range Name Create and Range Name Labels Right. Since we've already discussed these commands in some detail, we will not repeat descriptions of them here.

A third menu option will be particularly useful for developing macros that we wish others to be able to use but not examine, copy, or change. The Menu Format Other Hidden sequence permits us to hide the contents of the cells in which our SCL macro is stored. Its effect depends upon the current setting of worksheet protection, which is described in more detail in the following subsection. The sequence hides the contents of cells from view, but under some circumstances (described below) it will permit displaying the contents of the cells on the control panel line of the display.

Services Command Options

From the Services main menu, three sequences will be needed fairly often during our programming in SCL. Two of these — Settings Global-Protection and Settings Security Lock/Unlock — involve keeping prying eyes and tampering fingers away from our macro code. The third permits us to copy useful macros into worksheets from other files where they are stored.

Settings Global-Protection is a toggle. When we choose this option from the Services menu, we are given a menu choice of Yes or No. Choosing Yes puts global protection on the worksheet, making it impossible for anyone without the proper password to modify any cells in our worksheet. With Global-Protection Yes in effect, no cells will be alterable unless they fall within a range whose protection has been modified using the Services Range Protect Allow-Changes sequence.

An individual setting on a particular range will override the master selection for the worksheet.

The Settings Security Lock/Unlock option is also a toggle. When we invoke this sequence, we are given a choice between Lock and Unlock as the status of the worksheet. This is the "top" level of security in Symphony. Once we have issued a Settings Security Lock sequence, it is impossible to even alter the Global-Protection or Range Protect status. In other words, once we've locked the worksheet using the Settings Security Lock sequence, we cannot modify any other security setting without knowing the password to get past the lock.

Moving macros defined in one worksheet into another worksheet is the function of the File Combine Named-Area Read command sequence. This combination of commands will cause Symphony to read another Symphony file in part and bring it into the current worksheet. We are asked for the name of the range to be combined with the present worksheet, and the program reads that entire range into our current worksheet. The processing involved in this sequence is described in detail in the *Symphony Reference Manual* (Cambridge: Lotus Development Corp., 1984) under "FC".

Errors in General

One final concept with which you should be familiar is that of errors. A great variety of events can cause Symphony to generate an error. Sometimes a formula that calculates a value out of the range displayable in a particular cell produces a cell with the abbreviation "ERR" in it. Sometimes we try to read files that don't exist or execute nonexistent macros. Error handling is a big part of any program's job, and macros in SCL are no exception to that rule.

Besides error handling, there are a number of other fundamental programming techniques with which you should have at least a nodding acquaintance. These are the subject of the following section.

More About Macros

Before we can begin putting macros to real use, we should explore three more topics. This final section of the Prelude will cover the use of arguments in macros, the definition and use of subroutines in macros, and the designation of a macro as the startup macro for a particular diskette or application.

Macro Arguments

If someone were to say to us, "Divide," we'd be left in a bit of a quandary. We wouldn't know whether to "clone" ourselves or perform a mathematical operation. But we'd be sure of one thing: we need more information.

Many Symphony macro commands have a similar trait. They need to be given specific information about what they are to do or they cannot perform. The information that tells a macro statement exactly what to do is called an "argument". (Somewhere there's probably a very logical reason why a bit of data that *ends* arguments over what the command is to do is *called* an argument.)

How Arguments Are Used

When we wish to give a macro statement one or more arguments, we "pass" them to that part of the Symphony program that processes SCL commands.

Correct formatting of an SCL macro command line, including arguments, is shown and described in Figure 1 and the accompanying discussion.

Arguments are placed inside the braces that define the macro command and are separated from the command keyword itself by at least one space. If more than one argument is to be passed to the command, the arguments are separated from one another by a comma or semicolon. We can configure Symphony to use some character besides the comma as the second argument separator. The semicolon is a permanently affixed way of separating arguments from one another in a macro command line.

If we pass a string argument to a macro command and the string has a comma embedded within it, we must ensure that SCL knows what we are talking about when it gets the argument. To do this, we enclose the entire string inside quotation marks. In fact, it is a good practice to enclose *all* string arguments inside quotation marks; it is never wrong, and omitting them can sometimes have undesirable consequences.

Declaring Data Types

Sometimes it is important to ensure that the information stored in a particular location or passed to a macro command line is of a known type. In some cases, SCL takes care of this by limiting arguments that can be passed to a specific command to one type. Other commands, however, will permit any of the three types of data allowed by Symphony to be passed to it. In such cases, we will want to predefine the type of data passed if that is significant. The three types of data with which Symphony can deal are strings, numeric values, and ranges.

Strings are the easiest type of data to define. A string in Symphony is any group of characters put together as a single entry. The elements of a string can be letters, numbers, or even special characters like punctuation marks or symbols. A string consisting entirely of numbers is still a string. Strings cannot be manipulated using mathematical operations; an attempt to do so produces an error condition.

Numeric values, as their name suggests, are numbers that can be manipulated using mathematical symbols and operations. There are basically two types of numeric arguments, single numbers and expressions. A single number is an entry like "123.45" or "−11" (with the quotation marks omitted, of course). Most of the data we enter into a spreadsheet tends to be in this form.

Expressions that result in the calculation or formation of numbers are also treated as numeric values. These expressions may consist of a simple cell address that contains a number, a range name where the data are entirely numeric, or a formula comprising several mathematical steps.

Assuming that the cell D10 contains a numerical value and that we have defined a range called SALES_DATA containing only numerical values, any of the following would be a valid numeric argument to be passed to an SCL macro that requires or permits such arguments:

```
75.093
D10
D10*11.5+2
SALES_DATA
```

The third type of argument that can be passed to a macro command line is a *range*. A range may be defined in a command statement either by name or by providing the cell addresses of two opposite corners (upper left and lower right or upper right and lower left).

If we use a range *name*, it is *not* necessary that the name be defined at the time we write the macro command. But when we *invoke* the macro, the range must already be defined by the name provided or an error will result. In dealing with macros, Symphony treats a cell address and a range consisting of a starting and ending cell with the same address as if they were the same thing. In other words, telling Symphony to perform a particular operation on the data contained at cell address AA104 is the same as telling it to work on the data in range AA104...AA104. In Symphony functions, as we know, there are sometimes subtle but important differences in the way these two addresses would be dealt with.

Limiting Types of Data Entered

Generally, an individual command in an SCL macro will allow only one type of data to be entered into it. For example, Symphony will not permit us to enter a string in response to the {GetNumber} command.

But several SCL command statements will permit more than one type of data to be passed to them. When using those statements, we must ensure that our macro "knows" what kind of data it will be receiving as the result of that macro statement's execution. To provide such assurance, SCL allows us to use "suffixes", which tell the command statement to accept either values (that is, numeric arguments) or strings.

For example, look at the simple {Let} macro command. We'll discuss the command itself in more detail later in this book, but, briefly, it has two arguments: the first is a cell address and the second is a value to be stored at that cell address. In other words, the command line:

```
{LET GG8,54}
```

will store the value 54 at cell address GG8. Similarly, the command line:

```
{LET GG8,"54"}
```

will store the *string* consisting of the two characters "5" and "4" at cell address GG8.

If we supply the argument *explicitly*, as in the above examples, we needn't tell Symphony about the type of argument; it determines the type from the argument itself. But quite often we will supply information indirectly, for example, by cell reference. In such cases, we might want to convert a numerical value to a string value and store it in a specific cell.

To ensure that cell J14 contained a string, for example, we would write a command line to read:

```
{LET J14,AV99:STRING}
```

The word *string* following the cell location AV99 is a suffix to the command line that tells SCL to convert the contents of cell AV99 to a string. If AV99 already contains a string, Symphony simply transfers its contents.

If, however, it contains a numeric value, Symphony converts it to a string value, which it then places into cell J14.

To force the value to be numeric, we add the suffix "value" to the end of a command line. If we have already carried out the last statement above, we can convert the value 25, which is stored as a string in cell J14, back into a number and store it in cell X1 with the following command:

```
{LET X1,J14:VALUE}
```

Since the vast majority of SCL command statements require arguments, it is important that we understand these concepts thoroughly. As we move through the examples in the First Movement, pay particular attention to the passing of arguments and the declarations of types of data either explicitly (with suffixes) or implicitly (by command language rules).

Subroutine Usage

Our next topic is the use of subroutines within macros. A subroutine is simply a collection of one or more statements that is given a name and is needed relatively frequently inside a macro. The use of subroutines will save keystrokes in macro programming.

Example of Subroutine Use

If we are designing a macro that must frequently permit the user to examine some information on the screen and then go to another window display, we may want to do three things:

Print a message that says "Press RETURN to continue" in the control panel area

Change the upper right corner of the screen to indicate that the program is waiting for something

Change the indicator back to whatever Symphony would normally display there when the user has pressed the [↵] key

The command sequence to handle these tasks would look something like this (for now, just take our word for it; explanations will come in due course!):

```
{INDICATE "WAIT"}
{GETLABEL "Press RETURN to continue",JJ112}
{INDICATE}
```

This sequence requires that we type 73 characters (including the carriage return or pointer movement keys at the end of each statement). If we wanted to do this in a dozen places in our macro, we'd have to type 876 keystrokes!

Using a subroutine approach, we would write the above commands once and give the subroutine a label. Then, any time we wanted to make this sequence of events happen, we would simply type the label of the subroutine.

For example, we might call this subroutine USER_PAUSE. (Note that this subroutine name tells something about what the subroutine does.) Any time we wanted to use it, we would simply type:

```
{USER_PAUSE}
```

The macro would then look at the area labeled "USER_PAUSE" and, starting at that location, begin carrying out the instructions stored until encountering a blank line or a {Return} command. At that point, it would come back to where it left off when we told it to jump to the area called "USER_PAUSE" and continue executing commands.

As you can see, subroutines are powerful tools in any computer programming language that permits their use. They save a great deal of effort in writing programs.

Passing Arguments to Subroutines

SCL subroutines become even more powerful by allowing us to pass arguments to them much as we pass arguments to macro command statements. Doing so requires two steps, which we will illustrate by creating a variation on the theme of the subroutine from the previous section.

We could customize the message on the control panel line of the display when we called the subroutine USER_PAUSE, by writing the following SCL command lines:

```
USER_PAUSE      {DEFINE X99}
                {INDICATE "WAIT"}
                {GETLABEL X99,JJ112}
                {INDICATE}
                {RETURN}
```

To call this subroutine and have the program print a different message in the control panel area, we could write:

```
{USER_PAUSE "Hurry up, you slow human!"}
```

Symphony would store this message at location X99, where we told the subroutine USER_PAUSE to store its argument by the first statement, {Define X99}. Then, to use that message, we just refer to the address where we've told the program to store it.

We can pass multiple arguments to a subroutine as long as the {Define} statement has one cell location defined for each argument we are going to pass to the subroutine.

Summarizing, then, using subroutines and passing arguments to them requires us to take the following steps:

1. Write the commands that make up the subroutine into the worksheet, giving the sequence a label. Begin with a {Define} if arguments are to be included and end with either a blank line or a {Return} command.
2. Call the subroutine by writing its name inside braces, together with any arguments we have defined as being passed to the subroutine.

If we define a subroutine to require two or more arguments and then fail to pass it the number we've specified to enable it to carry out its tasks, we may either create an error condition (most often) or produce unanticipated results.

Autoexec Macro

Each worksheet in Symphony may have one macro sequence that it will automatically execute any time that worksheet is retrieved into the computer's memory. To define a macro as the "autoexec" (for AUTOmatic EXECution) macro for a particular worksheet, simply use the Services Settings Auto-Execute sequence.

When that sequence is carried out, we'll be asked whether we want to set or cancel the Auto-Execute setting. Use "S" to define a new macro as the autoexec macro for the sheet. Then tell Symphony the starting location of the macro by providing an explicit cell address or the macro's name.

Once we've taken these steps, the macro defined as the autoexec macro will always begin to execute as soon as we load that worksheet. This makes it possible to create applications that are very easy to use for people who don't necessarily know much about Symphony. It also provides yet another level of security against prying eyes finding our SCL programming code and copying or altering it.

Summary

We've covered a lot of ground in this Prelude. Before we take a deep breath and prepare for the First Movement of our orchestration of Symphony, it might be a good idea to list the ideas you've just encountered. You've learned a lot about:

Defining and structuring macros

Naming and saving macros

Using Symphony's Learn mode to create simple macros

Passing arguments to macros

Defining and using subroutines

Passing arguments to subroutines

Setting up an automatically executing macro

You've learned a *little* about:

Programming keystrokes and function keys in a macro

Important Symphony commands that will help you use macros

Programming techniques in general

We are now ready to progress to the next section of this discussion of SCL. In the First Movement, which follows, we will type, name, save, use, and analyze a few small sample macros. This is in keeping with the reality that we learn better by examples and analysis than by straightforward presentation of material.

Are you ready, maestro?

FIRST MOVEMENT

Slow and Easy

This section will present three short but useful macros to teach you two things. First, you will learn how to type, edit, save, test, and use a macro command. Second, you will learn to begin to look for Symphony applications that make efficient use of macros.

We will begin by presenting the macros themselves. Following the listing of each macro will be a set of brief instructions on how the macro could be put to immediate use, occasionally with some modifications, in your own Symphony work.

After the three macros have been presented and you've been instructed in their use, we will move to a more in-depth explanation of how each works.

The end of this First Movement will discuss how the ideas presented in the three macros can be extended to the database (FORM) environment of Symphony to assist you in performing even fairly complex tasks.

Reminders

Before we begin, let's review the important things you've learned in the Prelude about techniques for entering and using macros. Be certain that you understand and remember the following ideas:

1. Put macro definitions in a part of the working environment where they won't be disturbed by your work with the rest of the document or worksheet.
2. Follow naming conventions, including using single-character sequences (backslash followed by a single character) for quick use from the keyboard later.
3. Use the Step key ([Alt][F7]) to debug your macro if you run into trouble with it executing properly.
4. Remember that a blank row ends a macro definition, so don't double-space inside a single macro definition.
5. Use the Range Name Create Labels Right (RNCLR) sequence to assign label names to the macros so that they can then be used in your worksheet or document environment.

A Glossary Key for DOC Usage

Sometimes legal or technical documents require relatively long pieces of text that we will want to use many times in various documents or in different places in a single document. This kind of text is called "boilerplate". Other kinds of boilerplate include complex phrases or hard-to-spell words that keep recurring in a document.

One advantage of powerful word processors is the availability of a single-keystroke glossary command that allows boilerplate to be prestored on the system's diskette. We can then have the computer place the boilerplate into documents as we wish, eliminating the need for tedious retyping of materials. For technical and professional writers, the ease of use of glossary commands is one big advantage of using a word processing system.

The following sample macro affords a way of giving yourself this same power inside a Symphony DOC window. Simply by changing macro names and their contents so that they serve your own specific purpose, you can create a powerful tool for your Symphony work sessions.

Although we discuss this macro in terms of its use in a DOC window, it could be used in any kind of window where simple entry of boilerplate could be useful.

With that explanation out of the way, let's look at the macro itself:

```
\S   Symphony Command Language (SCL)
(blank line)
\O   Orchestrating Symphony, by Daniel G. Shafer
(blank line)
\D   agreed and entered into this {?} day of {?}, 1985.
```

When these macros have been put into place in a Symphony DOC environment, we can type any of the three long phrases that we've coded into the macro by simply holding down the [Alt] key with the single-letter key with which we named the macro. Thus, to insert the phrase "Symphony Command Language (SCL)" anywhere into a document, we just press [Alt] S. The letter can be typed in upper- or lowercase; SCL automatically converts all the macro-invoking commands to uppercase.

Defining a glossary of commonly used and long phrases in SCL can be a real timesaver in the preparation of contracts, sales letters, proposals, advertising copy, and other documents where repetitive appearances of such text are required.

The same technique can be used in the SHEET environment. There we might have a situation where a formula is used often but not in a sequence of cell addresses, so using Symphony's powerful repeating functions will not be as effective as we might like. Just define a glossary-type macro containing the formula as a literal string and then invoke it at an appropriate point in the spreadsheet.

As you work with SCL in this book, you'll find a great many occasions where the use of a glossary-type macro is of real value. Note, too, that we often create glossary-type macros by using keyboard macro definition techniques as described in the Prelude. Unless they incorporate some user input requirements — as in the contract agreement clause defined above as the macro "\D" — they are prime candidates for keyboard definition.

Quick Print Setup Macro

Users of Symphony generate a lot of paper. Spreadsheet summaries, database reports, documents, and graphs are all destined ultimately to be reduced to a printout so that they can be shared with others. The process of getting any document ready to print involves a number of steps, one of the most repetitive of which is the establishment of an appropriate format for a particular type of document. This preparation process may provide one of the most effective uses for short and simple macros in your use of Symphony.

The following macro sets up a document format for printing so that it is right-justified (called "even" justification by Symphony, in total disagreement with the rest of the industry!) and double-spaced. It then prints the document, ejects the page, and returns to the document environment.

The entire process requires 13 keystrokes when done from the keyboard. Defining it as a macro, then, will save 11 keystrokes each time it is used. Furthermore, we can invoke this macro and then leave the room while a long document prints, knowing that, when we return, the last page will have been ejected and the system will be ready for us to resume work on the document.

Here's the text of this short but highly useful macro:

```
PRINT_SET      {M}fsjes2q
               {S}pgpq
```

We chose a multicharacter name for this macro when we used it during the preparation of this book. (We decided to reserve one-keystroke macros for glossary applications.) You are obviously not constrained by that preference.

You could, obviously, use this little macro as a model for designing your own print setup routines, even storing more than one in a worksheet. Then you could print the document differently depending, for example, on whether you are preparing a rough draft or a final manuscript.

This macro also lends itself to keyboard capture definition in Learn mode.

Special Typing Format Needs

Particularly when working in a DOC environment, we may need to set up special, nonstandard formats fairly frequently throughout the text. An example would be in the case of writing technical or instructional manuals where we frequently want to call special attention to the importance of some step with a WARNING or CAUTION note. This last simple macro is the most complex of the three and adds a special feature that we'll discuss later to help guide the user through its use.

The macro sets up a special format line for such a note, automatically centering the text within a print line that has new margin settings so that the text will be offset from both original margins and thus stand out from the main flow of the text.

```
BOX       {Menu}fc~jcm{Insert}{Right 20}l
          {End}{Right}{Backspace 20}r~q
          {Indicate "Box"}
          {?}{Justify}~~
          {M}fc~jeq
          {?}{Justify}~~
          {M}fc~rq
          {End}{Left}
          {Indicate}
```

The resulting format would look something like this:

```
     The major part of the text is typed within the margins
selected.  Upon invoking the macro, however, the format changes.
Margins are indented 20 columns on both sides.

                      The   new  text  is
                      placed between  the
                      new   margins   and
                      right-justified.
                      When you change the
                      indicator,

the margins return to their original settings and normal keyboard
entry is resumed.
```

Invoking this macro will produce a flurry of screen activity, followed by a new format line like that shown above. This will appear at the line where the cursor was located when you called the macro. The cursor will be positioned at the newly placed left margin, and Symphony will be waiting for you to type in a heading line for the box material. You can tell this point has been reached because the indicator in the upper right corner of the display, which we would normally expect to read "DOC", "SHEET", or sometimes "ERR", contains instead the word *Box*.

After you type in the heading for this box (for example, "WARNING!") and press the ↵ key, Symphony will automatically center this heading in the newly defined space and set up another new format line immediately below where you put the heading.

At this point, type in the text to appear in the special box. As you type it in, it will all go continuously across one row of the document. Don't worry. The line will automatically reformat as soon as you press the ↵ key. Rather than being centered, however, the block of text will be justified on the left and right sides of the newly indented margin placements.

The last thing this macro does is reset the original margins and tabs, move the cursor to the left margin, and change the indicator in the upper right corner to read the more familiar "DOC".

As you can see, a relatively short and uncomplicated macro can carry out quite sophisticated operations. Defining a number of such special formats, as the one shown here for setting up a special text box, will save dozens of keystrokes. It will also avoid the problems that might be caused if we forgot the proper sequence or made a mistake in entering such specialized segments of text.

Before proceeding with the rest of this section, enter all three of these macros, store them on the disk, work with them until they are familiar to you, and perhaps experiment with the glossary macros for a while to gain some appreciation of what's involved in entering, editing, and designing SCL macros.

Once you've done that, you're ready for the following pages in which we will examine the above macros in some detail to find out what makes them "tick".

How the Glossary Macros Work

"Glossary" macros are the easiest and most straightforward macros to design. Yet, as we have indicated, they are also among the most potentially useful. The macros we wrote were only one line long. There is no reason, however, for that limitation. Glossary macros can consist of whole sentences, paragraphs, or even entire pages of text!

Text production macros simply place into the current worksheet all the text identified with their macro names, beginning at the current cursor location, until the end of the macro is reached. Since they function exactly as if we had entered the information at the keyboard, they will word wrap in DOC windows as we would expect. This, of course, means that we need not concern ourselves with formatting of the boilerplate or glossary information as we enter it. For example, we could as easily define the macro "S" in our sample as follows:

```
\S        Symphony Co
          mmand Langua
          ge (SC
          L)
```

It is not clear why we would *want* to define a glossary macro that way, but there is nothing illegal about it. SCL will treat this macro exactly as if we had put it all on one line.

We can get a great deal of mileage out of just this information about glossary-type macros. There are, however, a number of other possibilities for their use.

We could, for example, place an input request ({?}) in the middle of a sentence. SCL would then print the material up to the question mark, pause and wait for the user to type in something and press the ↵ key, and then go on with the rest of the sentence or paragraph. This approach could be used, for example, in designing and using blank legal forms where it is necessary to pause occasionally for the legal secretary or attorney to type in the name of a party, the address of a piece of property, the price of a sale agreement, or some other piece of information not known in advance.

A final warning: if the material in a glossary macro is being used anywhere but in a DOC window, be sure to take into account the window or field width involved. Don't make the text typed by the macro extend beyond the window into which it is being placed unless you are certain you have handled the implications of that for all the cells to the right of the input on the same line or row.

How the PRINT_SET Macro Works

The second macro we have furnished for the purposes of this discussion is a bit more complex than the simple glossary macros. It incorporates the use of two main SCL commands, each of which involves a number of option selections and data entry. In the following pages, we will take this macro apart a command at a time in order for you to gain a firm understanding of how it is assembled and what it does when it is called. In the process, you will learn a great many basic principles of SCL programming that will make the rest of your learning experience clearer and more direct.

An excellent way to follow the discussion below is to place the system into Step mode (by the [Alt][F7] combination) and then invoke the macro. At each step, you'll get a chance to observe the action of SCL as we describe it.

Invoking a Main Symphony Level: {Menu}

The first line of the PRINT_SET macro says simply and elegantly {M}. This is the shorthand equivalent of the command {Menu}. It is the equivalent of pressing the Menu ([F10]) key on the PC keyboard. {M} and {Menu} are interchangeable; there are no rules other than personal preference for when and where to use each. When this command is executed in a macro, the control panel displays the Menu prompts for Symphony.

Commands that invoke the Menu or Services control panel response, like most other main SCL commands, are enclosed in curly braces.

Selecting Subsequent Options: fsjes2q

The second line of this macro definition begins with the letter "f". This letter and all others in a macro can be in uppercase or lowercase without affecting how SCL operates and executes the ideas.

But what does the "f" mean?

If you're following along with us on the system, you'll notice that when you press the {Menu} key or call for its use by the SCL {M} or {Menu} command, a new control panel display appears. One option is Format, which you would call for from that point by pressing the f key or using an arrow key to position the cursor over the word *Format*. To carry out the same step in an SCL macro, simply code into the macro the letter of the option to be selected. In this case, our objective is to change a format for printing purposes, so we choose the "f", or Format, selection.

Doing that produces yet another control panel display. This one offers us the various formatting options available in Symphony at this level. We want to change some settings. If we were operating this function from the keyboard directly, we would type "s" at this point. In the SCL macro, we do exactly the same thing.

The remaining steps in this line are identical. The "j" calls on the Justification option, the "e" sets up "even" justification, the "s" puts us into a position to alter the spacing of the document, the 2 selects double-spacing, and the "q" tells the program to quit and move us back to the previous level.

Note that there are no carriage return symbols (tildes: ~) in this line of the macro. That's because at no point are we required to press the ↵ key on the keyboard. If we were, for example, asked to do so after entering the line spacing, we would have to include that command (~) in our macro line.

The Next Level: Printing the Document

The last line of this small macro begins by calling the Services option of Symphony into effect. It then calls for the Print function ("p") and tells the Print function to "Go" ("g") — that is, to begin printing.

Note that regardless of how long the printing process takes, the macro remains in charge until the printing completes. This confuses many SCL neophytes; there is no need to instruct SCL to wait for a process to conclude as long as the process is being invoked by the macro in question.

When printing completes, the next "p" in the last line of the macro calls for a Page-Advance by the Symphony Print menu and then uses the "q" (Quit) selection to return to the previous Symphony level. The program is now ready for us to do whatever we want.

How the Box Macro Works

The macro we called "box" is the most complex of the three short macros in this section. If carried out from the keyboard directly rather than through a macro, it would require no less than 37 individual keystrokes, and we would be unable to change the contents of the indicator box to the right of the control panel to indicate what is going on.

Writing a technical manual or instruction booklet might give us the occasion to use this special box formatting on every third or fourth page, so the macro could save us a tremendous number of keystrokes.

This macro introduces some new ideas, so it will be useful to take it apart. We will move quickly over things already covered in the discussion and spend more time on those subjects introduced here for the first time.

Setting Up the Left Margin for Indenting

The first line of the macro "box" calls the menu control panel into play and then goes into the formatting mode ("f"). At that point, Symphony asks which format line we want to work with. Since we haven't established any yet, we choose to work with the current one, which is the default. So we press "c" in response to the question (coded by the letter "c" in the macro line as well).

Symphony's next question relates to where we want the new line to be inserted. We want it in the current location, so we simply press the [↵] key (symbolized by the tilde, "~") after the "c".

When we've done that, Symphony inserts a copy of the current format line into the present active line of the document and displays a new control panel that allows us to choose from a number of modifications we can make to this line. We want to make changes in justification and in margins.

We take care of the justification first by keying the "j" followed by the "c". This combination results in centered justification of the text to follow the format line. We want to center the heading for the box we are writing.

Next we want to work with the margin settings. To do so, from the control panel for the formatting line editing, we simply type "m" for "Margins/Tab Stops". So we code an "m" in the next position on the macro statement line.

So far, this is largely the same material that we saw in the small macro for print-formatting setups. Now, though, it gets a little trickier.

Keyboard Keystroke Commands

The next word in the macro line is the word:

```
{Insert}
```

This is SCL's way of carrying out the process that would take place if the user pressed the [Ins] key on the PC keyboard. In this case the command is only precautionary, but it has the effect of putting us into Overwrite mode instead of the standard Insert mode for the next few text operations.

Almost all keyboard command keys can be coded directly into SCL macros using this same technique. Table 1 shows the various keys that can be handled this way and the commands needed in SCL to invoke their use. As we go through the rest of our discussion of Symphony's powerful Command Language, we'll need to frequently invoke various keystroke commands.

Table 1
SCL Commands for Keyboard Entries

Symphony Key Name	*On Keyboard*	*In Macro Coding*
Abs	F3	{Abs}
Backspace	BACKSPACE	{Backspace} or {BS}
Big Left	CTRL ←	{BigLeft}
Big Right	CTRL →	{BigRight}
Break	CTRL BREAK	{Break}
Calc	F8	{Calc}
Capture	F4	{Capture}
Center	Alt F4	{Center}
Delete	Del	{Delete}
Down Arrow	↓	{Down}
Draw	Alt F8	{Draw}
Edit	F2	{Edit}
End	End	{End}
Erase	F4	{Erase}
Escape	ESC	{Escape} or {ESC}
Goto	F5	{Goto}
Help	F1	{Help}
Home	Home	{Home}
Indent	F3	{Indent}
Insert	Ins	{Insert}
Justify	F2	{Justify}
Learn	Alt F5	{Learn}
Left Arrow	←	{Left}
Menu	F10	{Menu} or {M}
Page Down	PgDn	{PgDn} or {BigDown}
Page Up	PgUp	{PgUp} or {BigUp}
Return	Return, or ↵	~ (tilde)
Right Arrow	→	{Right}
Services	F9	{Services} or {S}
Split	Alt F3	{Split}

Symphony Key Name	*On Keyboard*	*In Macro Coding*
Switch	Alt F9	{Switch}
Tab	TAB	{Tab}
Type	Alt F10	{Type}
Up Arrow	↑	{Up}
User	F7	{User}
Where	Alt F2	{Where}
Window	F6	{Window}
Zoom	Alt F6	{Zoom}

Repeating Keyboard Command Keys: {Right 20}

The next command on the first line of the "box" macro demonstrates another aspect of the use of keyboard commands in SCL. It says:

```
{Right 20}
```

Not much imagination is required to figure out that this command means Symphony should react as if the Right Arrow key were held down for 20 cursor position movements.

Here is a list of all the Symphony cursor, or cell pointer, movement keys that can be used with a repeat factor.

Table 2
Commands that May Take Repeat Factors

{Right}
{Left}
{Up}
{Down}
{PgUp}
{BigUp}
{PgDown}

```
{BigDown}
{BigRight}
{BigLeft}
{Tab}
```

Repeat factors must be separated from key command words by at least one space and should be kept within a range that won't result in the cursor trying to move outside the boundaries of the current window.

Following the {Right 20} command in the first line of the SCL macro called "box" is the letter "l".

To reset the left margin of a format line in a DOC window, we position the cursor where we want to place the margin (which is what the command {Right 20} did for us) and then type an "l" or "L" to mark the new margin location. To do that in SCL, we code the "l" at the cursor position where we want the new left margin to appear.

Compound Cursor Movement: {End}{Right}

The first two commands on the next line of the "box" macro are designed to move the cursor to the right end of the line on which we are working in the DOC window. To do this in Symphony, we would press the End key followed by the Right Arrow key. The SCL sequence is virtually identical. We use the command {Right} to substitute for pressing the Right Arrow key.

Other commands that reposition the cursor to the beginning of a line, the end of a document, or other places requiring the use of the End key are coded in the same way. Thus, for example, to move to the end of the document on which we are working, we would write a macro command like this:

```
{End}{Home}
```

The rest of the second line of the "box" macro is much like the earlier macro commands we've examined. Having reached the end of the line we are working on, we move to the left 20 spaces using the command:

```
{BS 20}
```

This could also have been written with the word *backspace* spelled out. We then type an "r" to indicate the new position for the right margin and press the [↵] key (coded with the tilde). We then use the Quit ("q") option to return to the document-editing process.

Changing the Mode Indicator: {Indicate "Box"}

When we use Symphony, a small box is displayed in the upper right corner of the PC's screen that keeps us informed of what mode we are in. This position is called the mode indicator. Normally, it contains the abbreviated name for one of the window types (DOC, SHEET, FORM, or COMM) or, occasionally, the word WAIT or ERROR.

We can use the {Indicate} command in SCL macro coding to alter the contents of this mode indicator. This turns out to be particularly helpful in identifying a specific new mode so that the person using our macro will have some clue as to why the system is doing what it is doing.

For example, when someone runs the macro "box", the screen seems to go berserk for a few moments while a new format line is set up and the cursor is repositioned. If we don't provide some indication that something unusual is *supposed* to be happening, we could make people wonder if the program had "blown up".

To overcome this, we use the {Indicate} command to change the mode indicator so that users can be conditioned to look up in the right corner of the screen when a program does something unexpected.

In this case, we set up a command that said:

```
{Indicate "Box"}
```

We can change the mode indicator to read any way we want, provided we understand that, no matter how long the argument to the {Indicate} command is, Symphony will display only the first five characters. This means that if we code:

```
{Indicate "Something Peculiar Is Happening"}
```

SCL will change the mode indicator so that it says only "Somet".

Once again, quotation marks around characters to be displayed in the mode indicator are optional. We include them out of habit and because it makes it easier for us to spot where we've placed a literal string in our program, but you can safely omit them if you're comfortable doing so.

When finished, we return the mode indicator to its standard condition by coding the {Indicate} command with no arguments.

Accepting User Input: {?}

We have only one new concept in this macro to explain. It is often desirable in an SCL macro to pause in execution and permit people to enter some information before continuing. If that weren't the case, we would probably find it easier to place Symphony in Learn mode than to learn to program using SCL command structures. A number of commands enable us to get information from the user to the system via the keyboard. The simplest of these is the {?} command.

The {?} command simply pauses the SCL macro's execution and lets the user enter material from the PC keyboard followed by a [↵]. It places the information into the current cell position and continues executing the macro in sequence.

There are more complex ways of accomplishing this task, including displaying prompts in the control panel area, choosing to place the input into a different cell position from the current one, and capturing single-keystroke entries without requiring the user to press the [↵] key.

The Rest of the "Box" Macro

There is nothing new in the remainder of the macro called "box". We have anticipated that keyboard input will consist of a short (one or two words) heading that the user wants to center over the newly created box format. After receiving the input, we {Justify} the text. Remember that Symphony in a DOC window will not automatically justify our input as we enter it; we must explicitly instruct it to do so. Then we press the [↵] key twice to put a blank line between the heading and the text of the message to appear in the newly created box.

The next line looks like this:

```
{M}fc˜jeq
```

This line sets up another new format line identical to the one we just created, except that text placed into it is right-justified (thanks to the "e" option coded into it after the "j", for "Justification", selection).

It is interesting to note here, again, that when we are working in a DOC window and have defined a new format line that does not cause automatic word wrap, text typed into the newly created box gets entered as one long line with no carriage returns. When the user presses the ↵ key to indicate the end of the input, though, the {Justify} command in the macro results in the text being broken into appropriate-sized pieces and right-justified in the margins we've set.

Having filled the box with text, we want to return to the previous format conditions so that the user can go on entering text of a "normal" nature. We do this with the "r", for "Reset", option in the next line:

```
{M}fc~rq
```

The effect of this is to place a new format line into the document, with margins and tabs as they were before we began setting up our box. In reality, the Reset command returns the format to its *default* settings. If we are using a format that has been modified from the default, we must code an SCL macro statement to explicitly set up margins and tabs where they should be and not simply use the "r" option.

Without the next line, the cursor would remain positioned at the indented left margin from our previous special format, so we tell the cursor to move back to the new left margin by writing a macro statement like this:

```
{End}{Left}
```

The last line of the macro returns the mode indicator to read "DOC" again.

Always Leave Them Knowing, Not Guessing

An important programming principle taught by the last three lines of the SCL macro is that when we finish doing something special with the user's environment, we should return the environment to its original condition. Some programmers forget this principle and thereby cause consternation for people trying to use their macros and programs.

Besides this, the concept has a more selfish justification from the programmer's perspective. If we know what state the system is in when we begin a new macro, we can know how to manipulate and modify it to do what we want. If, on the other hand, we don't know where the margins are, resetting them in a macro is going to be one neat trick!

Using Macros in FORM Applications

The macro uses we've been discussing so far would find their best uses in DOC and SHEET environments. In fact, they are most useful in the DOC windows we use for creating word processing documents. But the same principles that apply to creating macros for DOC and SHEET windows can greatly simplify and streamline our use of the powerful database management aspects of Symphony found in the FORM environment.

This section will discuss three possible uses for macros in a FORM window and provide some directions and pointers to assist in designing and creating SCL macros for use in this environment. We won't attempt to provide complete, functional macros since database design and use are highly customized for each application, and since the proper use of macros in this environment requires the creation and existence of a database application. Instead, we will provide "skeletons" of such macros and indicate where you could or should modify them to meet your specific needs in a given application.

Repetitive Data Entry: A FORM Glossary

One excellent use for macros in a FORM window would be the definition of the glossary-type macros discussed earlier. These would be used to enter data for which we expect to have repeated need in our application. For example, if we were building a database of customers and all customer numbers started with a certain five-digit code sequence, had four unique identifiers, and had a single-letter concluding code depending on geographic region, we might define two glossary-type macros as follows:

```
\C        12345{?}C{Down}
\T        12345{?}T{Down}
```

In each of these cases, the operator entering information into the database would invoke the appropriate macro using the [Alt] key in combination with the letter key for the region involved ("C" or "T" in our examples). The macro would provide the first five characters and then pause and wait for the operator to enter the next four and press the [↵] key. The macro would then provide the last character plus a cell position movement key. We've selected a Down Arrow because we suppose the form is set up so that the customer numbers are in a column.

Obviously, much time and effort can be saved in a FORM application where repetitive portions of data are frequently needed.

There are at least two other areas where macros could be quite useful in a FORM window. The first involves setting up repeatedly used search criteria, and the second enables us to predefine commonly needed report formats. Both macros would permit an operator only vaguely familiar with Symphony to generate meaningful reports. We'll discuss each of these applications in the following pages.

Setting Up Search Criteria

In most cases, once we've defined a database and entered a number of records into it, we can predict most reports we're likely to want the system to generate and the order in which we'll want it to sort information. Some repetitive operations can be handled by designing and saving multiple Settings sheets of various kinds in the FORM environment, but this is not always the most efficient way to do the job.

This section will take a look at general principles for setting up an SCL macro that will guide an inexperienced Symphony user step by step through the design of an online database search. The macro will conduct the process of setting up a search strategy based on search criteria entered from the keyboard.

Criteria: A Quick Review

We assume you know about search criteria and their use in Symphony, but let's take a whirlwind review tour of the subject.

Criteria are the conditions that records in our database must meet to be selected for inclusion in a report or onscreen. For example, a database might consist of names of customers and invoice dates and amounts. We may want to look only at customers with bills older than 30 days. Or we might want to look at the bills of just our biggest customers to see what the ordering pattern is. To do these things, we set up search criteria.

Setting up search criteria in a database application using Symphony requires use of the Criteria Edit command from the Menu option in a FORM window. The Criteria Edit command produces a blank form that looks exactly like the form we use to enter data into the database and to review it. We type into that form the criteria we want the records to meet to qualify for selection from the database.

For example, to search our accounts receivable database for all bills for the Amalgamated Shippers and Receivers Co., we move the cell pointer to the blanks where the company name is being stored and type in the company's name exactly as it appears in the database. Then we press the [Ins] key, and this selection condition is stored in the criterion range of the SHEET environment that corresponds to our FORM window.

Having done that, we instruct Symphony to use this criterion for selecting records by executing the Criteria Use command from the Menu option. Thereafter, unless and until we tell the program to ignore our selection, only data that meet the conditions we have set up as criteria will be displayed on the screen or included in reports we print.

Know Your Database

It follows from the way databases handle the establishment of search criteria that we'll have to know the structure of the database in order to provide automated support for the operator. Otherwise, we won't be able to be any more helpful with an SCL macro than Symphony already is with its control panel prompting.

Let's assume we have defined a database that consists of a collection of records of three fields: company name, a 25-character string label; invoice amount, a dollar-formatted numeric field; and date. We enter data into this system through the FORM window. The accounts receivable clerk who usually operates this database frequently needs to look at one customer's bills because that customer wants to place a new order and the sales representative wants to ensure that the customer's bills are current.

We want to automate that process as much as possible using an SCL macro that the clerk can invoke from the keyboard with a simple [Alt] key combination. Then the clerk just needs to type in the customer name and page through the data form as it is displayed on the screen.

Symphony is not so difficult to run and load a FORM into that this process should require automation. We will assume that Symphony is running on the operators' terminals and that they are in the right FORM environment. Without that assumption, we'd have to do a lot of time-consuming and probably unnecessary up-front programming.

Given this limited assignment, the following macro would do the trick.

```
\Q    {M}ce{?}~{Insert}   Get the company name; insert record
      {ESC}u              Use the new criterion
      {Home}              Position at start of database
```

As you can see from the comments incorporated in this macro, we first position the user at the point where the {Menu} has been invoked and the Criteria Edit function called into play. Then the operator enters the name of the company. If we wanted keyboard entry of, say, the bills issued on a particular date, we'd have included a command like this in the macro before asking for the input with a {?} statement:

```
{Down 2}
```

Since the company name is the first field, that step is unnecessary. Notice that the tilde (symbol for the carriage return) is needed in the first line of the macro. When operators press the [↵] key at the end of the name for which they want the system to search, the tilde signals to the macro that input is complete.

Symphony requires an explicit carriage return to enable it to accept the {Insert} command or the pressing of the [Ins] key, so we must supply it.

Now whenever operators want to review a specific customer's bills, they need only press [Alt] Q, type in the name of the customer, and then use the [PgUp] and [PgDn] keys to browse through the database.

It might be a good idea to define a macro that restores the database to its original status with no customers selected. In this way, a subsequent search for a record that is present in the database but does not meet the criteria currently in the file won't come up empty and cause needless concern. This step may be unnecessary if the system is used only to inquire about the status of customers' bills.

Such a macro would be easy to code, however:

```
\X          {M}CI{Home}
```

This macro simply goes to the menu and invokes the Criteria Ignore command — in which Symphony usually works with data in a FORM window. It then returns the operator to the first record in the now unselected file (for example, the file in its natural sequence with all records visible for browsing).

These two macros are short and simple, which leads to two observations. First, short and simple doesn't mean useless. In fact, the macro we labeled "\Q" saves operators seven keystrokes every time it is used. If an operator receives half a dozen calls per hour, that's a savings of 336 keystrokes per day. Second, these two macros could become significantly more complicated if, for example, we wished to set up multiple criterion records or even two fields in one criterion record.

The two examples provide brief skeletons of such macros to give you an idea of how to design and code a useful SCL macro in a FORM environment.

As an example of how the idea could be extended, let's slightly modify the jobs of our hypothetical accounts receivable clerks. Suppose they will want to answer quickly questions about past-due bills. We could easily modify the macro "\Q" above to incorporate this additional criterion. Suppose we define as past due any bill that is more than 30 days old. After the clerk has entered the company name and pressed [↵], we add two more tildes, moving the cursor to the date field, and then enter the formula (being sure to include the tilde at the end):

```
+>(@int@now)-30~
```

We then code the {Insert} command. The rest of the macro "\Q" stays the same.

This additional information raises an additional point about macros: they can include Symphony @ functions. In fact, a great deal of the power in SCL can be attributed to the use of these functions.

Helping Sort Things Out

If the database application on which we are working requires a number of different sort sequences from time to time, we can respond with one of two solutions. We can code a macro that interacts with users to set up the sort criteria for a given run as required, *or* we can predefine our sort instructions in different Settings sheets and simply use the correct one for a particular situation.

In the latter case, we may still wish to use a macro to simplify the process of asking for the appropriate Settings sheet and getting it attached correctly to the database application.

The first method makes more efficient use of Symphony because it doesn't require additional memory or disk capacity to store additional Settings sheets. The second method is faster to execute, though both are fairly quick.

Let's look briefly at the principles involved in writing SCL macros for each of these approaches.

Dynamic Settings Sheet Modification

Sticking with our accounts receivable database example, let's say that we want the data sorted in two different ways: (1) alphabetically by company and, within each company, bills arranged by date beginning with the oldest, and (2) arranged by date beginning with the most recent.

When we redefine a Settings sheet, Symphony moves back and forth between a FORM window and a SHEET window. We begin in the FORM window and select the Menu option first. Then we ask for the Settings option and choose Sort-Keys. We must then define the first, second, and/or third sort keys by typing the numbers 1, 2, or 3.

Symphony then moves into the database range in the SHEET environment and asks us to point to the column containing the key we wish to use. We position the cell pointer appropriately and press the [↵] key. The system then asks if we want to sort this column in ascending or descending order.

After we define the sort instructions, we go back to the Menu level and select the Record-Sort option. When the sort completes, Symphony automatically positions us at the same record number we were at when we started; we usually want to use the [Home] key at that point.

As you can see, we need to know how the database is structured in the SHEET environment to code a macro that handles this process automatically for the operator. We do not, however, need to know where the database range begins; Symphony will take us there automatically when we ask it to redefine the sort keys for the file.

A macro that would set up the first sort sequence outlined above would look something like this:

```
SORT1          {M}ss1~a2{right 2}~d
               {ESC}r{Home}
```

The first line of the macro SORT1 calls the Menu, selects Settings and Sort-Keys, indicates that we wish to define the first sort key ("1"), presses the [↵] key since the first field of the database is the one we wish to use as the first sort key field, instructs Symphony to sort that field in ascending order ("a"), then asks for the second sort key field definition ("2").

We wish to sort on the date, which we've defined as the third field in the database, so we use two Right Arrow movements ({Right 2}) to position the cell pointer correctly, then press [↵]. Finally, we indicate we want this field sorted in descending order.

Invoking the sort is the function of the second line of the macro, which simply uses the [Esc] key (Escape) to return to the main Menu control panel point, then chooses the "r" (Record-Sort) option. The {Home} command positions us at the first record in this newly sorted set of information.

Creating the other sort macro involves a similar process, except, of course, we don't need a second sort key, so the line is shorter.

Here's the macro we created to handle the second sort — in ascending date sequence:

```
SORT2          {M}scss1{Right 2}~a
```

Notice two additional commands in this sequence. The added c's after the Menu command clears the present contents of any sort keys that may have been left over from a previous run. (Clearing such potential sources of problems is a good idea any time you set up an SCL macro.) We would suggest adding this same two-instruction set to the macro SORT1. The macro would then look like this:

```
SORT1          {M}ss1~a2{right 2}~d
               {ESC}r{Home}
               {M}scss1{Right 2}~a
```

Other FORM Uses of Macros

You will gain experience with Symphony's database management capabilities and become more familiar with SCL macro definition through this book and by programming macros. Expect to find dozens of places where a well thought out macro will be a real timesaver for the people using the Symphony systems you design.

Summary

This chapter has covered a lot of ground, primarily by examining examples of small but highly useful SCL macros. You've learned:

The basic principles of macro coding and design

How to implement keyboard commands inside a macro

How to get keyboard input while the user is running a macro

How to modify the mode indicator

In addition, you've learned some important principles of designing macros, such as ensuring that you always return the user to the most logical or expected place in the processing when your macro has ended its run.

The next chapter will examine each SCL macro command statement in depth — to ensure that you have a thorough understanding of the variety of available commands. Our examples will become more complex throughout the rest of the book. To save time and energy, we will explain the individual commands now so that we can concentrate later on the design and use of the complex examples we are providing.

SECOND MOVEMENT

The Tools of the Trade

This movement will fully discuss each of SCL's command statements. We will provide not only the rules about the use of these commands but also hints about their proper implementation in your macros, cautions about things you should consider when you use them, and examples of their use in macros.

To make the discussion of these commands easier to follow, we have organized the commands into several groups, as follows:

Special key indicators — use of PC keyboard key calls

Controlling the environment — commands that affect the display and the general processing environment

Getting data into the program — commands that handle data entry from the keyboard or other sources

Controlling program flow — commands that involve conditional processing, subroutine usage, and menu design

Function usage — instructions on the use of @ functions inside macros

Telecommunications — commands that are used only in the telecommunications environment (COMM windows)

Coda A is an alphabetical table of the commands covered in this movement. Coda C contains the commands that have been added with the release of version 1.1. Refer to either Coda if you are interested in a short explanation of the command while you are designing a macro.

Special Key Indicators

We have previously encountered this subject and dealt with it in some depth (see First Movement, Tables 1 and 2). Here, we will refresh our thinking about the subject.

Any special key on the PC keyboard can be simulated in a macro by placing its abbreviation or name between braces. Optionally, we can also place a number after the name of the key if it is one that is often used as a self-repeating key.

Actually, not *all* special keys can be invoked from macros; the [Num/Lock], [Scroll/Lock], and [Caps/Lock] keys and the [Spacebar] cannot be used except by pressing them physically on the keyboard.

Some keys (listed in Table 2) can be called upon a specified number of times without having to write their names or abbreviations more than once. To move the cell pointer down five rows, for example, instead of having to type the keyname {Down} five separate times, we can simply code:

```
{Down 5}
```

Obviously, when using this feature, we should keep in mind the boundaries of the windows and sheets within which we are working so that we don't create a situation where we are attempting to move outside those limits.

Some of the keys have two "names". For example, to invoke a backspace, we can code the name of the key or its abbreviation, "BS", in the braces. In other words, the following two commands are equivalent:

```
{Backspace 9}
{BS 9}
```

The function keys located in two rows along the left side of the keyboard are programmed using their functional names, not their function key numbers. Therefore, to cause the macro to move the cell pointer to location AA43, for example, you'd code the following macro command:

```
{Goto}AA43~    (don't forget the carriage return!)
```

One final point. The [↵] key, for mysterious reasons known best to Lotus Development Corp., is coded as a tilde (~), and is located to the right of the single and double quotation marks on the IBM PC keyboard as a shifted character.

Controlling the Environment

This section describes a dozen SCL commands whose purpose is to permit us to control the environment within which the application we are creating will be run. The following paragraphs will cover:

Enabling use of the [Break] key

Turning windows and panels on and off

Forcing automatic recalculation

Changing the contents of the indicator box in the upper right corner of the Symphony display

Sounding the system's audible bell to get attention

Erasing some data and causing the system to pause in its processing

{BreakOn} and {BreakOff}

There are times when using the [Break] key can cause serious difficulty for the person using a Symphony program or running an application. For example, during the time a file is being written to, interrupting processing may result in a data file that is not in the condition Symphony expects to find it in. This in turn may mean that the file is unusable by Symphony, or, for that matter, by any other program we might wish to use to examine or update it.

Perhaps the most common use of this key-disabling function will be to secure a Symphony macro from examination by people using it. This would prevent unauthorized copying or use by people who didn't pay for it or otherwise weren't permitted to have it.

Any time it is possible that users could cause a problem for themselves or us by pressing the [Break] key during processing, we should turn the key off — in other words, disable it — using the {BreakOff} command. There are no arguments to be passed to the command. It is simply coded as follows:

```
{BreakOff}
```

The {BreakOff} command stays in effect until the macro executes a {BreakOn} command. So long as it is in effect, the execution of the macro cannot be stopped by using the [Break] key; the only way to get out of the macro is to reset the computer or to turn it off. This, in turn, leads us to one of the important cautions about using {BreakOff}:

> Caution: If {BreakOff} is in effect and something goes wrong to cause the macro to go into an infinite loop, there is no way to regain control of the computer without restarting it. Doing so with diskettes in drives can damage data on the disks.

As a result of this potential problem, we always leave the {BreakOff} command out of the macro until we've completely debugged it and have it running. *Then* it can be safely added without being concerned about causing a serious problem.

We should also note one other caution in using {BreakOff}. If we forget to close our macro with a {BreakOn} command, the [Break] key remains disabled even outside the macro. So we won't be able to interrupt any processing in which Symphony might be engaged which uses the [Break] key. We always end our macros with a {BreakOn} command even if we never called {BreakOff}, just to be safe (we might add {BreakOff} later but forget to turn it back to "normal"). Another good idea is to have a one-line macro in our worksheet that simply reactivates the [Break] key so that we can execute that macro from the keyboard if we have forgotten to turn the key back on after leaving a macro.

Example 1

Here's a portion of a macro that demonstrates how we would use {BreakOn} and {BreakOff} in a "typical" situation.

```
Example1        {BreakOff}
                {MenuCall MyMenu}
*
*
*
MyMenu
*
*
*
                Quit
                Exit to Symphony
                {BreakOn}{Quit}
```

This skeletal macro invokes a new menu we've designed (a subject that is covered later under "Menu Creation and Use"). If we choose the Quit option from our menu and wish to return control to Symphony, we first execute a {BreakOn} command to ensure that control of the key is regained before returning to Symphony via the {Quit} command. While the macro is being executed, however, control of the system from the keyboard cannot be regained using the Break key because we execute a {BreakOff} command at the first line of the macro.

{WindowsOn} and {WindowsOff}

The commands {WindowsOn} and {WindowsOff} control the display of windows and their contents on the CRT. They are useful for stabilizing the screen display during large-scale updates of data affecting displayed windows. They are also used to create one or more new windows and have them appear seemingly spontaneously and simultaneously.

In some respects, we could think of {WindowsOff} as being a command that tells the system to go into what we call "background mode"; in other words, "Do the next steps without showing the user what you're doing".

Neither of these commands takes an argument.

The {WindowsOff} command in effect freezes the entire CRT display except for the control panel (which is separately controlled by the {PanelOn} and {PanelOff} commands discussed in the next section). To include it in a program, simply use its name as follows:

```
{WindowsOff}
```

Window updating consists of the creation and display of new windows or the updating of information that appears in the displayed portions of existing windows. Updating takes place without showing the effects. The display will remain static while a {WindowsOff} command is in effect.

In some ways, {WindowsOn} and {WindowsOff} act like the Windows Auto-Display setting in the SHEET environment, except that the setting affects only one window at a time, while {WindowsOn} and {WindowsOff} affect all displayed windows at once.

Obviously, if we left a {WindowsOff} command in effect, the person using the macro would never know what was going on on the screen! As with the {BreakOn} and {BreakOff} commands discussed earlier, we must place the windows back into normal operation at the end of a macro or the section of a macro where we have turned the windows off. It is a good idea to create a one-line macro in our worksheet that simply turns the windows back on. That way, if the macro gets "hung up" in the middle or terminates unexpectedly with the {WindowsOff} command in effect, we can still get the display back so that we can figure out what happened.

To turn the window display back to its normal mode in which all windows are displayed and updated as they are affected, we will code the command:

```
{WindowsOff}
```

Example 2

This small example macro freezes all the windows on the screen, creates a new one, isolates it from the others (with the Window Isolate command coded as "wi"), creates three more, and then unfreezes the display.

```
Example2  {WindowsOff}
          {S}wuMy Window #1~
          {S}wi
```

```
{S}wuMy Window #2~
{S}wuMy Window #3~
{S}wuSomeone Else's Window~
{WindowsOn}
```

The effect of this macro's execution will be that the screen will freeze, and in a few moments a new screen will appear with only the four newly designated windows displayed. (This assumes that we've defined them in such a way that they are all simultaneously visible.) The windows appear suddenly, with no flickering or intermediate display updating.

{PanelOn} and {PanelOff}

As we saw in the First Movement, when an SCL macro is running, it displays the commands it is carrying out in the control panel area immediately above the window display region of the screen. If the macro is quite long or complex, there can be a great deal of distracting flashing going on during its execution. The {WindowsOn} and {WindowsOff} commands help lessen this distraction. A similar role is played by the commands {PanelOff} and {PanelOn}.

If {PanelOff} and {WindowsOff} are both in effect during the execution of a macro command sequence, the screen is effectively frozen throughout the time the macro is running. It will remain frozen in the status it was in when the {PanelOff} command was called for. In other words, if we want the control panel region to be blank during a macro's execution, we must explicitly make it blank and *then* issue the {PanelOff} command.

Like the other environmental control commands, the control panel commands must be tracked during their use. It is essential that we reset the environment so that windows and the control panel are active when our macro completes its assignment. This is so that Symphony will be able to carry out its activities outside our macros.

Note that if {PanelOff} is in effect, using the commands {GetLabel} or {GetNumber} with screen prompts during input will not have the desired effect. In other words, if we want a prompt displayed at some point during the macro's execution, we must explicitly turn the control panel back on, use the routines to display the messages we want, and then turn the control panel back off when we are ready to proceed with other processing.

The following sample skeleton macro will clarify what we mean by this caution.

```
MACRO11        {PanelOff}{Windowsoff}
               statements
               statements
               more statements
               {PanelOn}
               {GetLabel "Enter the name of the party",G112}
               {GetLabel " ",G113}
               {PanelOff}
               statements
```

Note that immediately prior to the {GetLabel} command, we turn the control panel on so that the prompt "Enter the name of the party" will be visible in the control panel area. After receiving a response to our request for input, the {PanelOff} command freezes the display once again. Between the {GetLabel} command with the prompt and the {PanelOff} command, we use a {GetLabel} command with a blank prompt area to clear the control panel. That freezes it in an empty state, which is how we usually want things to be when frozen on the display.

{Recalc} and {RecalcCol}

These two commands are the first ones we have seen in the Second Movement of our Symphony orchestration that require an argument to be passed to them. Both commands expect to find the definition of a location immediately to the right of the commands themselves when they are coded into an SCL macro. That location definition can be a cell address range (for example, A1...I38) or an area that has been given a name (TOTALS).

We use these two commands when carrying out tasks in a large worksheet that requires several seconds to recalculate in its entirety but we need to update only a small portion of it.

For example, let's assume that we have a region of our SHEET window where the totals for accumulated cash flow requirements are stored. We have just entered a great deal of new information into some of the key locations in the spreadsheet; some of these figures affect the total cash flow needs. We want to know what those needs are now, but we don't want to wait a minute or two while Symphony updates the entire worksheet of complex formulas and interrelationships.

To deal with this problem, the SCL command {Recalc} can be used as follows:

```
{Recalc CUM_CASH}
```

This command recalculates the region defined with the name CUM_CASH while the rest of the worksheet is left alone.

The only difference between {Recalc} and {RecalcCol} is the order in which the recalculation takes place. {Recalc} performs its recalculation on a row-by-row basis, while {RecalcCol} recalculates column by column.

There are several additional key things to remember about the use of these commands.

First, it is unnecessary to use either of these commands or their keyboard relative {Calc} (equivalent to the F8 key being pressed) after we call a Symphony command that automatically performs such a recalculation. For example, Symphony Copy and Move commands automatically recalculate when they are carried out, even if they are invoked from inside a macro. An exception to this rule arises if we have placed the worksheet's recalculation method to Manual. In that case, we must explicitly code {Recalc} or {RecalcCol} instructions into the macro if they are to be updated before the recalculation method is changed.

Second, neither command performs any calculations outside the range affected, which means that formulas in other parts of the worksheet that use this information may no longer have the current data when the macro is finished. It is a good idea to include a {Calc} command at the end of any macro that uses {Recalc} or {RecalcCol}.

Finally, it is almost always irrelevant whether we use {Recalc} or {RecalcCol}; only when the order of calculation is significant should we occupy the extra space and keystrokes needed to specify column-by-column calculations with the {RecalcCol} command.

{Indicate}

As you have used Symphony, you have undoubtedly noticed the mode indicator in the upper right corner of the screen. This small box of inverse video characters is provided by the program to indicate where in the processing you are at any point. The most common contents for that mode indicator are the names of the environments or window types (SHEET, FORM, COMM, DOC, or GRAPH) or special notices like WAIT and ERROR.

The {Indicate} command lets you control the contents of the mode indicator. The first five characters of the string argument that follows the word *Indicate* in the command will replace the current contents of the mode indicator. For example, if you are writing a macro that maintains a telephone list, you might want the mode indicator to show that the macro is in use by displaying the word *PHONE* in the upper right corner. To accomplish this, you would simply code:

```
{Indicate PHONE}
```

As soon as the command is executed, the word *PHONE* will appear in the upper right corner of the screen, in inverse video, to indicate that the telephone macro is in use. If you provide a string longer than five characters, only the first five are used by Symphony. In other words, coding:

```
{Indicate TELEPHONE}
```

would result in the mode indicator containing the letters *TELEP*. On the other hand, if you use fewer characters than five, the program will fill the rest of the mode indicator area with blanks. The command:

```
{Indicate TEL}
```

will result in a mode indicator containing the letters *TEL* followed by two blanks. To *center* the letters *TEL* in the space, put them inside quotation marks and include a blank on either side of the letters, like this:

```
{Indicate " TEL "}
```

Since the spaces are inside quotation marks, they are considered by Symphony to be part of the label itself. Without the quotation marks, Symphony simply ignores extra blanks.

You should know that if you use the {Indicate} command to change the mode indicator's contents, the new characters stay in the box until you explicitly change them. Even if the user leaves your macro and begins working in a DOC window outside your macro, the mode indicator is still going to say "TEL" (or whatever you put into it last) unless you restore it to its original condition. You do this by using the {Indicate} command without any string argument. The effect is to return control of the mode indicator to Symphony.

You can also use the {Indicate} command to cause the mode indicator to be blank by using an "empty" string or one that consists only of any number of blanks. An empty string consists of two quotation marks immediately adjacent to each other, without anything, including spaces, between them. Either of the following commands will result in a mode indicator box that is simply an inverse video block in the upper right corner of the screen:

```
{Indicate ""}  ←Empty string
{Indicate "              "}  ←Some arbitrary number of spaces
```

If you blank the mode indicator, you will still need to use the {Indicate} command without any argument to return control of the mode indicator to Symphony. As far as Symphony is concerned, you have put something in that region of the display, even though you have only put in blanks.

{Beep}

People using your macro may wish to know when a particular step in the processing is completed. For example, a particularly long update process might be involved, and users may want to do something else until it completes. Or you might want to alert users to the occurrence of an error condition, for example, if they enter a string response you don't have a program condition to handle. In either circumstance — and in many others that will occur to you as you work with Symphony — you can use the {Beep} command to sound the speaker's tone on the computer.

Most of the time, you'll just use the command {Beep}. Despite what the *Symphony Reference Manual* says in its description of this command, however, you *can* vary the pitch and duration of the tone by using a number as an argument. Using a 2, as in

```
{Beep 2}
```

creates the same tone as using {Beep} without an argument. But an argument of 1 creates a lower tone, while 3 yields a very short "chirp" that is much higher in pitch than the usual tone.

We don't know what all the possible values are. Just for fun, we coded a macro that included the command:

```
{Beep 100}
```

and got an altogether different-sounding tone. If you want to experiment and see what kind of beep you prefer, try this short macro:

```
\b          {GetNumber "Enter a number for BEEP",AA3}
            {Beep +AA3}
(blank line)
```

We haven't yet dealt with the {GetNumber} command, although you can probably figure out what it does. This macro permits you to enter any number you want to try, puts that number into cell address AA3 (an arbitrary choice), and then uses that value as an argument to the {Beep} command.

Why would you want to use a {Beep} different from the usual one provided by Symphony? You may want to provide different kinds of feedback depending on the reason for the tone. For example, you might want a low-pitched tone to indicate that a process has been completed and a high-pitched, easily heard beep — or a series of beeps — to signal an error. To code a series of {Beep} tones, you'll have to provide them explicitly, like this:

```
{Beep}{Beep}{Beep}{Beep}
```

SCL probably doesn't afford enough range and duration possibilities to permit you to use it to play music, but we haven't really *tried* all the combinations, either!

{Blank}

The {Blank} command operates identically to the SHEET Erase command but can be used outside the SHEET environment, which makes it particularly useful as an SCL macro command. For example, to erase the contents of the Main Report range from within a FORM window, you could write the command:

```
{Blank MAIN_DB}
```

To accomplish the same thing using the SHEET window's Erase command from inside a FORM window, you would have to first switch to the SHEET environment, issue the Erase command, and then return to the FORM window. Using {Blank} is obviously far more efficient.

The argument supplied to the {Blank} command must be a range or cell address. Predefined labels can be used, as we saw in our example above.

You might be tempted to use the {Blank} command any time you are going to put some new data into a cell by using a {Get} command or one of its variations. That is not necessary; Symphony automatically blanks the cell before it puts new data into it.

You might want to use {Blank} to erase the contents of a cell you've been using as a temporary holding area for data entered when you leave the macro. This would allow you to restore the window to the condition it was in before your macro was invoked and then erase the cell that you used to remember the restore information.

Like Erase, {Blank} does not alter the display format or protection settings on the cell or range affected.

{Wait}

There are two common sets of circumstances under which we might want a macro to pause in its execution of our instructions.

First, we might want a macro to pause for some arbitrary number of seconds, to allow us to examine something on the screen, and then continue processing without anything being done on the keyboard. This technique is particularly useful in demonstrations of macros where we are training people to use a system and want simply to show them what a particular sequence looks like.

Second, if we are using the powerful communications facilities of Symphony in a COMM window from an SCL macro, we might want to set up a routine that automatically calls another computer at some preappointed time. For example, if we live on the West Coast, we might want our computer to call Dow Jones News/Retrieval® service and gather information about our ten top stock interests a half hour before we get up in the morning. We can use the {Wait} command to set up a macro that waits until a specific time has arrived and then executes.

Each of these situations requires a slightly different use of the {Wait} command's arguments. Both require us to use @ functions, which are more fully discussed later.

{Wait} for a Specific Time

We'll show you the second situation first, because waiting for the arrival of a specific time is more straightforward than the other option. Using the @TIME function built into Symphony, we can explicitly define the time we want the macro to execute. To make our hypothetical phone call at 6:30 a.m., for example, we would code a macro statement like this at the beginning of our macro program:

```
{Wait @TIME(06,30,00)}
```

This macro puts the word *Wait* into the mode indicator box (assuming that we haven't put something else there) and then begins a loop in which the program compares the current time to the one we've told it to wait for, determines if they are the same, and, if so, carries out the instruction that follows this statement.

This application of the {Wait} macro statement could be particularly useful for automatically dialing and retrieving information from databases that charge less for access during hours when it may be inconvenient for us to use our systems.

{Wait} for Some Specific Period of Time

The other approach to the use of the {Wait} command is one in which our objective is to cause the macro to pause in its execution for some *relative* amount of time. In other words, we don't want to wait until 1:33 p.m. for the next step, but we want to pause 15 seconds from the time the last statement was executed until the next one is carried out.

To do this, we need to add the @NOW function to our macro. As you probably know if you've used @ functions in Symphony worksheet design, this function returns the current time. We take advantage of that to tell Symphony to pause for the arrival of a time that is 15 seconds later than @NOW, as follows:

```
{Wait @NOW+@TIME(0,0,15)}
```

Notice that we *still* define a specific time of day for the macro to wait for before continuing. For example, if the time when we invoke this macro is 12:45:30 p.m., macro execution will pause, *Wait* will be displayed (again, assuming that we haven't explicitly changed it with the {Indicate} command), and the macro will begin to look for a match between the current time and our requested time of 12:45:45 p.m. At that point, macro execution will resume.

We could obviously build longer pauses into our programs. To stop a macro for 10 minutes and 30 seconds, for example, we could code:

```
{Wait @NOW+@TIME(0,10,30)}
```

The {Wait} macro command *always* looks for a specific time of day to arrive. We "fool" it into waiting for a relative amount of time by providing it with a future time based on the current time, as reflected in the @NOW function.

Getting Data into the Program

This section will discuss all the SCL macro statements that result in data being entered into the worksheet in which we are operating. There are essentially two ways of doing this: (1) asking for entry from the keyboard and then storing it in a cell address or (2) explicitly putting a value in a location by providing the data in the macro. The former is a far more frequent need than the latter, though the latter will clearly be used from time to time.

Commands that fall into the first category are {?}, {Get}, {GetLabel}, and {GetNumber}. Commands that allow us to provide data explicitly through the macro include {Let}, {Put}, {Contents}, and {Look}. We will discuss each of these eight commands in turn in this section.

General Input Command: {?}

If your macro needs information to be placed from the keyboard into the current cell location and no prompting is needed and no editing of the input is desired, the simple use of the {?} command will do the trick nicely. The {?} command causes Symphony to pause in its execution until receiving a [↵] from the keyboard. When that happens, Symphony places whatever the user enters into the current cell of the worksheet and proceeds with the rest of the macro.

One drawback of the {?} command when compared to other input commands ({GetLabel} and {GetNumber}—which we will discuss shortly) is that no definite indication is given that Symphony has paused and is waiting for input. Unless the person running the macro is quite familiar with the processing it governs, confusion about why the program has halted could result.

Still, the {?} command is so convenient to use that it may be helpful to know a way around this problem. If we use the {Indicate} command in conjunction with the {?} command, we can have our cake and eat it, too. Try this kind of approach:

```
{Indicate Input}
{?}
{Indicate}
```

This macro segment will pause Symphony's execution only after displaying the word *Input* in the mode indicator location. After the input has been entered, the next {Indicate} command clears the indicator and passes control back to Symphony. Obviously, this approach is not so valuable if it avoids writing only one {GetLabel} or {GetNumber} command. But if we are doing a string of entries, perhaps with some intervening cursor movement, we might find it quite useful.

Controlled Input: {GetLabel} and {GetNumber}

We deal with these two commands in one discussion because they are virtually identical. As you can probably tell from their names, one requires numeric data only while the other accepts any input and treats it as a label. Other than that, they are identical.

Each of these commands takes two arguments. The first must be enclosed in quotation marks. It is the message that will appear in the control panel when the macro executes this line and pauses to wait for an entry. The second argument provides the cell address into which the input should be placed by the macro. Note that the window display does not change to *show* this location if it is not presently on the screen. You can, of course, force it to do so prior to making the entry (if that is important) simply by using [F5], the {Goto} key command.

The prompt string you provide to the {GetNumber} command must be enclosed in double quotation marks. They are optional with the {GetLabel} command unless the prompt contains a comma (or the command separator character if you've changed it from a comma to some other character). However, it's good programming practice to use double quotation marks with either of these commands so that there won't be any unexpected errors during macro use. If you forget to put the quotation marks around the prompt in a {GetNumber} command, you will encounter an error message that says:

```
Macro:  Illegal string in GETNUMBER
```

While there is no theoretical limit to the size of the prompt string, you should note two things. First, the total size of the string is limited by the size of the control panel area. If you code a prompt string that won't fit into the control panel, Symphony simply scrolls the whole message to the left and eliminates characters from the beginning of the string. Second, if the combined total length of the prompt string and the expected keyboard input is longer than the control panel's space allows, the same thing will happen (that is, the data in the panel will scroll off to the left). Neither of these conditions affects what is placed into the cell in the worksheet, but it can lead to difficult-to-understand prompts during macro execution.

If anything other than a number is entered in response to a {GetNumber} command, Symphony puts the value "ERR" into the address of the cell involved and proceeds with execution of the rest of the macro. As we will see later in this movement, this is a case where conditional processing using the {If} command is quite helpful in getting around the problem.

It is important to code a tilde, symbolizing a ↵, at the end of each {GetLabel} and {GetNumber} command. If you fail to do so, Symphony will not immediately place the entered value into the appropriate cell. Depending on what subsequent processing takes place, this can be either a major problem or a mere inconvenience. Also, don't place a space after the comma and before the cell location to which you want the input assigned. Doing so will result in an error condition. This is true in all macro commands but is particularly tempting in {GetLabel} and {GetNumber} when we have been typing spaces into the prompt line and may not be as conscious as we should be of the need to keep the arguments together from SCL's perspective.

Unlike the {GetNumber} command, the {GetLabel} command doesn't care what information is entered in response to it; an ERR condition will never result from any input made. However, the *result* of the entry might not be what was intended. For example, if a number is entered in response to a {GetLabel} command prompt, Symphony merely stores that as a command string. If an @ function is entered, Symphony stores *that* as a string.

```
AA1: 'GetDemo                                                            SHEET

     AA        AB        AC        AD        AE        AF        AG        AH
1  GetDemo  {GetNumber "Please enter a number: ", AG1}~
2           {GetNumber "Please enter another number: ", AG2}~
3           {GetNumber "Please enter a date: ", AG3}~
4           {GetLabel "Give me a string: ", AG4}~
5           {GetLabel "Another string.... ", AG5}~
6           {GetLabel "One More Time! ", AG6}~
7
8
9
10
11
12
13
14
15
16
17
18
19
20
                                                                          MAIN
20-Feb-85  06:43 PM
```

Figure 7
Get Demo Macro Listing

Figures 7 and 8 will help clarify this discussion about how {GetNumber} and {GetLabel} handle various kinds of input. Figure 7 is a macro that we have called GetDemo. Figure 8 shows the contents of cells AA10 through AA15 after the macro GetDemo has been run. The macro uses {GetNumber} three times and then {GetLabel} three times. We entered the following answers, in the sequence shown, for each of these sets of three requests for input: alphabet soup, 1097.98, and @now. (This last is an @ function that produces a representation for today's date.)

Notice in Figure 8 that {GetNumber} produced an ERR in response to the first input because it was alphabetic. It did as we expected, however, with both the numeric input and the function input. In the case of the @ function, it evaluated to a number, in this case 31098.78, so {GetNumber} dutifully stored the result at the location it was instructed to use.

{GetLabel}, on the other hand, handled the first input, alphabet soup, as expected. It *seems* to have handled the second input of a number, 1097.98, correctly as well, but if we tried to do any mathematical calculations with the result stored in cell AA14, we'd find that it stored that value

```
AA1: 'GetDemo                                                          SHEET

         AA        AB        AC        AD        AE        AF        AG        AH
1    GetDemo  {GetNumber "Please enter a number: ",AA10}~
2             {GetNumber "Please enter another number: ",AA11}~
3             {GetNumber "Please enter a date: ",AA12}~
4             {GetLabel "Give me a string: ",AA13}~
5             {GetLabel "Another string.... ",AA14}~
6             {GetLabel "One More Time! ",AA15}~
7
8
9
10        ERR
11   1097.98
12  31098.78
13  alphabet soup
14  1097.98
15  @now
16
17
18
19
20
                                                                        MAIN
20-Feb-85  06:55 PM
```

Figure 8
Results of Running Get Demo Macro

as a string, not as a number, and a straight math manipulation would not work. It simply treated the @ function as a string and put it, "@" symbol and all, into the cell location it was told to use.

Single-Keystroke Entry: {Get}

There are times during a macro execution when we want the processing to pause until the user is ready for it to proceed. There are other times when we want the macro to look for a one-character response — like "Y" for "yes" or "N" for "no". In either case, we would prefer not to require that the [↵] key be pressed after just one character is entered. This kind of input can be obtained by means of the {Get} command.

You must furnish the location at which you want the response to be stored. If this location is a range, Symphony stores the response in the upper left cell of the range.

The input in response to a {Get} statement can be any single key — a standard typewriter key, a special key (like the [Calc] key), or a COMPOSE key sequence. Notice that the {Get} command does not permit a control panel prompt. To show that the macro is waiting for input, use the same technique discussed above when we presented the {?} command.

A typical usage of the {Get} command might be in a macro where a window is used for display of a request for a response rather than using the control panel. Look at this macro as an example:

```
{Goto}AA10~
Are you ready to proceed?  (Y=Yes, N=No)~
{Get AB10}
{IF AB10="y". . .       ←Incomplete statement; details later
(continued processing steps follow)
```

This macro first positions the cell pointer in location AA10, where it displays the message "Are you ready to proceed? (Y = Yes, N = No)". The macro then pauses while the user types in any single key in response. The rest of the macro would check the response and take action based on which answer was given or whether the answer given was an unexpected one. (We'll have much more to say about conditional processing and error handling later.)

Before we depart from the subject of keyboard input statements, we should point out that although we have used explicit cell references for our input destinations, we can also use a named location. Thus the above macro, instead of explicitly placing the input in cell AB10, could have used any of several Symphony techniques to name AB10 "REPLY", for example, and then used the command:

```
{Get REPLY}
```

which is more readable and more generalized than the statement in the original macro.

Explicit Data Assignment to a Cell: {Let}

The {Let} command provides a means of storing a value in a cell by providing the value itself, either explicitly or indirectly through a cell reference or a formula. The {Let} command is quite powerful in that it is one of the few SCL macro commands that permits the use of string values. (In case you haven't worked with them much, "string values" are text strings that can be dealt with using Symphony's powerful string manipulation techniques, including concatenation — putting strings together — with the "&" operator. They are a kind of cross between labels, which cannot be manipulated, and values, which are numeric.)

In its simplest form, the {Let} statement provides Symphony with a cell address and an explicit value. For example, the macro statement:

```
{Let AB43,709}~
```

places 709 in cell AB43 as a numeric value. If we have a macro statement later in the macro that looks like this:

```
{Let I12,AB43}~
```

then cell location I12 would also contain the numeric value 709.

If we furnished a string as the value to be stored in a location, for example, by writing:

```
{Let Q11,"Jones"}~
```

SCL would first attempt to convert the string "Jones" to a string expression. If it could do so — which in this case it could — it would store at location Q11 *not* the label "Jones" but the string expression "Jones". In most cases, this is acceptable.

But the {Let} command offers two special forms that can be used with Symphony to be explicit about how we want arguments handled. If we want Symphony to carry out the calculation of 32 multiplied by 16 and store the result as a numerical value, we can write a macro command like this:

```
{Let AA1,32*16:value}~
```

The added argument, a colon followed by the word *value*, clarifies any confusion SCL may have when it encounters this macro command. Similarly, if we want the result of the calculation stored as a label and not as a string expression, we can write:

```
{Let AA1,32*16:string}~
```

SCL will override its normal inclination to try to use the second argument to the {Let} command as a numeric or string expression and store it as a simple label because of the addition of the colon and the word *string*.

This same special coding can be used to convert stored labels to string expressions for manipulation. For example, let us assume that cell Z1 contains the label "Symphony" and we want to store the title of this book, "Orchestrating Symphony", in cell AA23. Even though the label "Symphony" cannot be used in string manipulation, we can achieve this result by coding a macro command like this:

```
{Let AA23,+"Orchestrating "&Z1:value}~
```

This macro instructs Symphony to take the contents of cell Z1, convert it to a string expression, concatenate (add) it to the end of the string "Orchestrating", and store the result in cell AA23. (The plus sign calls for concatenation of strings.)

Placing Data in a Specified Range: {Put}

The {Put} statement is almost identical to the {Let} command we have just finished discussing. It processes its arguments and evaluates expressions in precisely the same way. The difference is that {Put} requires the location it is given to be a range, not an individual cell, and it must be told the column and row position in which to place the data provided as the fourth argument. These column and row locations must be coded as offsets from the starting cell of the range. An example will help clarify this difference between {Let} and {Put}.

Figure 9 shows three macros — put1, put2, and put3 — arranged in locations AA10 through AB14. Each of them acts upon a range defined in the {Put} command itself as beginning with cell AA1 and covering through cell AF8.

After these three macros have been executed, the window looks like Figure 10. The first macro, put1, instructs Symphony to place the value 409 into the cell that is zero columns and 2 rows from the upper left corner of the range. Column AA plus zero leaves the cell pointer in column AA, while adding 2 to the row number brings us to row 3. Symphony places the value 409 in cell AA3. Similarly, put2 places the string "Alexander" in location AD6, which is three columns and five rows from the upper left corner of the range. The macro put3 uses the "string" modifier to place the label "18*36" into location AA8 (zero columns and seven rows from location AA1, the upper left corner of the range affected).

```
AA1:                                                                SHEET

     AA          AB          AC          AD          AE          AF          AG          AH
1
2
3
4
5
6
7
8
9
10   put1        {Put AA1..AF8,0,2,409}~
11
12   put2        {Put AA1..AF8,3,5,Alexander}~
13
14   put3        {Put AA1..AF8,0,7,18*36:string}~
15
16
17
18
19
20
                                                                    MAIN
20-Feb-85  08:41 PM
```

Figure 9
{Put} Example Macro

```
AA1:                                                                SHEET

     AA          AB          AC          AD          AE          AF          AG          AH
1
2
3          409
4
5
6                                        Alexander
7
8    18*36
9
10   put1        {Put AA1..AF8,0,2,409}~
11
12   put2        {Put AA1..AF8,3,5,Alexander}~
13
14   put3        {Put AA1..AF8,0,7,18*36:string}~
15
16
17
18
19
20
                                                                    MAIN
20-Feb-85  08:42 PM
```

Figure 10
Execution Results of {Put} Macros

Copying a Cell: {Contents}

The purpose of the {Contents} command is to copy a (usually) numeric value from one cell in a worksheet and place it into another cell as a left-aligned label, optionally with a specific format and perhaps changing its width in the process. Though the command *may* be used with cells containing labels, this is not its best use, and {Contents} is not the most efficient method of accomplishing such a move. This discussion concentrates exclusively on the use of {Contents} with a numeric field.

{Contents} requires two arguments and optionally allows one or two others. The required arguments are the first in order. The first identifies the destination for the copying, that is, the cell into which the left-aligned label should be placed. The second defines the source cell, that is, the cell containing the numeric value to be manipulated.

Using the optional third argument, the width of the numeric value can be altered as the copy is made. If you supply this argument, Symphony acts as if the destination cell has the same width as you specify. If you supply a fourth argument, it is interpreted as a format code that determines how the numeric value will be *formatted* in its new position. The meanings of the format codes are discussed below. Though it is perfectly acceptable to supply a width argument without a format code, the opposite is not true. In other words, if you provide only three arguments, Symphony will interpret the third value as a width, regardless of your intent that it be a format code.

For the sake of discussion, assume that cell AA43 contains the value 963.02. If we code a macro statement that says:

```
{Contents AA1,AA43}
```

Symphony will place the label '963.02 into cell AA1 using the default width of 9 (or the current width of column AA1 if it's been changed from the default). It will also display the number in the default numeric display format or the current format for the range in which AA1 is found.

If we want to copy the contents of cell AA43 to location AA1 and we think we want to reduce its width to 3 in the process, we would write the macro:

```
{Contents AA1,AA43,3}
```

which would result in three asterisks being placed in cell AA1. This is because we have essentially told Symphony to treat cell AA1 as if it had a width of 3 and have then tried to place a number with five digits and a decimal point into it. As you know if you've run into this problem with Symphony, attempting to do this results in an undisplayable result, which Symphony handles by putting asterisks in the fields it cannot display properly.

On the other hand, if we expand the size of the field, for example, by writing the following macro statement:

```
{Contents AA1,AA43,18}
```

SCL places the value '963.02 — followed by 12 blank spaces — into cell AA1.

Format Codes

In the process of copying a numeric value, we often want to convert its format. To do so, we can choose one of two methods. First, we can move the number into a cell location whose numeric display format has been preset to be the one we wish to use. Second, we can explicitly redefine the numeric display format of the destination cell by coding a value from Table 3 in the fourth argument position of the {Contents} command.

For example, to move our value from cell AA43 to cell AA1 and in the process convert it to currency format with three decimal places, we would write:

```
{Contents AA1,AA43,9,35}
```

This command places the left-aligned label '$963.020 — followed by a single blank space — into cell AA1.

An interesting "trick" can be performed using a source cell that contains a calculated value. We can retrieve its formula and move it to the destination cell by using format 117, Literal. For example, if cell AA43, instead of containing the value 963.02, contained the formula +A12*A4/.8, we could recover that formula and put it into cell AA1 by coding this statement:

```
{Contents AA1,AA43,10,117}
```

The left-aligned label '+A12*A4/.8 would completely fill the ten-character space allotted in the {Contents} command for cell AA1.

Checking for Unsolicited Keyboard Input: {Look}

The {Look} statement is designed to check and see if the keyboard is entering information into the macro outside the context of normal requests

Table 3
CONTENTS Statement Format Numbers

Code	*Corresponding numeric format*
0	Fixed, 0 decimal places
1	Fixed, 1 decimal place
2	Fixed, 2 decimal places
15	Fixed, 15 decimal places
16-32	Scientific, 0 to 15 places
32-47	Currency, 0 to 15 places
48-63	%, 0 to 15 places
64-79	Punctuated, 0 to 15 places
112	+/-
113	General
114	D1 (DD-MMM-YY)
115	D2 (DD-MMM)
116	D3 (MMM-YY)
121	D4 (Full Int'l – varies with Configuration settings)
122	D5 (Partial Int'l – varies with Configuration settings)
119	T1 (HH:MM:SS AM/PM)
120	T2 (HH:MM:SS AM/PM)
123	T3 (Full Int'l – varies with Configuration settings)
124	T4 (Partial Int'l – varies with Configuration settings)
117	Literal (cell formula text)
118	Hidden (the result is a label consisting of the same number of spaces as the width)
127	Window's default numeric display format

for data entry, which makes it different from the other commands in this section, which deal with means of getting data into a macro. Nonetheless, like the other commands in this section, {Look} can furnish a keystroke for later use.

The {Look} command takes a single cell location as an argument. If a range is provided, Symphony uses the upper left cell of the range as the location in which to store the result. To understand how {Look} works and how to use it effectively in a macro, you must understand Symphony's "type-ahead buffer".

If you've used Symphony extensively and you're even a moderately fast typist, you've found yourself keying in commands for the next step just before Symphony changed the control panel to show the request for that input. Symphony incorporates a small buffer into its operating area in which it can store several keystrokes at a time. If we type more characters than this buffer can handle before Symphony has a chance to react to the first one, Symphony simply beeps and ignores us.

The {Look} command stores the *first* key entered into the type-ahead buffer into the location specified. We can then later retrieve it and program our macro to respond accordingly. This technique is often used to get a macro to stop executing without requiring a [Ctrl][Break].

We usually put the {Look} command into a loop (which we'll discuss in the next section) where the macro continues processing until a key is pressed. Here's an example.

```
COUNT_IT  {Let AA12,1}~          Put the numeric value 1 into AA12
LOOPIE    {Let AA12,+AA12+1}~    Increase the value of AA12 by 1
          {Look AA14}            See if a key has been pressed
          {IF AA14<>""}{Quit}    If a key has been pressed, stop,
          {Branch Loopie}        Otherwise go to LOOPIE again.
```

There are a couple of things here that we haven't discussed yet, but the macro should be fairly easy to follow. The first line puts a value of 1 into cell AA12, to give us someplace to start. The next line increments that value by 1, so that when the macro portion called LOOPIE starts executing, cell AA12 actually has the value 2 stored in it. The third line stores the first key pressed in location AA14 (so you can see the result; normally, you'd put this someplace outside the visible window range on the screen).

The next line, translated into English, would read something like this: "If cell AA14 is not empty (that is, is not equal to nothing, which is what two double quotation marks side by side mean), then a key has been pressed. This means that someone wants my attention, so let's stop and see what he wants''. If, on the other hand, the {Look} command checks location AA14 and finds it empty, it simply increments the value of cell AA12 by 1 and goes through the process again.

Try running the macro COUNT_IT and you'll undoubtedly get a quick understanding of how {Look} is used in such situations.

Controlling Program Flow

Left to their own devices, computer programs simply execute one statement after another, sequentially through the list of instructions of which they are composed. Any valuable program requires that this course of action be altered. Even in some of the relatively simple example macros we have discussed, we have had to use such techniques.

This section will examine a series of SCL macro commands designed to give you control over the flow of the program. These commands will permit you to:

- Use subroutines for repetitive execution of groups of commands
- Test for the presence or absence of a condition and alter the course of the program accordingly
- Carry out one set of instructions several times before continuing with the execution of the program
- Jump from one part of a program to another
- Set up a customized menu and take action based on menu selections
- Change program flow based on the occurrence of a specific type of error

We will discuss each of these methods of controlling program flow in the rest of this section of the Second Movement.

Using Subroutines

The subject of subroutine usage is common to most programming languages. The basic concept is discussed in the Prelude of this book. In the following discussion, we assume that you understand what a subroutine is and why subroutines are used in computer programs.

To use a subroutine in SCL, we simply use the name of the subroutine as if it were a command, placing it inside braces in the main SCL macro that calls it. The subroutine itself is defined exactly like any other macro, except that it must end with a {Return} statement. The effect of the {Return} statement is for the macro to pass program control back to the macro statement immediately following the one that calls the subroutine when the subroutine has finished execution.

For example, if you have a subroutine called ADJUST that establishes a correct decimal point and format for a value entered at the keyboard, you would use it simply by a macro code segment that looks something like this:

```
{macro1}        instruction 1
                {?}
                {ADJUST}
                instruction 2
                (etc.)
```

This macro would carry out whatever was required by instruction 1, then wait for the information to be entered from the keyboard. (In practice, we'd be more likely to use a {GetNumber} command here, but the principle is the same.) The subroutine ADJUST is then called by the statement that says {ADJUST}. When ADJUST has finished its assignment, program control returns to instruction 2.

In one sense, this use of subroutines by simply calling them by name makes SCL a language that you can extend with your own vocabulary. If you begin to do this, store these often used macro subroutines in a separate file from which they can be easily retrieved. Then by using the File Extract command, you can bring those "favorite" subroutines into any macro you are creating.

If all subroutines didn't require any information before they could be used, then there would be nothing more to learn about the design and use of subroutines in SCL. Many subroutines, however, require that some arguments be sent, or passed, to them to work.

For example, consider a macro that takes the two adjacent sides of a right triangle and calculates the length of the hypotenuse using the standard high school geometry formula $c^2 = a^2 + b^2$, where a and b are the adjacent sides and c is the hypotenuse. This function is simple enough to write in an SCL macro command. If we have the need to carry out this operation several times in a program, we could design a subroutine like this one:

```
Pythag1         {Define AE1:value,AE2:valuc}
                {Let AE3,+@SQRT((AE1*AE1)+AE2*AE2)}~
                {Return}
```

(We chose the name "Pythag1" because the name of the rule involved here is the Pythagorean Theorem.) To *use* this subroutine in a macro, we would write a section of code that looks like this:

```
label           {Let AB1,3}{Let AB2,4}
                {Pythag1 AB1,AB2}
                (Perform some calculation with value at AE3)
```

Notice that the second line of this macro segment calls the subroutine "Pythag1" and has two values following it. This line could be read to mean, "Use subroutine called Pythag1 on the values stored in cells AB1 and AB2". The first line of this segment stores specific values at those locations. We could, optionally, explicitly provide the values by coding:

```
{Pythag1 3,4}
```

Usually, however, we either don't know the values in advance or are having them entered from the keyboard or from some other macro or subroutine.

Notice that the first line of Pythag1 uses the new SCL keyword {Define}, followed by two arguments that are cell locations followed by colons and the word *value*.

{Define} tells SCL to set up following cell locations to contain information being passed to the subroutine by the macro that calls on the subroutine. Note that the number of cell locations in the {Define} command must match the number of arguments passed to the subroutine by the macro call, or an error condition will result.

The second line of the subroutine performs the calculation and places the result in cell AE3. The calling macro can do whatever it needs to with the result.

Step by Step Through a Subroutine's Use

It may be easier to follow what happens when a subroutine like Pythag1 is invoked if we simply walk through the process described above.

With Pythag1 defined and stored at some arbitrary location, assume that we are now executing a macro and have reached the point called "label". The next line of the macro we encounter says to store a 3 at location AB1 and a 4 at location AB2. The next line calls the subroutine Pythag1, passing to it as arguments the values contained at cell locations AB1 and AB2, which we know are the numbers 3 and 4, respectively.

The subroutine Pythag1 takes the value 3 stored in cell AB1 and puts it in cell AE1, then takes the number 4 stored in cell AB2 and puts it in cell AE2. The cells provide storage areas for these values while the subroutine works on them. The next line performs the calculation, squaring the value 3 to get 9, squaring the value 4 to get 16, adding the two together to get 25, and taking the square root (using the @SQRT function) to get 5. It stores this answer in location AE3 according to the instructions of the {Let} command. Control then returns to the macro, which performs whatever calculation is required on the value 5 stored at location AE3.

Any subroutine that uses arguments will usually be written as described above. The {Define} statement tells Symphony where to store the values passed to the subroutine by the calling macro. Notice that the "value" modifier ensures that SCL would store the *numbers* 3 and 4 in the cell locations indicated. Without the use of this modifier, SCL assumes that we want to store a *label* in the cell following the {Define} statement.

Conditional Processing: {If}

In most programs, we sometimes will want to take one of two alternate courses of action depending on whether a particular condition is true. For example, if a value is negative, we might want to print the word *Loss* on a report, and, if positive, to print the word *Profit*. The SCL {If} command provides the capability for this kind of processing. If you need to review the concept of conditional processing, the Prelude contains a brief discussion of the subject.

Essentially, an {If} command contains within its braces the condition to be tested. If that condition is found to be true, the macro commands appearing immediately adjacent to and on the same line as the {If} command will be executed. If the condition is found to be false, the macro skips the rest of the line and continues its execution with the next line in the macro.

Let's take the profit-loss example we sketched above and see how we would code a macro segment to do as described. We'll begin with a forthright implementation of the description. In a few moments, we'll find that we have one minor problem with this approach, and we will discuss how to fix it.

```
{If +A12>0}Profit
Loss
```

Assuming that we have stored the value we are interested in checking in cell address A12, the above macro segment looks at that value and compares it to the value zero. If it is greater than zero (that's what the ">" symbol means), the macro prints the word *Profit*. If the contents of cell A12 are either zero or negative, then the word *Loss* is printed, because the macro skips the rest of the line containing the {If} when it encounters a false condition.

As indicated earlier, there is a problem with this design. When SCL reaches the end of the first line and prints the word *Profit* — assuming that a profit was shown — it is not told what to do next. Because of the way Symphony behaves, the macro will simply go to the next line in order and execute it, resulting in a very confusing report, indeed, since the word *ProfitLoss* would appear where we really wanted only one or the other.

When we do not want the next line to be executed after the rest of the {If} command line is carried out, we end the {If} line with a command that alters the macro's flow of execution. Usually, this means a defined {Branch} command, which we will discuss shortly.

You may be wondering why Lotus didn't design the {If} statement so that if the condition is true, execution would automatically skip the next line. The reason is that quite often we design such code segments so that the second line is intended to be executed regardless of whether the condition is true. What we are trying to accomplish is to carry out some *additional* step or steps if the condition *is* true. Again, an example will help to clarify. Look at the following macro segment:

```
Testing         {GetNumber "Type a number smaller than 100",AE1}
                {If AE1<100}{Let AE2,+AE2+(.25*AE1}
                {Beep}{Blank AE1}{Branch AB1}
```

When it is run, this subroutine asks for a number smaller than 100. It then tests that number. If it is smaller than 100, as requested, it adds 25 percent of this new value to the value already stored in cell AE2. Whether the number is smaller than 100 or not, the system then beeps, erases the contents of cell AE1, and passes control to the line stored in cell AB1. Any value less than 100 will thus affect the content of cell AE2, while any other values will be ignored.

The point is that we often to want to carry out the second line of an {If} group regardless of whether the condition in the {If} command is true or false.

What Is Meant by "True" and "False"?

We have gone blithely along assuming that it is entirely obvious what we mean by saying that the conditional statement is true or false, but it is not quite that simple. Here are the clinkers.

The conditional expression we give SCL to interpret can be any numeric or string-valued expression or entry. The condition is determined by SCL to be false *only* if its evaluation results in a numerical zero answer or if the result is an empty cell. If the answer is a numeric value other than zero, *or* if it is a cell containing any value at all (even an empty string), the condition evaluates to true.

It is almost always true that the condition is the outcome of a logical comparison — that is, comparing two values to one another to see if they are equal or, if unequal, which is greater than the other. The technicality in the above paragraph is therefore seldom important.

We sometimes, however, use a noncomparative expression as the condition. For example, we might store a value in a particular cell as a result of a calculation and later wish to alter program flow based on whether that cell contains any value.

If the cell involved is QR111, then we could use this kind of statement:

```
{If QR111}{Branch DoIt}
{Branch ForgetIt}
```

Upon encountering this line, Symphony would examine cell QR111. If it was empty or contained a zero, the macro would drop to the second line and branch to someplace called "ForgetIt". Otherwise, control would pass to a place labeled "DoIt".

Interestingly enough, {If} statements often work together in these situations. For example, the value placed in cell QR111 might be the result of a conditional statement group like the one below:

```
{If result=14}{Let QR111, 0}{Branch xyz}
{Let QR111,1}
```

This group of statements checks a value in a cell location named "result", and, if the value is 14, it puts a zero in QR111. Otherwise, it puts a 1 in that cell. Later, when we test the contents of cell QR111, the result will depend originally on the value of the cell location named "result", which may in fact have changed in the meantime. But the importance of the original value has been, in effect, saved for later use.

Another interesting way {If} statements can work together is in a process called "nesting". We may want to test a particular cell's contents and compare it against several different values. In that event, we might code a statement group that looks like this:

```
{If +A14=1}January{Branch Elsewhere}
{If +A14=2}February{Branch Elsewhere}
etc.
```

This group of statements will put the name of a month into a report or cell location based on the number stored in cell A14. Notice that each statement ends with a {Branch} statement so that the next line doesn't have to be checked. This is not required because cell A14 certainly cannot contain more than one number to deal with, but it results in slightly more efficient execution of the macro segment.

Combining Logic Tests

Sometimes the test we need to carry out and evaluate in an {If} command must check for more than one particular condition. For example, if we want to see if the value contained in cell AA14 is a "y" (or a "Y"), and if it is, we want to see if cell AA15 has a zero in it. If *both* conditions are true, we want to do a particular thing. We could write an SCL macro to do this as follows:

```
Start     {If AA14='y'}{Branch Step2}
          {If AA14='Y'}{Branch Step2}
          (instruction1)
```

```
Step2       {If AA15=0}{Branch Step3}
            (instruction2){Branch End}
Step3       (instruction3)
            (instruction4)
End         (instruction5)
```

This is a fairly complex set of {If} statements. The first two check location AA14. If that location contains either a "Y" or a "y", then the macro branches to the step named Step2. Otherwise, instruction 1 is carried out (and should end with a branch to somewhere else in the program to avoid the "fall-through" to Step2). If AA14 is *either* a capital or lowercase letter "y", then the code at the label Step2 checks location AA15 to see if it is zero. If so, it passes control to the location named Step3; otherwise, it passes control to the label named End. In the former case, instructions 3 and 4 are executed before instruction 5; in the latter case, only instruction 5 is executed.

If we were to put all of this into an English sentence, we would say, "If cell AA14 contains a 'y' *or* a 'Y' *and* cell AA15 is zero, then pass control to Step3; otherwise, jump to the label called End."

It is practically as straightforward in SCL using the logical operators #AND# and #OR#. The above example reduced to a more usable form would look like this:

```
{If (((+AA14='y')#OR#(+AA14='Y'))#AND#(+AA15=0))}{Branch Step3}
{Branch End}
```

Notice the use of parentheses to force SCL to first evaluate the expressions that check cell AA14 and then AA15 and then combine the results to determine if control should be passed to the routine at label Step3 or the one at label End.

Use #AND# and #OR# to string together combinations of conditions that must be met for a particular processing step to take place. Other than remembering to use the parentheses correctly, this is both more efficient to write and easier to understand. Correct use of parentheses comes with careful thinking about what you want examined, in what order, and with practice in writing SCL macros.

Jumping to Another Location: {Branch}

Up to this point, we have used the {Branch} command several times without explaining it. Now we will turn our attention to this useful and very straightforward SCL command. The {Branch} statement functions like a GOTO statement in many other programming languages (see the Prelude for more detail). It unconditionally transfers control of the program from the line it is currently executing to one located elsewhere in the worksheet area containing macros. Its most common use is in conjunction with the {If} statement.

Let's examine a fairly common use of the {Branch} command in conjunction with an {If} command group. If we want SCL to execute several lines of instruction when the condition we provide is true and several other lines of code if the condition is false, we might handle it as follows:

```
startit         {If AB123<0}{Branch Negative}
                (instruction1)
                (instruction2)
                (instruction3)
                {Branch NextStep}
Negative        (instruction 4)
                (instruction 5)
                (instruction 6)
                (instruction 7)
NextStep        (instruction 8)
                etc.
```

This macro segment instructs Symphony to look at the contents of cell AB123. If the value there is less than zero (that is, negative), the macro will pass control to the location called "negative", four lines below. In other words, if AB123 is negative, the macro will execute instructions 4-7 and then continue processing with instruction 8. If, on the other hand, cell AB123 is zero or positive, the macro will carry out instructions 1-3 and then jump to the location named "Next Step" and carry out instruction 8.

Where is "NextStep"?

SCL will permit us to use *names* for places to send control with a {Branch} instruction only if we have used the Range Name command to inform Symphony which labels are associated with which sheet locations. In the above example, we would have used some technique, probably the Range Name Label Right sequence, to inform SCL of the existence of all of the labels in a macro group. We can then use the labels in place of the cell addresses themselves. It is, however, perfectly valid to use the cell address in a {Branch} command, as in:

```
{Branch AJ44}
```

The real danger in using cell addresses rather than range name labels is that, if we later modify the sheet by inserting or deleting rows in the range where the macro is stored, we can cause ourselves considerable headache with macros that used to work but no longer do! We *strongly* recommend using range-naming techniques to prevent the occurrence of such problems.

It may be obvious to you, but let's reiterate that the only difference between a {Branch} instruction and a subroutine call is that the latter returns to the place from which it was invoked, while a {Branch} is irrevocable. The only way to get back to the neighborhood from which the {Branch} occurred is with yet another explicit {Branch} command.

Repetitive Processing in Loops: {For}

When writing SCL macros, you will often want to carry out a specific set of instructions a defined number of times before proceeding with the straight-ahead macro processing. This process is called "looping" because the program seems to loop back onto itself some number of times before continuing.

In SCL, as in most other programming languages, the expression that triggers such a loop is the {For} instruction. It will be easier to understand how SCL handles this if we first digress a bit and discuss how BASIC handles FOR loops. In BASIC, if we wanted to have ten values entered into a location, we would write a loop that looks something like this:

```
FOR COUNTER=1 TO 10
PRINT "Enter a value:"
INPUT VALUE
(do something with VALUE)
NEXT COUNTER
```

The key words to look at here are: *FOR, COUNTER, TO* and *NEXT*. Translated into English, this program segment would read as follows: "Start a counter called COUNTER with a value of 1. Do the steps between here and the NEXT statement. When you get to the NEXT statement, add 1 to the value of the counter called COUNTER. If it hasn't yet reached 10, do the same thing again. When it reaches 10, jump to the line just below the NEXT statement and continue the program."

It should be noted that we left out one feature of what for obvious reasons is called a FOR...NEXT loop. We could add a value called STEP to the first line of this group of BASIC statements so that instead of incrementing the counter by 1 each time through the loop, we would increment it by 10 or some other arbitrary value. There are times when we wish to do this, though they are relatively infrequent.

SCL handles {For} loops in much the same way, except that it compresses the ideas of the counter's starting and ending values, the step, and the steps to be carried out all into one statement. The above BASIC routine could be written in an SCL macro as follows:

```
{For COUNTER,1,10,1,GetNames}
```

The location named "GetNames" would then contain the steps necessary to request ten values to be entered (probably just a {GetLabel} command or a {Get} command combined with some cursor movement to change the current position of the cell pointer).

The first argument in the {For} loop command is the location where the counter is to be stored by the program. You do not need to put anything in the counter location. You do need to use the Range Name Label Right technique (or the equivalent) to give the cell location a name or else use the cell address explicitly. The next argument is the starting value for the counter, the third argument is the finishing number at which processing should stop, and the next number is the value by which to increment the counter each time through the loop (the equivalent of the STEP option in BASIC). In SCL, this fourth argument — the STEP equivalent — is not optional; it must be provided explicitly.

The final argument in the {For} loop construction is the starting location of the routine to be carried out by the {For} loop. Again, we can use an explicit cell reference or a prenamed location's range name. We recommend the latter.

Let's look at how we might use such a {For} loop in a realistic application involving SCL. If we wanted users of our macro to provide labels for ten consecutive cells in the sheet — which we might do to permit customizing the layout for the user's own needs — we could write a macro segment that would look like this:

```
Count          (empty cell)
Loop           {For Count,1,10,1,CustomNames}
               (instruction 1)
               (instruction 2)
               (blank line)
CustomNames    {?}~{Right}
               (blank line)
```

This macro segment will store a 1 in the location labeled "Count", then execute the routine at the location named "CustomNames". That routine uses the {?} to get some keyboard input for the current cell location, then increments the location by one to the right.

The main macro segment then adds 1 to the value at the location labeled "Count", resulting in that location having a 2 in it, checks to see if it's a 10 yet, then executes the line at location "CustomNames" again. This process continues until all ten labels have been entered by the user.

Menu Creation and Use

In one sense, designing and using menus in SCL is another means of controlling program flow. But in a broader sense, it is the "stuff" of which your own special SCL macros can truly be made. By making your own menus and controlling the program's flow based on the user's interaction with them in the same way that Symphony does, you can give your macros a polished, professional look.

This section begins with an overview of menus and their use in macros. We will then explain how to set up a menu in a worksheet for later use by your macros. Next, we will discuss the two special SCL commands, {MenuBranch} and {MenuCall}, that enable us to manipulate the environment and control macro execution via menu selections.

Menus: An Overview

Figure 11 provides a general look at how a menu is usually designed and used in an SCL macro environment. In that figure, the macro called "mainl", after carrying out several instructions, executes a {MenuBranch}

```
main 1  instruction 1
        instruction 2
        {MenuBranch}
        (blank line)
```

address of menu = upper left corner

choice 1	**choice 2**	**choice 3**	**choice 4**	**choice 5**
	(text explanations of each choice here)			
command	command	command	command	command
command	command	command	command	command
command	command	command	command	command

Last command in menu macro is often {Branch} or {Return}

Figure 11
Menu Macro Diagram

command that names the starting location of the menu to be used. The address of this menu is the upper left corner of the menu itself.

Each row of the menu contains something specific. The top line contains the menu selections' names, that is, the choices that will be displayed in the control panel. The second row contains the longer explanations of each menu option. This is the text that will be displayed across the top line of the control panel when that menu selection is highlighted by cursor movement or by typing the first letter of the menu option.

Below each menu choice is the set of macro commands that will be executed if that particular selection is made.

Figure 12 provides a specific example of the generalized menu operation shown in Figure 11. If you have access to Symphony at the moment, type in the screen shown in Figure 12, proofread it carefully, save it, and then begin to use it. Notice that we begin with address AA1 so that your addresses will match ours.

After you have typed in the menu macro shown in Figure 12, use the Range Name Label Right option to define "start", "Help", and "Test" to be valid range labels. Then save the macro for later use.

```
AB3: '{GetLabel "Main macro.  Press RETURN.",AA20}~{Branch Start}              SHEET

         AA                AB                      AC            AD        AE
1    start            {GetLabel "Press RETURN to start things.",AA20}~
2                     {MenuCall AA5}
3                     {GetLabel "Main macro.  Press RETURN.",AA20}~{Branch Start}
4
5    Help             Test                 Quit
6    Get Help Here    Carry Out Test       Return to Main Macro
7    {Help}           {Test}               {Return}
8    {Return}         {Return}
9
10   Help             This routine could be set up~{Down}
11                    to provide the user with help screens~{Down}
12                    or additional menus.~{Down}
13                    Press any key to go on.
14                    {Get AA20}
15
16   Test             Here again, we could provide some~{Down}
17                    testing input, display or check ~{Down}
18                    a value, etc.~{Down}
19                    Press any key to go on.
20                    {Get AA20}
                                                                           MAIN
22-Feb-85   10:10 PM
```

Figure 12
Sample Menu Macro

Now position the cursor outside this range (using the [Home] key) and press the [F7] key to invoke the macro. Type the macro's name, "start", and press [↵]. The control panel should read "Press RETURN to start things". (If it doesn't do so, use [Esc] to return to the place where you can use the [F5], or the [Goto] key to get back to cell AA1 and check to see if you have produced exactly the macro shown in Figure 12.)

Press the [↵] key, and the control panel will be replaced by the following:

```
Get Help Here
Help  Test  Quit
```

The word *Help* is highlighted on the screen; that is, the cursor is presently positioned on it. Press the [↵] key and the message that appears in the macro called "Help" is printed first in the control panel area and then, row by row, in the sheet area beginning with cell A1. In the final implementation of such a menu, we'd probably use a {PanelOff} command

```
A4:                                                                    LABEL
Press any key to go on.
┌──────A──────B──────C──────D──────E──────F──────G──────H──────┐
1   This routine could be set up
2   to provide the user with help screens
3   or additional menus.
4
5
6
7
8
9
10
11
12
13
14
15
16
17
18
19
20
└─────────────────────────────────────────────────────────MAIN┘
22-Feb-85  10:11 PM                  Macro
```

Figure 13
Results of Selecting Help Option

here to speed up the processing and make it look cleaner, but for now this is easier to use to see what is going on, and the whole macro fits in one screen.

Notice that the last line of the macro displays in the control panel so that when the Help menu option has been selected and its run has been completed, the screen looks like Figure 13.

At this point, pressing the [↵] key will result in the message "Main macro. Press RETURN." being displayed in the control panel. Pressing [↵] will start the process over again. As we've designed this (and we do not suggest you do this as a rule) the only way to stop the macro is by pressing the [Ctrl][Break] keys.

Try each menu choice and you'll be able to see what is happening as you trace through the macro listing shown in Figure 12.

All in all, this is an awfully slick way to give your macros the Symphony-like feel that makes users comfortable with the operation of them because they're doing the same kinds of things they do all the time when running Symphony.

One other point about menus must be made. If we use a {PanelOff} command to suppress displays in the control panel area during macro execution and then call a menu into effect, the menu call *overrides* the {PanelOff} command and writes the menu information into the control panel anyway. When the menu processing is complete, the {PanelOff} situation returns to the expected state (that is, nothing is displayed in the control panel area) until we explicitly change it or call another menu.

With this overview behind us, let us examine in greater detail the rules for setting up the macro in the sheet in the first place.

Setting Up the Menu

As we saw in Figures 11 and 12, the menu itself is simply a group of labels stored in a particular format in the sheet environment within which we are creating the menu and its associated macros. There, because it made it easy to display all in one screen, we placed the menu in the same set of rows and columns as the macro itself. But we suggest that you put the menu(s) off to the side in an area of its (their) own. This will make your programs much easier to follow.

The first line of the menu definition area contains the names of the menu options as they will display when the menu is executed. There are several important things to remember about this menu design; some are really common-sense considerations when you stop to think about them, but they are worth stating explicitly.

1. Keep these names short. The total number of characters made up of all these names must fit across the control panel.
2. Start each menu selection's name with a different uppercase letter or a number. This will enable users to pick the menu option the same way they do in Symphony, by typing just the first letter of the option's name. Don't use lowercase letters because Symphony will then let that option be chosen only by cursor positioning. And don't use the same initial letter for menu choices, because Symphony will always assume that the user wants to choose the first one that appears (from left to right) each time that letter is typed.
3. There is a maximum of eight menu choices in any one menu.
4. Do not leave any cells across the first row of a menu blank until you reach the end of the menu line. The next cell to the immediate right of your menu line must be blank. If SCL encounters a blank cell in, say, the third position, it will assume that the menu ends there.

Aside from these simple rules, use your imagination to create powerful and easy-to-understand menus. They will be a very helpful guide to the use of your macros.

The *second* line of the menu definition area contains the textual explanation for the menu option. This information will display across the top line of the control panel when the user or Symphony highlights the menu choice. These explanations can be as long as one screen width, though you will usually keep them somewhat shorter than this.

One problem caused by the presence of longer than usual labels is that they are seldom entirely visible, and seem to run into each other if the normal column widths are used. We suggest that you widen those columns in the menu definition area to permit you to see all of the textual information. This technique is useful when programming the macro and designing the menu. Once the macro is implemented and in use, condensing the columns back to normal size will not cause a problem.

There is only one other rule about these top-line explanations. Every menu option choice must have an explanation area associated with it. Empty cells in the second row of a menu definition area will produce an error. If you don't wish to provide a textual explanation, simply use a blank as the explanation. Blank cells are permitted; totally empty ones are not.

Once these two lines of the menu definition area are completed, simply code the macro statements you wish the macro to execute in the event a given choice is selected. Sometimes, these will be short macros that are complete in themselves. More often, however, you will program a {Branch} or call a routine name in these areas because this technique keeps your programs easy to read. As you will see in the next portion of our discussion about menus, you can use a {Return} as the last line of any or all of these macros if you use a {MenuCall} to invoke the menu instead of a {MenuBranch}.

As with all macros, the last line between these menu-selected macros and any following text must be blank. Otherwise, SCL will simply attempt to keep executing macro statements in the column until it finally runs into a blank or an error condition.

{MenuBranch} and {MenuCall}

With the menu definition area properly set up, to cause a menu to appear magically in the control panel and give the user control of the macro via a menu we need only issue either a {MenuBranch} or a {MenuCall} command. Both commands take a single argument, which is the address of the upper left corner location of the menu. This can obviously be either the specific cell address (as in AA5 in Figure 12) or a name.

If you want to use names rather than explicit cell addressing to point to a menu, don't place a name in, for example, cell AA4 and the first line of the menu itself in AA5 and then use a Range Name sequence to name the range from AA4. The result will be a menu being displayed with one choice, the name of the range, and one text explanation, which is the first line of what you intended the menu to be. Instead, use the Range Name Create (instead of Label) sequence and give the menu range an easily remembered name. Then code this into the {MenuBranch} or {MenuCall} command line.

The only difference between {MenuBranch} and {MenuCall}, as you can probably guess, is that {MenuBranch} carries out a *branch* to the menu control area, while {MenuCall} treats the control passage as a subroutine from which a {Return} command can cause control to return to the next line. Which one you use is mostly a matter of personal preference. You can always force a return to the location you wish, even if you use a {Menu-Branch} command, by using an explicit {Branch} instruction with the appropriate address.

If the person using your macro should press the [Esc] key when your menu is displayed, control passes to the next line after the call to the menu, whether that call is a branch or a subroutine execution. That is why in our example menu macro in Figure 12, we could not get out of the menu by pressing the [Esc] key. When we did, the next statement was executed, which simply required pressing the [↵] key and then branching back to the beginning of the macro. This technique, combined with the use of the {BreakOff} instruction, can secure your macro from a user ever breaking out of it without using the method you've provided in your code.

Error Handling

In virtually every program, someone can find a way to make a fatal mistake while using it. That is an adage among programmers — and is mainly true.

This section will primarily discuss the use of the SCL {OnError} command. But before we do that, let's discuss how to avoid creating situations in which errors are likely to occur and then explain how to handle errors in general. Then we'll be ready to look at SCL's provision that enables us to manage error conditions wisely.

Anticipating Misunderstanding

People who design and program SCL macros or BASIC programs (or any other kind of computer program, for that matter) assume too much knowledge and understanding on the part of the person using the program or macro. The first cardinal rule of avoiding errors in programming is:

> Don't assume anything about what people who use your program will know or understand about the program, how to use it, or what the terminology means.

The control panel (where most of our helps will be displayed in most of our macros) permits a relatively limited number of characters to be displayed. But don't be so terse that users will have no idea what you expect them to do next.

For example, "Type RETURN key" may have an entirely different meaning from "Press RETURN key". The first message may give the impression that you expect the words *RETURN key* to be entered at the keyboard. That is almost certainly *not* what you intended. The second message requires only one additional character and is far clearer. Most users of the IBM PC will understand it.

Another source of problems can be avoided if you design your macros to be explicit about how they obtain data from the keyboard and how they ensure that the data is what they expected to receive. For example, if you *need* a number between 1 and 10, and any other number will have unanticipated or dire consequences, *check* the input after it's received. A macro segment something like the one below will do nicely.

```
Input  {GetNumber "Enter a number between 1 and 10".,AA20}~
{If AA20>0#AND# AA20<11}{Good}
{Bad}
```

Don't just assume that because you *asked* for a number between 1 and 10, your instructions will be followed. It isn't always a matter of misunderstanding — sometimes a key sticks or a finger slips. Don't create needless problems by failing to provide such useful checks on keyboard input.

A final hint about error anticipation will suffice to make the point clear. If an option in a macro will have disastrous consequences if invoked by accident, build in a second level of safety.

For example, suppose you have a menu option that erases a whole range of data in one keystroke. When the option is selected, you might add a segment of code something like this:

```
Are you SURE you want to erase all that data (Y/N):
{Get AA20}~
{If AA20<>"Y"}{Branch TryAgain}
{DeleteIt}
```

Symphony does a good job of handling these kinds of situations. If you use the program a lot, you'll gain a feel for when to use such techniques.

How to Handle Errors

Given that you have anticipated all the errors you can by the methods described above, how do you handle the mistakes encountered by Symphony, whether you have created proper conditions for handling them or not? It is easiest simply to acknowledge that the error has occurred and request the entry again, this time in accordance with the macro's needs.

An example will help clarify the meaning of this advice.

We just created a situation in which a number between 1 and 10 was requested. We provided part of the macro segment that would handle the problem by checking input to ensure that it was between 1 and 10. If so, it branched to a location called "Good"; if not, it went to another location called "Bad". Here is a sample of the kind of code you could have placed at the location called "Bad" to handle the error:

```
Bad        {Beep}
           Oops! The number must be between 1 and 10.  Try again.
           Press RETURN. ←Should be one line in SCL macro
           {Get AA123}~
           {Branch Input}
```

Now when a number outside the acceptable range is entered, a message will be displayed in the control panel area. When the ↵ key is pressed, the program will again ask for a number between 1 and 10, the input will be checked again, and the same process will be repeated.

This is the usual method for handling errors. To provide more assistance, move to an unused area of the worksheet, display a more detailed "help screen", and then clear that area and return to processing. The technique is the same; the only difference is in the amount of information furnished.

An infuriating way of handling errors is to cause the macro simply to {Beep} and reask the question. This approach is used by more programmers than we'd like to meet and is an unsatisfactory way to solve the problem. It leads to frustration on the part of users who can't understand what they're doing wrong.

A more sophisticated way to manage input errors is simply to ask for reentry of the information unless the error recurs some arbitrary number of times. At that point, a more detailed explanation of the problem is given. The following skeletal macro segment provides insight into this idea.

```
        {For Tracker,1,3,1,Input1}
        {MoreHelp}
Input1  {GetNumber "Give me a number less than 100".,AA99}~
        {If AA99<100}{Branch Continue}
        The number MUST be smaller than 100.  Press RETURN.
        {Get AA98}~
        {Return}
```

In this example, the {For} loop causes the input process labeled Input1 to repeat three times. Each time through the loop, the program checks the input in cell AA99. If acceptable, it branches out of the loop with the branch to the {Continue} routine. If the {For} loop executes three times and program control has not transferred to {Continue}, the line after the {For} loop executes and calls a subroutine called MoreHelp.

These are the *general* methods for dealing with errors caused by input mistakes we should be able to anticipate. But another class of errors is composed of program errors that produce Symphony error messages. That is the subject of the next section.

Handling Symphony Errors: {OnError}

The best example of a Symphony error that a macro might encounter while executing is a "File Not Found" mistake, which occurs when we try to open a file the first time someone uses a macro and the file has not yet been created. This is a common problem plaguing programmers in *any* language. SCL provides a straightforward way out of such situations.

If Symphony encounters an error such as "File Not Found", and our macro does not have an {OnError} command telling Symphony what to do if it encounters such a mistake, Symphony simply halts the execution of our macro. That is known as a "fatal error".

Use the {OnError} command to suppress the printing of the error message on the screen and the inadvertent termination of the program.

The {OnError} command has one required argument and one optional argument. The *required* argument is the first one that follows the word *OnError*. It tells Symphony where to begin executing your macro if an error condition is encountered. In effect, it is a {Branch} command that is used by Symphony only if it runs into an error condition.

The *optional* argument is an address where you'd like Symphony to store the error message it would normally have displayed at the bottom of the screen if it had not intercepted that message because of your {OnError} command. We will almost always want Symphony to store that error message, because without it we cannot know what error occurred.

Let's use our "File Not Found" error as an example. Since we intend to create the file if it doesn't yet exist and will save the sheet under that filename later, we want to ignore that error if it is encountered. We may also wish to place a value in a location so that, when we later do a File Save command, we won't accidentally code a tilde for a ↵ when asked for the filename since none has been provided.

```
         {OnError Handler,MessageSpot}
Step1    (instruction1)
Step2    (instruction2)
Handler  {If MessageSpot='File Not Found'}{NewFile}
         {Beep}{Beep}Fatal Error.  Call Programmer.
         {Wait @NOW+@TIME(0,0,30)}{Beep}{Beep}{Quit}
NewFile  {Let AA5,1}{Blank MessageSpot}
         {OnError Handler,MessageSpot}
         {Branch Step2}
```

In the above example macro segment, we assume that the instruction called "instruction1" at location Step1 is the one that causes the error to occur. As a result, thanks to the {OnError} statement, Symphony stores the message "File Not Found" in the address named MessageSpot and then passes control to the routine labeled "Handler".

"Handler" checks to be sure that the message is what we anticipated. If it is a "Disk Full" or any other error we had not anticipated, we may want to react differently to it. If it isn't what we anticipated, it beeps a couple of times, displays a frightening message (we don't recommend scaring people this way, but in an example, it's kind of fun!), beeps again after a 30-second delay, and ends the macro.

But if the error is the one we expected, we pass control to the area labeled "NewFile". There, we store a number 1 at a location to be used later to determine if we created a new file this time or worked with an old one, reset the {OnError} conditions (we'll explain why in a moment), and then branch to the next line we want the program to execute.

When we finally call for the File Save procedure, we can check location AA5 to see if it has a 1 in it. If it does, then we won't press ↵ with a tilde to indicate that we want to save the file under the same name we retrieved it from earlier. We also won't have the macro include the "y" we'd normally supply as an answer to the next question about replacing the existing file of the same name. That code segment could resemble these lines:

```
          {S}fs
          {If AA5=1}FILE1~{Step3}
          ~Y
Step3     (instructions)
```

We invoke the File Save option from the Services menu and then, if AA5 has a 1 in it, meaning we created this file with this macro run, we type in the filename FILE1, press ↵ with the tilde, and pass control to the instructions at Step3. Otherwise, we simply press ↵ to accept the filename by which we retrieved the file "Y" to indicate that it's okay to replace the old version, and then continue processing with the steps beginning at the next line, labeled "Step3".

Why the Second {OnError}?

Recall that when we discussed the {OnError} example above, we had the error-handling routine include another {OnError} command. This is necessary because SCL uses each {OnError} command it encounters only once. If an error occurs, Symphony does as it is instructed but cancels that {OnError} instruction. We want to ensure that if a similar error occurs, we exit the macro in an orderly manner, so we give the macro another {OnError} command in the error-handling routine itself. This is excellent programming practice.

The {OnError} command should always be placed in the macro before the place at which the error could occur. It is perfectly acceptable to include more than one {OnError} command in the macro, even though some of them are never executed.

Any {OnError} situation remains in effect until another is encountered or an error is handled. Thus we may have a situation in which we want to check for a "File Not Found" error, and then, some lines later, we might be more concerned about a "Disk Full" condition. We could put separate {OnError} statements in both places to handle the errors if they should arise.

One error condition can arise during execution of a macro that we may always want to check for. If the Ctrl Break key sequence is pressed during macro execution, that creates an error condition. No error message is produced, which makes this sticky to handle. The best solution is to issue a {BreakOff} command (described earlier in this chapter) at the beginning of the macro. The Ctrl Break key sequence cannot then be used to interrupt the macro.

Using @Functions in Macros

We have shown several example macros that use the powerful Symphony @functions. All of Symphony's @functions may be used inside macros exactly as if they were simply typed into the SHEET environment. In most cases, they are part of formulas and must be preceded by a plus sign, but that is not always the case.

Detailed instructions on the use of @functions are covered in Chapter 13 of the *Symphony Reference Manual* and in Chapter 7 of the *Symphony How-To Manual* (Cambridge: Lotus Development Corp., 1984).

Telecommunications Macro Instructions

We have now discussed all but two of SCL's macro commands. They are specialized macro commands used only when we are using Symphony as a communications program to link our home computers to other systems. This discussion will assume that you already understand how to establish communications, use a modem, access other computers, and the like. If that is not the case, these two macro commands are not likely to be part of your current programming requirements.

{Phone}

The {Phone} macro is straightforward and useful. As you might expect, it causes Symphony to dial the phone connected to your modem. Naturally, it assumes that you have connected the modem to the computer and to the phone line and that you have configured Symphony properly to use the modem. If those assumptions are not correct, no connection will be established.

{Phone} requires one argument, either a number or a reference to a cell containing a number. The number must consist only of digits, commas, and the letter "T" or "P". All but the numbers are optional. Commas are used to cause the phone dialing process to pause: one comma produces a one-second pause. This is often necessary if you are dialing out through a central PBX system where you must dial 9 (or some other number), wait for a dial tone, and then dial the outside number.

The use of "P" and "T" defines for Symphony whether the phone should be dialed using "pulse" or "tone" techniques. Most phones today are tone phones, and Symphony assumes that you want it to use tone dialing unless you tell it otherwise.

Although the {Phone} command is identical to the COMM menu Phone Call command, it has a distinct advantage: it can be used outside the COMM environment.

An obvious use of this command would be in a database (FORM) application where you have stored the names, addresses, and phone numbers of your clients and friends. You could write a macro that finds a specific individual, retrieves his or her telephone number, places it into a cell, and then automatically dials the number.

If the {Phone} command successfully connects with the phone on the other end of the line, the statements following it on the same macro line are executed. If no connection is made, processing skips to the line below the {Phone} command line.

{Handshake}

This is a confusing and relatively useless SCL macro on which we will not spend much time. It is identical in use to the COMM menu's Log-in and Settings Capture Range commands and cannot be used outside the COMM environment, so it is difficult to see what advantages it offers.

{Handshake} takes three required arguments and an optional fourth one. The first two are the send string and receive string, respectively. Both must be enclosed in double quotation marks and may be up to 240 characters long. The third is the number of seconds Symphony is to wait after transmitting the send string before it receives the receive string or times out. The final argument is an optional Capture Range where any data received by the system between the transmission of the send string and the receipt of the receive string will be stored.

This command can be used to automate a log-in sequence to a computer where we want the system to place the call at a nonpeak or preassigned hour, perform a certain task, capture certain data, and log back off. As we have indicated, these same activities can be managed from SCL macro commands inside the COMM window, which makes the {Handshake} command seemingly useless.

At least *we* haven't found any particular use for it. If you have, let us know!

Summary

This concludes the Second Movement of our Symphony orchestration. In this section, we have dealt with every SCL macro command in some depth. Using examples and format definitions, we have provided you with complete information on the use of the more than 30 commands. We have also discussed error-handling techniques and the use of menus.

The new commands that Symphony 1.1 adds to your repertoire can be found in Coda C. You will find a discussion of how to use them, and how to incorporate them into your applications there. You may want to go through Coda C before moving on to the Third Movement.

We are now prepared for the Third Movement, in which we will examine the creation of several real-life, useful macros and analyze them step by step.

THIRD MOVEMENT

Integrated Diversions

This third movement of our orchestration of Symphony will begin to combine various aspects of different kinds of windows and work environments to create truly integrated applications. The chapter is divided into three parts:

1. It begins with a discussion of windows, which are the real key to understanding and implementing integrated applications.
2. Then it presents some basic ideas about organizing our work so that integration becomes easy to manage.
3. Finally, it presents discussions of three potential applications where integration would be significant.

Discussion of the three applications does not include full-blown macros. Instead it focuses on providing basic design clues and partial macro listings of some of the more complex and/or interesting ideas incorporated in them. The discussion also provides hints for how to take the ideas and create full applications macros from them.

Windows: Key to Integration

It would be difficult to think of Symphony as an "integrated" program if not for the fact that a large number of several different types of windows can be created and manipulated on the screen at one time. That facility easily demonstrates the highly integrated nature of the program itself and provides for the integrated products we create using it as the base.

This section undertakes three important tasks:

1. It reviews the window management techniques with which you are probably already familiar from your work with Symphony outside the macro world.
2. The section then presents some important considerations to take into account as you create integrated applications that use combinations of SHEET, DOC, and FORM windows.
3. Finally, the section offers guidelines on the use of GRAPH windows with the other types of windows.

The section deliberately avoids discussing COMM windows in the integration phase of presentation. COMM environments are an important part of the integration process, but no significant design considerations connected with their use concern us at this point.

Review of Window Management Techniques

If you've had much experience dealing with Symphony outside the current experience of macro creation, you've undoubtedly created, used, manipulated, sized, restricted, and moved around among various windows on the screen at once. The following section will constitute a good review for you. If, however, you feel a little bewildered about the use of windows in Symphony, this information will prove essential to understanding the rest of the discussion of Symphony in this book.

One Worksheet, Many Windows

The most fundamental idea in Symphony is sometimes difficult to convey: **everything we are doing on the screen at any one time is all taking place inside one gigantic worksheet.**

No matter how many windows we create and use, of how many types, showing how many parts of the sheet environment, there is but one work-

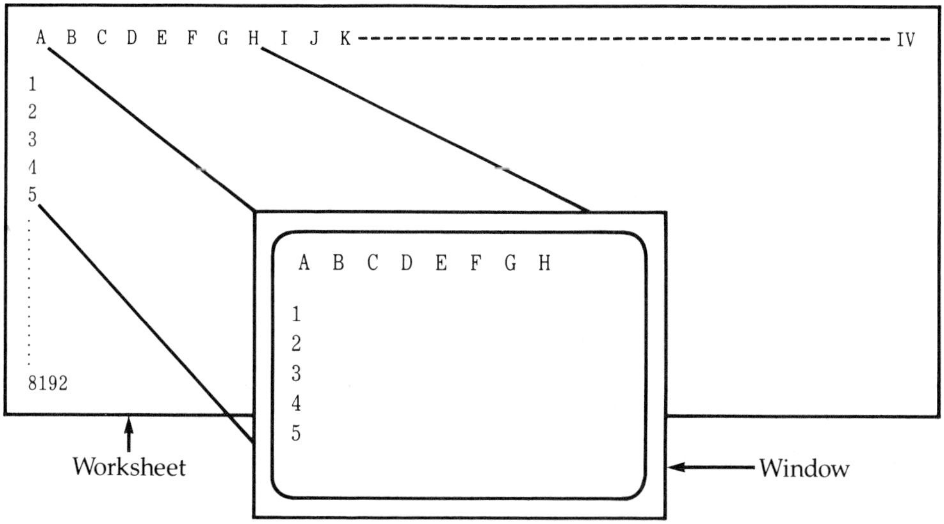

Figure 14
Symphony Worksheet and Window

sheet in memory at a time. This restriction can be overcome through the use of the Macro Library Manager add-in though (See Coda C).

Symphony can make use of up to 10 files of information at one time with this add-in. This is done by loading information that had been saved to a library (.MLB) file using the Macro Library Manager Menu.

Windows are openings into the worksheet as in Figure 14; they don't look into the library environment which is separate from the worksheet.

The various types of windows, or environments, each take a somewhat different *view* of the same data. This can be primarily seen in the way the [Menu] key operates in each environment. The commands available for dealing with the same data differ from one environment to the other. There is, of course, a good reason for this: if data is viewed differently, it is also manipulated differently.

For example, the Justify option on the DOC environment's menu would be useless in a SHEET environment. Paragraph justification doesn't mean anything in an environment where information is stored in rows and columns rather than in sentences and paragraphs.

If you have not worked collectively with at least the DOC, SHEET, FORM, and GRAPH environments, you may want to pause here and do a little experimenting. You can gain an appreciation for how different environments deal with common data if you will undertake this little process:

1. Bring up Symphony in a SHEET environment. Unless you've explicitly changed the starting environment, this one will automatically come up when you start Symphony.
2. Enter some data into the SHEET environment. Give yourself several rows of information, several cells wide, to manipulate. It will then be easier to see how the various environments deal with this data.
3. Use the Menu [F10] key to display the major options available in the SHEET environment. These may be familiar to you, but take a moment to refresh your memory about them.
4. Now use the Type key, [Alt][F10], to change the window type. When you press this key, a new control panel display appears, listing the five types of window. Move the menu pointer to one of these and press [↵]. The window will change to the new type. The mode indicator in the upper right corner of the display will change to reflect the new window type.
5. Again, use the Menu [F10] key to explore the available possibilities.
6. Notice that when you choose the GRAPH, FORM, or COMM environment, no data is displayed in the window called MAIN with which you are working. In each case, you must define other parameters before such a display will be shown. In the GRAPH environment, for example, you must tell Symphony where the data to be graphed are located, what kind of graph you want to use, and so on. In FORM mode, you must define for Symphony where the various *ranges* containing the data are located, describe them, format them for reporting purposes, and so on. We assume you already know how to do all those things. If you don't, learn them or else determine not to use these environments in your macro programming.
7. After exploring all the menus, clear the worksheet with a {Services}n(ew)y(es) sequence. You will then begin your work with a clean worksheet.

Creating, Naming, and Using Windows

There are two ways to create a new window on the Symphony display. The first uses the {Services}w(indow)p(ane) options to split the current window into two or four "panes". This leaves the original window intact (though reduced in size) and produces one to three additional windows, which Symphony automatically labels with the numbers 1, 2, and 3, clockwise from the upper right. You can then rename, change the type of, resize, and otherwise manipulate the three new windows created in this way.

A second way to create a new window uses the {Services}w(indow)c(reate) sequence. For most of the purposes we have in creating new windows, this is the preferred method. It maximizes flexibility in dealing with the various windows, and it forces us to consider what kind of windows and environments we want to deal with and where in the sheet environment we should locate them.

You've already seen how to create a window by using a macro in the first macro example presented in the Prelude of this book. Even though you may already understand how to create new windows, the following brief discussion will serve as a refresher. If you don't need a refresher, turn to the section labeled "Sizing and Moving Windows", which you should read regardless of how experienced you are in using Symphony windows.

Having chosen the {Services}w(indow)c(reate) sequence to set up a new window on the display, you must go through a series of steps to complete the definition of the window. These steps are discussed in the following instructions.

1. Enter a new window name. Just type in the new name. It is illegal to attempt to create a new window having the same name as one that already exists in this sheet environment.
2. Select a window type. This type can be changed at any time. You should plan this step and know exactly which type of window will best serve the purpose you have in mind for creating this window.
3. Describe the window's shape and position on the screen. Use the pointer movement keys and the [⇆] and period keys to anchor various corners. Use the [Scroll/Lock] key to move the entire shape of the window around. Tell Symphony where you want this window to display and what size to make it when it appears.
4. Optionally, you can adjust any of several window settings by using the {Services}w(indow)s(ettings) sequence. Here you can change the window's name (which you will probably seldom want to do), type (another infrequent change made at the Settings sheet level), borders, automatic display instruction, or Restrict Range. We will have such frequent need to work with Restrict Range that we devote an entire section to it later in this chapter.

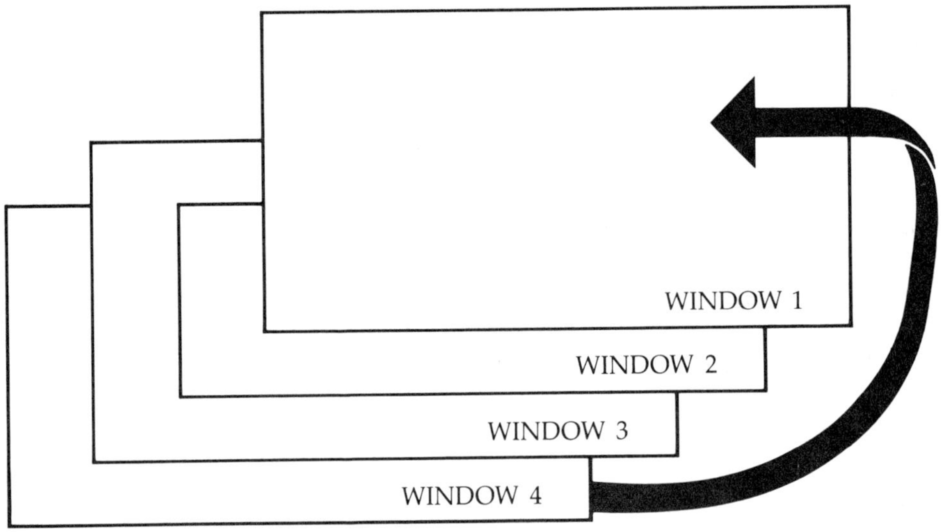

Figure 15
Stack of Windows and [F6] Key

You will usually name a window during the creation process. In fact, the {Services}w(indow)c(reate) sequence *requires* that you name it. However, even if you use the {Services}w(indow)p(ane) command sequence, you may wish to rename the window from the unimaginative "1", "2", or "3" assigned by Symphony. Do this with the {Services}w(indow) s(ettings)n(ame) option. Once you have carried out this sequence of instructions, either at the keyboard or in a macro, type the new name for the window and press [↵] (or code a tilde if you are in a macro).

With more than one window on a particular screen, the next problem is one of using the right one at the right time. There are two basic ways of accomplishing this.

First, you can use the Window key, [F6], to move from window to window. Symphony keeps all the windows you've defined in a stack. Windows below the top of the stack are sometimes temporarily invisible because they are completely covered up by windows higher in the stack. When you press the [F6] key, the bottom window of the stack is brought to the top and all the other windows are pushed down one level.

Figure 15 depicts this window-stacking process. There four windows of different sizes are named, unimaginatively enough, WINDOW1,

WINDOW2, WINDOW3, and WINDOW4. With the windows arranged in numerical order, top to bottom, pressing the Window key results in WINDOW4 becoming the top and current window, with WINDOW1 immediately below it, followed by WINDOW2 and WINDOW3.

As long as you either have very few windows or wish to use them in this kind of sequence, using [F6] is a very efficient way of moving from one window to another. Quite often, though, you will prefer to go from WINDOW1 to WINDOW2 without having to press (or code into a macro) the Window key three times. To do that, use the {Services}w(indow)u(se) sequence to select the current window.

When you use this set of commands to move around in the windows, you must give Symphony the name of the window to make the current window. You can do this from the keyboard by using the menu pointer to highlight the name of the desired window or by typing the name of the window. A macro will always use the explicit name technique of using a window since we can't guarantee that the order of the windows hasn't changed for some reason on the display.

Sizing and Moving Windows

Sizes and relative positions of windows on the display screen are always under your control. When creating windows with the {Services}wc sequence, you must notify Symphony of the size, shape, and position of the window when it is on the top of the stack.

If you use the {Services}wp technique to set up a new window, you must provide explicit information about the size, shape, and position on the display of the new window(s).

To change an existing window's size, shape, or placement, use the {Services}w(indow)l(ayout) sequence.

Both methods used for defining or redefining a window's display characteristics use similar techniques to carry out that definition. The pointing techniques are familiar because of their use in defining data ranges. The [⇆] or period key is used to determine the dimension of the window area to be adjusted. Cursor keys are then used to relocate that particular border position. If you've gone through this process often enough to be comfortable with it, skip to the following section, "Restricting a Window's Range". Otherwise, follow along with a small example of how window sizing and positioning are handled.

In Symphony, begin with a new worksheet (either by bringing Symphony up fresh or by using the {Services}n(ew)y(es) sequence). Carry out the operations below:

1. Create a new window by using the {Services}wc instructions. Name the window NEWONE. (Upper- and lowercase are immaterial because Symphony will use only uppercase in window names.)
2. When you have given Symphony the window's new name, the whole display area inside the borders of the SHEET will be highlighted as Symphony asks you to show it where and how you want this window displayed.
3. A small underscore is blinking in the lower right corner of this highlighted window. This symbol tells you which corner you are working in during the redefinition process. Move it by using the [⇆] or period key. Use one of those keys to move this cursor four times and watch it progress from its origin at the lower right to the lower left, then upper left, then upper right, and finally back to lower right corner.
4. With the cursor in the lower right corner, press the Left cursor arrow 15 times. The display should look something like Figure 16.
5. Now, leaving the cursor where it is, press the cursor Up arrow ten times. The display should now look like Figure 17.
6. Press the [⇆] key twice to put the cursor in the upper left corner of the window and press the Down arrow five times. The display should now look like Figure 18.
7. Now press the [Scroll/Lock] key once and notice that at the bottom of the display the word *Scroll* appears in inverse video to let you know that you've done this.
8. Now press the cursor Right arrow seven times and watch the entire highlighted window area move to the right three positions. Press the [↵] key, and Symphony will display the Window Settings sheet. For now, just Q(uit) and observe that the window display on your screen now looks like Figure 19.
9. Pressing the [F6] key will move you to a place where you can see both MAIN and NEWONE, as in Figure 20.
10. To keep things orderly on the screen, we sometimes create windows that are quite small. We can make such a window occupy the entire display area of the screen by using the Zoom, or [Alt][F6], key. Try that now by making NEWONE the current top window and pressing the

Figure 16
Adjusting Horizontal Window Size

Zoom key. Be sure to return the window to its "unzoomed" position when you're done.

Remember, you can change the position, size, or shape of a window at any time by making it the current window and using the {Services}wl sequence. Doing this does not change the data available in the window, though it may change the amount of data you can see at one time.

Restricting a Window's Range

One of the most useful (indeed essential) techniques for dealing with multiple environments in a single worksheet is that of restricting the range of the windows used to peer into the contents of that worksheet. The *process* is quite simple, but the *concept* requires elaboration.

If you've worked with Symphony applications where you've had multiple windows into a worksheet, you've probably made the mistake of deleting data in one place because you thought you had a "copy" of the data in another window, only to watch the other data disappear just as

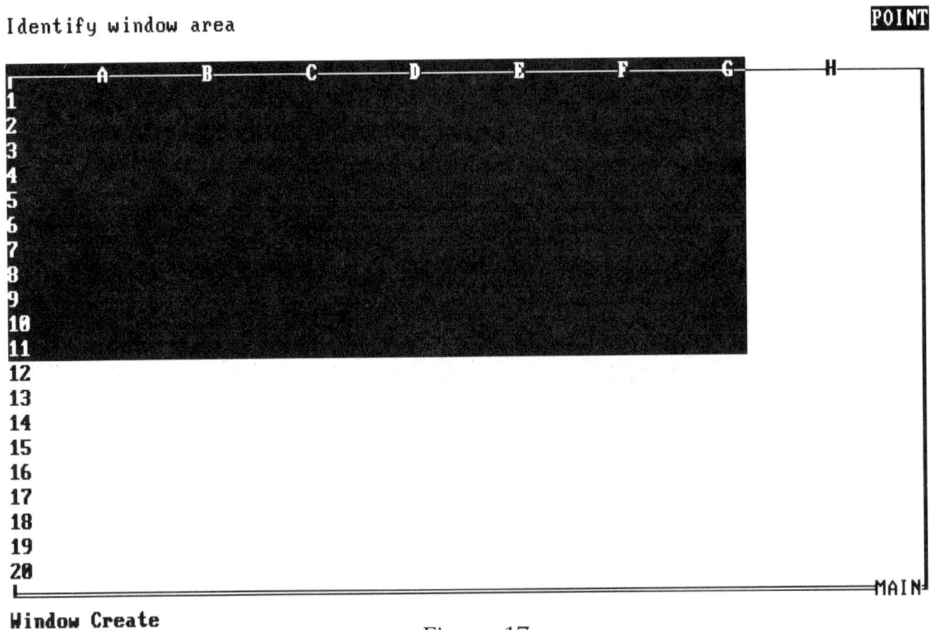

Figure 17
Adjusting Vertical Window Size

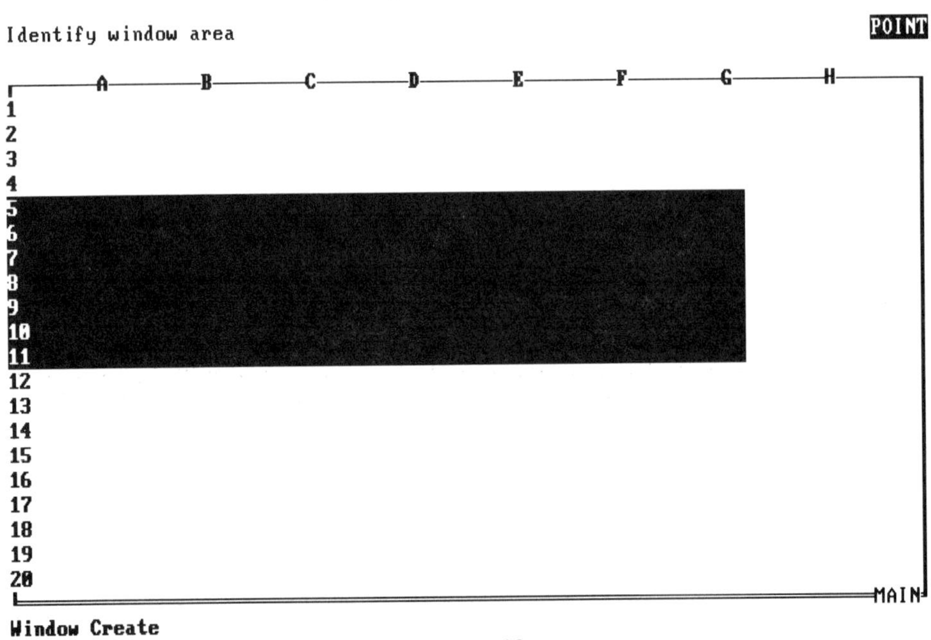

Figure 18
Narrowing the Window Vertically

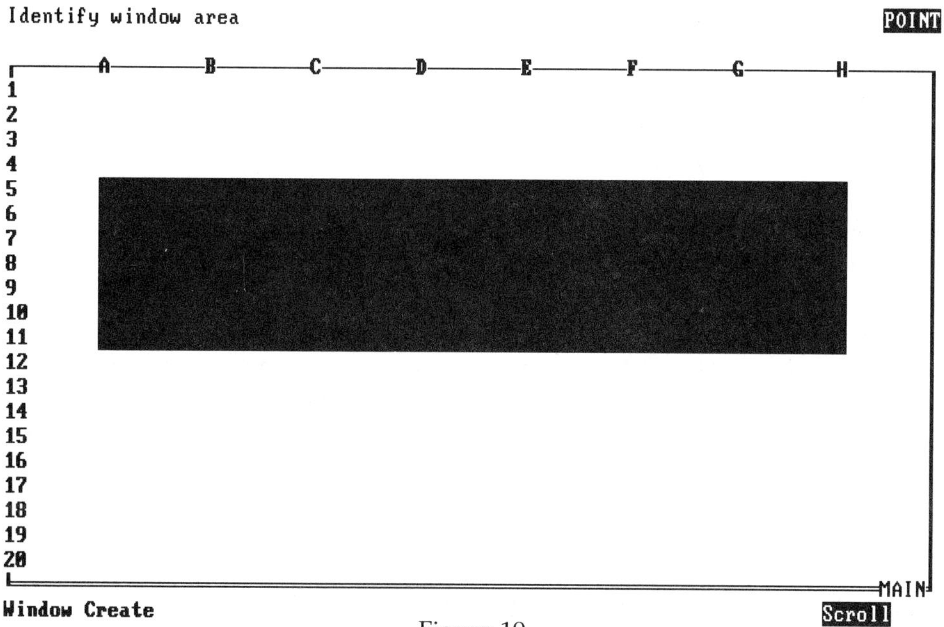

Figure 19
Moving Window

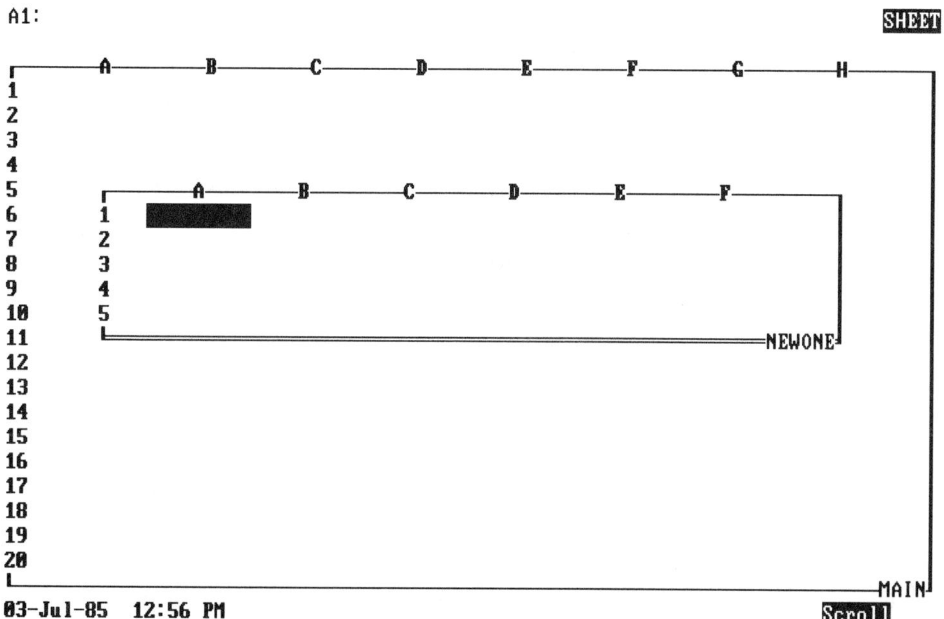

Figure 20
[F6] Window Key Results

quickly. Or you may have designed a model that relied on some absolute addressing of cells and then, a few days later, changed the sheet's structure by deleting some rows or columns, only to find that the application no longer worked correctly.

All the dozens of problems we have all grappled with as we learned the complexities and intricacies of Symphony's size and power result from a simple fact: what we do in one window of Symphony affects the same data in all other windows, *unless we specifically prohibit it from doing so*. You will learn about this prohibition in this section.

When working in the SHEET and DOC environments, and particularly in the FORM environment, we will often define ranges within windows for specific purposes. This enables us to use them easily without having to remember where they are located in the worksheet. It also enables us to identify a range with a particular purpose (assuming that we name the ranges meaningfully).

In the FORM environment, Symphony creates a number of such ranges for storing the database, report data, and selection criterion. If your database application is complex, you have probably defined several other such ranges to produce all the types of reports with all the selection options you need.

The use of ranges inside worksheets makes Symphony easier to use and understand. The same is true of defining windows within the worksheet in such a way that *their* ranges are limited to the areas of the environment in which we expect them to operate.

As you will see when we discuss how to "think integrated", planning and laying out a worksheet environment to accommodate all the activities in which we may want to engage in that environment are critical elements of success in a multiwindow application in Symphony. Restricting the ranges of the various windows we intend to use inside the worksheet will enable us to ensure that:

1. All the work done inside a particular window will be confined to that window and will not inadvertently affect some other area of the worksheet. This extends even to column and row insertion and deletion.
2. We can keep track of what kind of activity is being performed at any given point in the program or application by virtue of the nature and (if we are smart about it) the name of the window we are currently using.
3. Our macros can be organized in a methodical and easy to follow way.

```
Restrict pointer movement                                                   MENU
Name  Type  Restrict  Borders  Auto-Display  Quit

  Name:          MAIN
  Type:          SHEET
  Restrict:      A1..IV8192
  Borders:       Standard
  Auto-Display:  Yes
                                                              Window Settings

Window Settings
```

Figure 21
Restricting Pointer Movement

4. People who *use* our macros won't be able to cause catastrophic errors by moving or manipulating data outside the range we want them to be able to work with.

So much for the sales pitch. You'll see for yourself the soundness of the advice about using window range restriction as we move into more complex macro applications.

As we said earlier, the process of imposing restrictions on a window is quite simple. Use the {Services}w(indow)s(ettings) sequence to access the Window Settings sheet as shown in Figure 21. Once there, use the Restrict Range sequence to inform Symphony that you want to restrict the current window to a particular range of data.

Symphony will move you to the current window, highlight the entire thing, and place you in Point mode (as shown in the mode indicator in the upper right corner of the screen). From there, you can use the ⇆ and period keys to anchor and change beginning points, or simply typing in the actual cell addresses to which you wish to restrict this window.

Using the latter method is quick if you've preplanned the worksheet and know precisely to where you want to confine this window's range. If you use it, though, be sure to include periods between the beginning and ending cells (for example, AA1...AG144).

Once you've defined the range by either method, press [↵] to go back to the Settings sheet. If you finish changing information about the current window, simply use the Q(uit) option to return to the Symphony desktop. But if you wish to change parameters of other windows, use the Window or [F6] key from the Settings sheet screen and Symphony will cycle to the next window, as described above. With this method, you can set up the range restrictions for all your windows without having to re-enter the Settings sheet area each time.

We strongly recommend that you always have one window that can access the entire worksheet, that is, one unrestricted window. Once you've completed and checked out a macro application for someone else's use, you may delete or restrict this window. During macro programming, however, it will often be a problem if you cannot, for example, access some part of the worksheet where an inadvertent error has occurred.

Other Window Management Ideas

There are a few more hints and suggestions that you might find useful before we move on to specific suggestions for using the techniques we've been describing in macro applications situations.

One suggestion is to keep track of which windows you have in a particular application environment and what their restricted ranges are. We know two ways to do this; you may find others.

One way is to create an actual map in a corner or segment of your worksheet that depicts (or at least lists) the windows and their bounds. This technique works well as long as you update the list each time you change the window settings. It would be helpful to give the list itself a range name, particularly if you are making frequent changes and additions to the list or map as you develop an application. That way, you can easily go back to it to make a modification.

An alternate way to handle this is a bit more complex but more "foolproof" in terms of keeping your list of windows up to date. Create a macro that, when executed, creates a new window you have asked it to create and adds the window to the Range Name Table kept by the computer. Have the macro then store the table in a remote corner of the worksheet (not *too* remote, or you'll run into a memory management problem!).

Your macro should require that you enter the parent window's name as well as the new window's name, size, position, and restrict range and then update the Range Name Table accordingly. The macro is relatively easy to design and create in its simplest form. You could, however, add many bells and whistles to it and make it more useful.

For example, you might add an automatic prefix to all your created windows so that they will group together on the list, which is displayed alphabetically. You might prefix your window names with the characters "AA_" so that they will be displayed first on your list.

Another idea is simply to store and display the Range Name Table that Symphony maintains. Symphony automatically keeps track of your windows and their restricted ranges in its own memory. Incorporate this list into your worksheet by using the {Services}r(ange)n(ame)t(able) command, positioning the cell pointer where you want the upper left corner of the table to be displayed, and pressing [↵]. The table will then be displayed in your worksheet but *will not be automatically updated.* To achieve that result, consider using a macro.

There is a simple way to permit moving from window to window on command during both program development and the use of your macros by others. Create a series of one-line macros that can be invoked by a single keystroke from the keyboard, each of which moves to a different window. For example, if you have four windows on the desktop called MAIN, ACCOUNTS, CLIENTS, and LETTER, the following macro would permit moving into each window by pressing the [Alt] key and the first letter of the window name.

```
\m          {S}wuMAIN~q
(blank line)
\a          {S}wuACCOUNTS~q
(blank line)
\c          {S}wuCLIENTS~q
(blank line)
\l          {S}wuLETTER~q
(blank line)
```

This is a simple but effective tool that proves again how powerful macro programming can be. Since in your final version of a macro you will know which windows are involved and when to use them, this macro can save substantial amounts of time.

One last hint is worth mentioning. Whenever you are in Point mode, you can use the Window key to switch from one window to another. This means that it is quite easy, for example, to move or copy data from one window into another. Remember, however, that both windows must be the same type if you want to move data between them.

Thinking Integrated

An integrated Symphony application uses more than one type of window or environment. For example, a database using a FORM environment (and often also a SHEET environment) that is related to a DOC environment containing a form letter is an integrated application. Another example is a SHEET environment that handles financial analysis tied to a GRAPH environment that produces graphs of the results.

Many companies and individuals buy Symphony because of its integrated nature. But integration does not simply happen; it is planned and carried out intelligently. This section will assist you in developing macros by helping you think in terms of integration.

One reason why integration doesn't just "happen" is that data is viewed and manipulated differently from one environment to another. Another is that if we lose track of the "big picture" of the worksheet, changes made to one portion of it can often have inadvertent and negative consequences for information stored elsewhere.

If you've ever carried out a Move operation in a SHEET environment and then watched a recalculation produce unexpected ERR conditions in cells, you know what we are talking about. When data involve different types of environments or windows, the problem can be even more mysterious and difficult to find.

The moral is that to create truly integrated applications involving two or more types of environments and multiple windows, begin with a design that takes into account the idiosyncrasies of each type of environment. Planning in advance, combined with judicious use of range restriction techniques, will result in simplification in the implementation of even very complex macros.

Planning the Application

There is no substitute for good planning. A few years ago a book was published about planning whose title was a pithy commentary on the subject, *If You Don't Know Where You're Going, You'll Probably Wind Up Someplace*.

Be prepared to take two steps in designing systems and Symphony macros of even medium complexity. First, describe all inputs and outputs you expect the system to work with and produce. Second, write or diagram a structured way to produce the outputs from the inputs. This should be a step-by-step description from which you can write an SCL macro with very little additional thought being given to the process.

By forcing you to focus on the best way to accomplish a particular step, such a design approach will make your macros easier to write and more efficient to run.

Each portion of such a macro can possess a number of alternative solutions. For example, if we were designing a scheduling program that attorneys could use to set up appointments for the next few months, we could have each date entered into the system manually. This would ensure that all weekends and holidays were omitted, since the person doing the entry could eliminate them in the process of entering the dates. But that involves a great deal of typing and hardly takes advantage of Symphony's powerful date-handling capabilities. So we might design another way to get this input information into the system.

We might, for example, simply ask users to enter:

The starting date for the calendar

The ending date for the calendar (checking to be sure they haven't tried to cover more dates than the design accommodates)

A "yes" or "no" response to a question about including Saturdays and/or Sundays in the schedule

A list of the nonweekend holiday dates that occur in the period

With that information, we could automatically generate the valid appointment dates for the period.

Obviously, a scheduling program will require many more inputs than the dates to be covered. But for each type of input the system needs, we should think through the process of how to get the information entered. One consideration in coding an SCL macro is the issue of the appropriate environment in which to carry out a particular task. This is not usually a factor in designing such systems in more conventional programming languages.

For example, staying with our date entry problem, we might conclude that this information could be entered through and stored in either a SHEET or a FORM environment. Then we would want to think about the advantages of each.

A FORM environment would certainly be easier to enter information into for people unfamiliar with spreadsheets.

However, remembering that each row in a FORM environment is a record and each column a field, we may want to consider whether a horizontally laid out schedule — dates on the left, time slots arranged to the right — would be the easiest way for users to work. Might they not be more comfortable with a system in which the dates are arrayed across the top (a more traditional calendarlike approach) and the time slots are vertically aligned under the date? If so, would a SHEET environment be better?

Or should we switch from one environment to another, using FORM for the entry of the information and SHEET to represent the data on the screen when asked to do so?

You get the idea. There will be many such considerations to settle in the course of designing a complex macro in SCL.

Dividing the Worksheet

The following pages will discuss how to best use the worksheet into which your macro application is placed so that structuring your application to fit the worksheet environment will make more sense to you than it does now.

The most complex macro application in SCL would involve one or more of each of the five types of windows (SHEET, FORM, DOC, GRAPH, and COMM), along with a region that holds the macros that actually run the application program. Each type of environment has its own advantages, needs, and limitations. SHEET is by far the most flexible and general, with DOC not too far behind, and FORM requiring the greatest attention to structure and format.

Let's look at these three environments to see what specific design issues should concern us. We'll then be better able to explore the combinations of these environments and the implications of more complex applications.

The SHEET Environment

Data stored in a worksheet in the SHEET environment consists of labels, numbers (values), and formulas. Each cell in the SHEET environment is either empty or contains one of these types of data. A cell that contains only blanks and *looks* empty is actually a label containing no displayable characters.

If the SHEET environment in which you are working is restricted to a particular range, then to insert or delete rows or columns that you don't want to affect other parts of the worksheeet, use the Insert or Delete function rather than the Insert Global or Delete Global function. The global functions will affect all the data, formulas, and contents of the rest of the worksheet, which is almost never what you really want to do.

When working with a macro application that you intend to make available to others, consider protecting cells in the SHEET environment that must remain constant for the macro to operate correctly. Do this by using the {Services}g(lobal-Protection)y(es) sequence. All cells in a worksheet begin with a Prevent-Changes status. This status, however, is not invoked unless you specifically call on it by using this method.

Consider using manual recalculation to speed up data entry into a SHEET environment. When a SHEET gets very large, recalculation that takes place after each entry made by the user can dramatically slow data entry. This is true even when much of the information is for use in only one of the other modes. Set the S(ettings)r(ecalc)m(anual) sequence before saving the application macro for someone else to use for data entry; then use the SCL {Recalc} or {RecalcCol} command to perform the calculations as needed. You will greatly improve the efficiency of your program.

The DOC Environment

A DOC environment stores data as a collection of long labels beginning in the left-most column of the range in which the DOC environment is active. In most cases, where the DOC environment is the only one present, this means that labels start in Column A, usually in cell address A1. In SCL macro programming, however, we may find it beneficial to use some other starting position for the DOC portion of our application. Whatever column we start with as our left-most is where the text entered is aligned as a label.

This idea is important. As we look at a document stored in a DOC environment, it *seems* that each line of text, which corresponds to a row in a SHEET environment, in fact spans a number of columns. As we enter the text, Symphony shows us, in the control panel, the names of the underlying worksheet cell boundaries we are crossing. But if we enter several lines of text in a DOC environment and then change that environment to SHEET, we will notice as we move the cursor through the document's area that the control panel shows us the entire line of text. Further, if we move the cell pointer to the right (to cell B1, for example, if A1 is our starting point), the control panel shows this column to be empty.

Keep in mind this lack of correspondence between entries made in the DOC environment and their counterparts in the SHEET environment. The DOC environment can't be used simply to enter label information for a worksheet intended for use in the SHEET environment. When moving from one of these environments to the other, keep this difference in data storage in mind to avoid results that are unexpected by us or our macros.

In almost every case we will examine, it is important that the Restrict Range be nonoverlapping with other windows for each type of environment that occurs in a macro application.

This caution is crucial in the case of SHEET and DOC environments. If, for example, we have data stored in cells Q1-Q14 in a SHEET environment and we define a Restrict Range for a DOC environment so that it encompasses those cells, we may move a line or paragraph in our document and later find that we've also moved information in the SHEET. This can have disastrous consequences that we may not find out about until much later, when it may be difficult to remember how we might have caused the problem.

One way that a DOC environment can work together with SHEET data is by including spreadsheet segments in a report being written in the DOC environment. There are at least two ways to do this. The first is simply to copy the needed data to the worksheet area where it should be printed. The copying will work fine if this region is a SHEET environment. To print, you merely encompass the SHEET region in the definition of the area to be printed when you define the printing source.

As you learned earlier, you must be sure that the region to which you copy the data *is* a SHEET environment, at least while the copying takes place. Later, you can switch back to a DOC environment, but that may cause other problems.

The trouble is that this report results in a sloppy, hard to follow layout for the macro application. We have a DOC environment with a SHEET environment stuck arbitrarily in the middle, followed by more DOC environment region. It isn't nicely structured and is therefore subject to strange errors when we later try to modify or edit the material.

Further, we can't edit the SHEET environment data using DOC commands and techniques. In the middle of editing a document, we shouldn't have to shift mental gears to work in a small portion of the document in a different way. This is inelegant, to say the least.

A smoother way to do this same thing while retaining control over the whole situation is to use the Print command from the SHEET environment and print the desired section of the worksheet into a destination range rather than to the printer. When using this technique, set the Margins option to No so that you don't end up with only a portion of the SHEET data being printed in the region.

The SHEET environment segment you want to insert cannot be safely moved into the DOC environment because any formulas or numeric values in the left-most column of the SHEET environment area being used will appear to the DOC environment to be blank lines. Try this on a small segment and then move into the DOC environment. Move the cell pointer through the area and watch the control panel; you'll see what we mean.

You may already have encountered another relationship between the SHEET and DOC modes. To enter printer initialization strings in a DOC environment, we must first switch to a SHEET environment, because when we enter text into a DOC window, Symphony automatically precedes it with a single quotation mark. However, a control character sequence designed to cause the printer to do something special must not have a single quotation mark as its first character; it must begin with two special characters, like this: ||\015. The "|" characters are produced by entering shifted backslashes on the PC keyboard. They signal to Symphony that it is about to receive control character information. If this sequence is preceded by a quotation mark, Symphony will merely print the character sequence and ignore the command it is intended to carry out.

One other use for storing a document in a DOC environment that involves interaction with other types of windows is the creation of a personalized form letter, sometimes referred to as mail-merging. To design and create such letters, we must enter formulas into our DOC environment. We can do this only by entering the formulas into SHEET mode.

Creating a form letter, then, usually involves a two-step process. First, we type the letter itself into the DOC environment, leaving blank spaces where we will want to instruct Symphony to insert individual names, addresses, balances, or other personalized information. Then we shift the entire document to SHEET mode and enter the formulas that call for the extraction of information from some other location — usually a database.

This necessity of switching back and forth from one type of environment to another can be quite confusing if we don't keep it straight in our minds and in our region maps.

Finally, we sometimes will enter tabular information into a DOC environment that we later decide to move into either a FORM or SHEET window for use by those more structured environments. This is done by using the Query Parse command sequence. If you need to make these kinds of moves, review this complex and powerful command and its use in the *Symphony Reference Manual.*

The FORM Environment

In some ways the FORM, or database, environment is the most complex of the various Symphony modes in which we can work. Data stored in a FORM environment consists of such things as a number of ranges that define the contents of the database, its structure, criteria in use for selecting data from the database, reporting formats, and requirements. Each such range consists of a group of cells containing information relevant to that particular range's function in the database environment.

As you may know if you've worked with database management in Symphony, we move back and forth between the FORM and SHEET environments, using the former for entering, retrieving, updating, and browsing through the database a record at a time and the latter for manipulating the entire database at once. In addition, the FORM window through which single-record management takes place can be edited using a DOC window approach. As if all that weren't sufficiently complicated, information can also be added to a database by filling a COMM environment's Capture Range with data over a telephone link.

In dealing with the contents of the database itself, a potential problem for a macro programmer arises if the database is updated in SHEET mode. In that event, Symphony does not keep updating the database range, the range Symphony uses to keep track of where the database information is stored.

When entry is made through the FORM environment, Symphony automatically adds the location of each new record to the range that defines the database. However, if the user enters data directly through the SHEET environment, the database range must be updated to reflect the existence of the new records. Otherwise, Symphony simply doesn't understand that those records exist and will be unable to retrieve them or include them in reports.

Because each record of data in a database occupies a row and each field within each record occupies a column, the database is laid out horizontally in the worksheet environment. This means that database starting locations should be defined to allow sufficient room for expansion down and to the right of the starting point. Therefore, take into account the locations of other environments or windows in the worksheet area and position the database environment where space for such expansion exists.

As with the other types of environments we've examined, it is important to define a window Restrict Range for your FORM environment that does not overlap other windows. This particularly applies to DOC or SHEET windows where a lot of cutting, pasting, inserting and moving will be carried out.

Occasionally a formula will be entered as one of the database fields. To do this directly, convert to SHEET mode, enter the formula, and then convert back to FORM mode. It is not possible to enter a formula in FORM mode, although we *can* enter a computed field and get a similar result.

FORM environments also permit us to redesign the data entry form that Symphony creates if we use the Generate command. To do so, simply place the window into DOC mode and type the names of the fields and the appropriate number of underscores to represent data entry points. This enables us to customize data entry forms to coincide with how a macro user has typically handled such processes manually or when using another computer system. It also allows us to avoid the problem caused when more fields occur in the database than will fit onto one entry screen in the vertical format Symphony uses as its default method.

A more serious problem arises when we attempt to use a macro for database management. Symphony is designed so that when a user moves into a FORM window, the user is placed in complete control of the processing. The macro is, in effect, suspended. This is almost never what we want in a macro (though we could conceivably design a macro to accommodate this idiosyncrasy).

One way around this problem, first suggested by Dick Andersen in his book *Symphony Encore: Program Notes* (Berkeley: Sybex Computer Books, 1984), is to create a simple macro that retains macro control when the program moves into a FORM environment. The macro that Andersen designed looks like this:

```
BEGIN      {type}f
           {Loop}
(blank line)
```

```
LOOP      {Get INPUT}
          {If #not#@iserr(@vlookup(INPUT,KEYS,0))){branch EXIT}
          {INPUT}
          {Branch Loop}
(blank line)
EXIT      {type}s
```

This macro requires that the user define a lookup table called KEYS, which contains a list of all the keys we don't want the user to be able to activate. In this case, that list would include {Services}, {Switch}, {Type}, and Window, since any of those approaches could be used by the user to exit FORM mode.

The way this macro works, any such key results in the system returning control to the user. This solution was first designed by Barry Spencer shortly after Symphony was released. In your design, you might change the line labeled EXIT to read:

```
EXIT      {Beep}{Loop}
```

This will work particularly well if it is important that the macro stay in charge of data entry throughout the process to ensure the integrity and consistency of the information in the database.

The GRAPH Environment

There are two facts about graphs in Symphony. First, they are very powerful tools. A number of flexible formats are available for creating graphs, and graphs can be designed to present information with a great deal of impact. Second, they cannot be integrated directly into a document. Unlike the SHEET or FORM areas of the worksheet, the area where a graph is displayed, for example, cannot simply be pasted into a DOC environment. The only way to print a graph is to run the external program PrintGraph, which must be done outside Symphony itself.

Additionally, if we have some data in a SHEET window and we switch the window type to a GRAPH window, we will not see a graph pop up on the screen. Advance setup of layout, design, graph type, range, labels, and a few other details must be completed before a graph can actually be displayed.

The COMM Environment

The only interactions to take place between a COMM environment and the others in an SCL macro application will usually involve dialing of telephone numbers and retrieval of information stored at a remote computer. Otherwise, the COMM environment remains somewhat separate from the rest of Symphony.

Strictly speaking, a Restrict Range is not usually applied to a COMM window. Instead, a Capture Range is designed for the COMM environment through the Settings sheet. You should, however, think of this range in much the same way as a Restrict Range. In other words, don't overlap a COMM environment's Capture Range with the Restrict Range of another window.

When we define a Capture Range, we will *usually* define just a single column, with a number of rows equivalent to the number of lines of information we expect to capture from the host computer. COMM then captures the data in a form suitable for use in a DOC environment. In other words, each line of incoming text is treated as a long label, left-aligned in the column.

Sometimes, however, the data we are capturing are tabular in nature, or potentially so. For example, capturing stock quotations for analysis by a macro we design for portfolio examination might involve having Symphony retrieve several numeric fields transmitted by the host computer and place them into a SHEET environment.

To accomplish this, we define the Capture Range as being more than one column wide. In that situation, Symphony "parses" the input and breaks it up into pieces the size of each column.

For example, if we know that Dow-Jones News Retrieval service lets us receive stock quotations in ten-character blocks, we can set up the columns in the Capture Range to be ten characters wide and then define the Capture Range to be as many columns wide as we have quotations to capture.

Some General Principles

Out of the above discussion and lots of experience in writing SCL macro applications, we have come up with a few suggestions for how a worksheet environment should be laid out. These are only suggestions; what works for us may turn out to be cumbersome for you. But the underlying principle of separating the various kinds of environments from

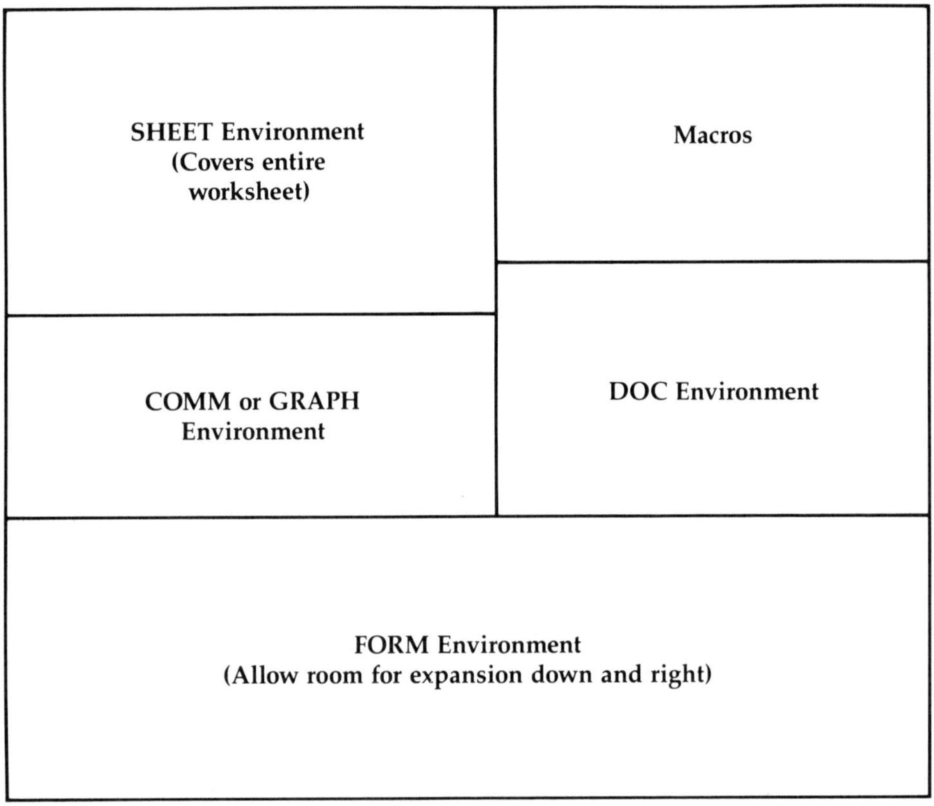

Figure 22
General Macro Layout

each other as much as possible is valid. So, too, is the general idea that certain kinds of environments are best placed in certain relative positions in the worksheet.

Figure 22 shows a generalized map of an SCL macro application worksheet as we would typically lay it out. Notice that we place the SHEET environment in the upper left corner. Actually, we *usually* leave the SHEET environment window so that it encompasses the whole worksheet; that is, we do not restrict its range.

Storing macros in the upper portion of the worksheet is a good idea. This will typically be to the right of the SHEET environment's main work area. Putting our macros in the range of AA1 as a starting point works well; most SHEET designs don't need more than 26 columns, and it's easy to remember the AA1 address. However, if you need more horizontal room for your worksheets, simply move the macro area to, say, BB1 or DD1.

The bottom area of the worksheet is reserved for database management functions. This does not include the entire worksheet, extending to address IV8192, but only the area we will be using for this application. Since databases expand downward and to the right, we tend to allocate the entire bottom portion of the worksheet to FORM uses.

DOC, COMM, and GRAPH windows can then be placed anywhere in the worksheet. In the interest of efficient memory usage, however, they should not appear outside the boundaries defined by the upper left corner of the SHEET, upper right corner of the macros area, or lower corners of the FORM environment. In other words, they should be "surrounded".

Generally, you'll find that this approach results in the fewest problems and the most manageable working conditions.

Next Up: An Example

This concludes our discussion about the various Symphony environments and key issues to consider when designing macro applications that use them.

To pull the entire concept together, we will now present an example that includes a few macros; a SHEET, a DOC, and a FORM window; and a number of Settings sheets. Although the example does not illustrate all the principles and concerns outlined in the past several pages, it does provide insight into the design issues involved in an SCL macro that uses multiple windows.

The example macro provides the beginnings of a usable teacher's gradebook system written as a collection of SCL macros. A view of the macros on screen is shown in Figures 23a and 23b. For the complete listings for this macro see Coda B.

We should note here that not all of the functions listed in menus have been implemented in the macros provided. Instead, we have provided you with a nearly complete framework within which to continue the design and programming. We suggest that you finish implementing this application example as a way to learn more about how SCL macro coding really works.

The following pages examine the macros presented in this listing in some detail. But first we will describe how we mapped the application's layout and use of the worksheet environment.

```
AA1: 'Macro to be used by a teacher to                                   SHEET

          AA           AB           AC           AD           AE
1  Macro to be used by a teacher to
2  maintain class lists, mailing lists, etc.,
3  calculate grades on a curve basis or enter
4  letter grades and print various reports.
5  (C) 1985, The Waite Group
6  Macro by Dan Shafer
7
8  GRADES        {MenuCall Main_Menu}
9                {ESC}{ESC}{ESC}{S}
10
11 Student       Grades        Reports       Quit
12 Work with studeEnter grades, cProduce lists, Return to Symphony
13 {MenuCall Stu_M{MenuCall Grade{MenuCall Repor{S}
14
15 Add           Change        Drop          Quit
16 Enter New StudeCorrect StudentDelete a StudenReturn to Gradebook Menu
17 {AddStu}      {FixStu}      {DropStu}     {MenuBranch Main_Menu}
18
19 Enter         Modify        Curve         Quit
20 Enter Grades  Correct a StudeCalculate CurveReturn to Gradebook Menu
                                                                     MAIN
03-Jul-85  01:02 PM
```

```
AA21: '{AddGrades}                                                       SHEET

          AA           AB           AC           AD           AE
21 {AddGrades}   {FixGrades}   {CalcGrades}  {MenuBranch Main_Menu}
22
23 Class_List    Mailing_List  Grade_Report  Poor_Work     Quit
24 Print a Class LPrint a MailingPrint Grade RepSend Poor Work Return to Grade
25 {Class_List}  {Mail_List}   {Grade_Report} {Poor_Work}  {MenuBranch Mai
26
27
28 DropStu       {S}wuSTUDENTS~{m}ce{?}~{Insert}{PgUp}{Delete}{Get a1}
29               {S}wuMAIN~{Home}{MenuBranch Main_Menu}
30
31
32
33
34
35
36
37
38
39
40
                                                                     MAIN
03-Jul-85  01:03 PM
```

Figure 23a
Gradebook Application Macro

```
AA41:                                                                    SHEET
      AA           AB              AC              AD              AE
41
42
43
44
45
46
47                 AddGrades       {GetNumber "Exam Number (1-5): ",a1}~
48                                 {if a1<1#or#a1>5}{beep 100}{addgrades}
49                                 {S}wuBOOK~
50                                 {if a1=1}{goto}b104~{getscores}
51                                 {if a1=2}{goto}c104~{getscores}
52                                 {if a1=3}{goto}d104~{getscores}
53                                 {if a1=4}{goto}e104~{getscores}
54                                 {if a1=5}{goto}f104~{getscores}
55
56                 GetScores       {for a2,1,40,1,input1}
57                                 {S}wuMAIN~{home}{menubranch main_menu}
58
59
60                 Input1          {?}~{Down}
                                                                          MAIN
03-Jul-85  01:03 PM
```

```
AA81:                                                                    SHEET
      AA           AB              AC              AD              AE
62                 FixGrades       {GetNumber "Which Exam? ",a1}~
63                                 {GetLabel "Which Student (Last Name)? ",a2}~
64                                 {goto}a3~+@vlookup(a2,a104..a143,0)~
65                                 {S}wuBOOK~{Home}
66                                 {Down +a3+3}{right a1}
67                                 {?}~
68                                 {GetLabel "More grade changes? ",a101}~
69                                 {if a101="y"#OR#a101="Y'"}{S}wuMAIN~{home}{fi
70                                 {blank a1..a3}{blank a101}{menubranch main_me
71
72  Class_List     {PanelOff}{WindowsOff}{S}pssrA293..C296~
73                 ota292..c292~qgpq{S}wuMAIN~
74                 {PanelOn}{WindowsOn}{menubranch main_menu}
75
76  AddStu         {S}wuSTUDENTS~{ESC}
77
78
79  \e             {S}wuMAIN~{Goto}BOOK~{?}~{Home}
80                 {MenuBranch Main_Menu}
81
                                                                          MAIN
03-Jul-85  01:03 PM
```

Figure 23b
Gradebook Application Macro

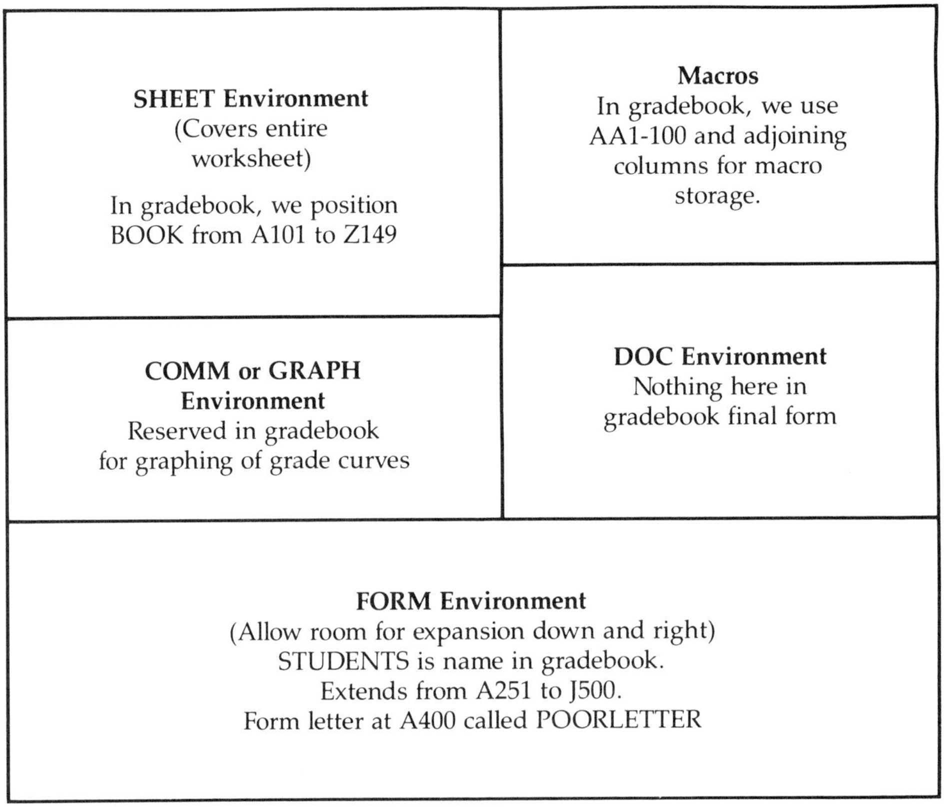

Figure 24
Map of Gradebook Application Layout

Mapping the Example

Figure 24 is a map of how we allocated the space in the worksheet environment for this application. Notice that we placed the macros themselves in the upper right corner and the FORM where the database information is stored at the bottom of the area. We left the upper left corner in SHEET mode and inserted a DOC window below the macros and above the FORM. We also allocated the region between the bottom of the SHEET area (which we ended at row 149) and the top of the FORM environment for a GRAPH window.

A form letter is stored inside the FORM area, not as a separate window but as the main report range of the database. Table 4 provides the range names for the key ranges and windows in the application environment.

Table 4
Important Range Names in Gradebook Application

Range Name	*Cell or range*
ADDGRADES	AC47
ADDSTU	AB76
BOOK	A102..Z150
CLASS_LIST	AB72
DROPSTU	AB28
FATHER	D293
FIRST NAME	B293
FIXGRADES	AC62
FIXSCORES	AC71
GETSCORES	AC56
GRADES	AB8
GRADE_MENU	AA19..AD21
INPUT1	AC60
LANGUAGE	H293
LAST NAME	A293
MAIN_MENU	AA11..AD13
MOTHER	E293
NICKNAME	C293
NOTES	I293
PHONE	G293
POORLETTER	A400..G430
POOR_WORK	AA200..AG229
REPORT_MENU	AA23..AE25
STREET	F293
STU1_AB	A284..I284
STU1_CR	A287..I288

Range Name	*Cell or range*
STU1_DB	A292..I293
STU1_DF	A274..H282
STU1_EN	A263..A271
STU1_MA	A285..I285
STUDENTS	A252..J500
STU_MENU	AA15..AD17
WORK PHONE	H295
\E	AB79
\Z	B1

Menu Structure of Example

A cursory examination of the macros in Figure 23a-e reveals that the first several lines of the macro region are occupied by some plain-looking text that describes the macro. Make it a habit to use this technique to denote where the macro section begins and describe briefly the purpose of the application. The text can be entered directly from the keyboard as any other label. Since we don't associate a macro name with it, Symphony won't try to execute these lines as if they were instructions.

The next several lines of the macro region are occupied with four menus. We used labels that are not part of the menu display, so you can't tell, but the menus are called MAIN_MENU, STU_MENU, GRADE_MENU, and REPORT_MENU, reading from the top of the menu listings. Figure 25 diagrams the main menu for the gradebook system.

We have completed implementation of the following menu options: Add Students, Drop Students, Add Grades, Modify Grades, and Print a Class List. The remaining options can be implemented by following the examples provided here, along with some basic knowledge of Symphony. The one exception is the Graphing function, which is discussed later in greater detail.

Adding Students: FORM and Macro Control Problems

We begin with the first option on the first subsidiary menu, Add Students. This macro has two portions: AddStu and \e. The first portion

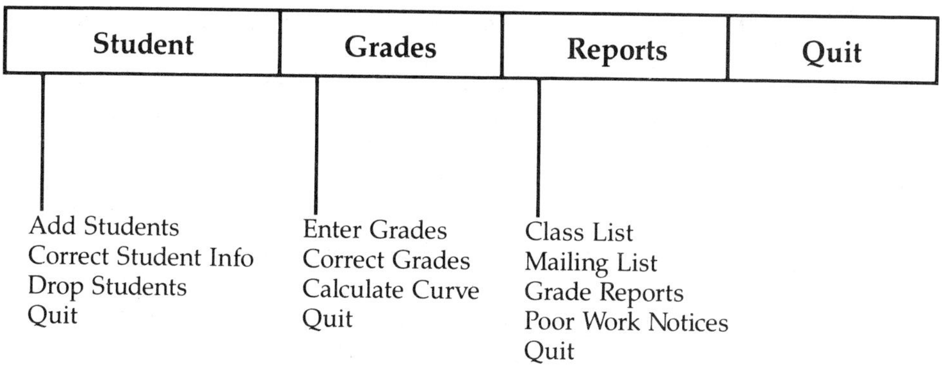

Figure 25
Menu Structure of Gradebook Example

is a one-line macro that simply calls up the window STUDENTS, which is the range name for the database area. Since it is a FORM window, Symphony takes control of the system as soon as it is entered unless we prevent it from doing so. A technique for retaining control is described earlier in this movement, but we chose here to let the user remain in control of operations at this level.

The second part of the macro is invoked by pressing the [Alt]e keys on the keyboard when a new student has been entered into the database by using the above macro.

Pressing these keys has two effects. First, invoking the new macro returns control to our application program for the continuation of the processing. Second, notice that the first line of this macro moves control to the area called BOOK with a {Goto} command. This is where we store the gradebook containing the examination scores. A student being added to the school must obviously be added to the gradebook as well.

This method has some disadvantages compared to a more automated method that would simply add the student to the BOOK area without any keyboard intervention, but coding it this way makes it easier to follow and understand the processing.

At the end of this gradebook addition, the macro returns to the top left corner of the worksheet, which is where we chose to start all operations, and displays the Main menu again.

Dropping a Student: Full Control Returns

Even though the process of dropping a student requires use of the FORM environment, we don't lose control of the macro's execution this time because the process is not adding people to the database. Instead, it is deleting them, a process SCL permits us by its design to automate. Notice the macro called DropStu, which carries out this processing.

We have purposely somewhat limited the process of deletion; the teacher can only delete people by entering their last names. Once he has done that, the system takes over control. If he had two students with the same last name, this process would not work as well, since it would require flipping through all the Browns until Suzie came up. Nonetheless, it works and is straightforward enough that it is easy to understand at this stage of your learning about SCL macro programming.

The first line of the DropStu macro brings the window called STUDENTS into use, brings up the FORM environment menu, and chooses the Criteria Edit option. It then permits entry of the student's last name. (We could easily key off some other field in the database by using a {Down} statement at the beginning to position the cursor in the field we want to use as the criterion.) It then simulates pressing the [Ins] and [Del] keys on the PC keyboard, resulting in the first record that meets the criterion being displayed and the question "Are you sure you want to delete this record?" being displayed in the control panel.

Based on the teacher's answer, the database program will either delete the student from the database or leave her there. It will then return to our usual beginning point.

Adding Grades

The macro called AddGrades provides an interesting example of editing input, branching to a point in the application based on an entry, and looping.

When the Grades Add option is selected from our macro application, the macro asks first for the examination number. We have arbitrarily allowed five in the database and five in the macro; obviously, that would be simple to modify for a particular user's needs during setup of the macro. When the examination number has been entered, we check to ensure that it is between 1 and 5. If not, we send a special audio message to the operator and redisplay the question.

Assuming that we have received a valid value for an exam number, the next several lines check for the correct position in the gradebook for entering the grades. Each examination begins in a different column but in the same row.

Notice that we make the macro's execution efficient by adding a {GetScores} command to the end of each line that checks to see where it should position the cell pointer. Consequently, if the answer is "1", the program doesn't have to check for 2, 3, 4, and 5; it heads for the right place to begin data entry.

We arbitrarily set the number of students in the class at 40, which would be easy to modify at installation for a particular class. The routine called GetScores simply does a 40-iteration loop. This loop in turn calls on the macro Input1, which simply accepts one score and moves the cell pointer down to get ready for the next one.

When all 40 scores have been entered (or if the loop is interrupted from the keyboard before it is complete) control returns to the usual point at the Home position in the MAIN SHEET window with the Main menu displayed.

We should make a final observation before moving on in our discussion of the gradebook application. We *could* have placed the gradebook itself in the database we call STUDENTS. Alternatively, we could have made it its own database. In fact, if you were to design a program like this for commercial use, that is probably the way you would do it, since it would permit the teacher using it to enter scores through a FORM entry sheet rather than directly into the worksheet. However, such an approach would have defeated one of our main purposes here, which is to show you a number of macro programming techniques.

Correcting Grades

This little macro has two useful techniques worth discussing in some detail. Notice that before transferring control of the macro to the area where the grades are stored, the program reports both the exam number and the name of the student whose grade has been incorrectly entered. This enables us to set up our first technique, the use of table lookup to position the cursor.

The third line of the macro FixGrades says:

```
{goto}a3~+@vlookup(a2,a104..a143,0)~
```

This has the effect of placing into cell A2 the relative position of the student's last name in the gradebook. If the student entered by the teacher

```
A102: 'Student Name                                                          SHEET

    ------A----------------B-----------------C-----------------D-----------------E------
102 Student Name      Exam 1            Exam 2            Exam 3            Exam 4
103 ==================================================================================
104 Allen                    100                98                90
105 Brown                     65                65                65
106 Smith                     82                78                75
107 Xerxes                    95                90                87
108 Barnhart
109
110
111
112
113
114
115
116
117
118
119
120
121
    ===============================================================================MAIN
03-Jul-85  01:04 PM
```

Figure 26
Gradebook Layout Showing Top Lines

is named Brown and that happens to be the third student in the list, the number 2 will be placed in cell A2. (Remember that FORM treats the first element in a list as the zero-th element, not the first. It's confusing, but at least it's consistent throughout Symphony!)

It also happens that examination grades are aligned in columns that start immediately to the right of the student's name in our design. This permits us to use the second technique, a cursor movement that uses information stored in cells rather than direct values (like {Down 3}). The line in question is the fifth one in the macro FixGrades and it reads as follows:

```
{Down +a3+3}{right a1}
```

When this line is executed, the program looks at the value in cell A3, which we have theorized is a 2, adds 3 to it, and moves down that many places. This accounts for the two lines of "heading" information we've inserted at the beginning of the gradebook, as shown in Figure 26.

Once we've positioned the cursor in the appropriate cell for the correction, we simply use a {?}~ command to get the corrected input. We then ask if the user has any more grade changes to make. If the answer (stored in cell A101) is affirmative, we return to FixGrades; otherwise, we return to our usual starting point, this time after blanking cells A1-A3 and A101, where information has been temporarily stored during processing.

The last step isn't necessary, since the application will never be saved, but it's left over from our fastidious period, so bear with us. Actually, it's probably a good habit to get into. Extraneous information appearing on computer displays results in lots of questioning telephone calls for the macro designer (that's you).

Printing a Class List

The macro Class_List provides a good example of how most reports prepared in Symphony will be handled. There is no need, as there is in most programming languages, to store a whole bunch of code describing the report, since Symphony thoughtfully furnishes us with print Settings sheets. All we do is modify the Settings sheet to reflect the current reporting need and tell the procedure to Go.

Here, we turn the windows and panel off so that we can freeze the display during the printing of the report. (You might want to leave those out during experimentation, or delete them if you've already typed them in before reading this far.) The screen does a great deal of flashing and shifting during this processing, so it is a good place to freeze the display. Notice that we turn the windows and panel back on in a few lines.

The {Services}P(rint)S(ettings)S(ource) sequence initiates the printing setup. We've supplied the address range explicitly here (for a reason we'll explain in a moment) rather than using a database range, which would be preferable in most cases. We've also set up the top titles on the next line with the O(ther)T(op-Title) sequence, again providing an explicit address range from which titles should be drawn by the program.

It would usually be a good idea to use a database as the source range for a print routine. However, with the Class List we want only the students' names, not their addresses, phone numbers, parents' names, and the other data we store in the database. An Output Range function could limit the fields to be printed, but this seems to be far simpler when the cells we want to use are adjacent to one another. It's a matter of taste.

The same can be said for the titles; normally, we'd use a range that included the titles and leave this part of the Settings sheet blank, but in the interest of further education, we've included this command sequence in the macro.

Poor Work Notice Form Letter

Embedded in the database STUDENTS is a form letter called POOR-WORK. Locate its position from the list of range names in Table 4. This letter was created in DOC mode by using usual word processing techniques. Ampersands were used to bracket the names of the fields to be taken from the database and inserted into the letter when it is printed. The first part of the letter, then, looked like this when we finished processing it as a document:

```
To the Parents Of:
&First Name& &Second Name&
&Street&

Free Spirit, CA  90998

Dear &Father& and &Mother&:
```

Before the letter could be used as a form letter, though, we had to tell the database that this was its main report range. We did that through the FORM Settings sheet and defined POORLETTER as the Main Report range.

After we finished writing and editing the letter, we used the Type (Alt F10) key to switch to SHEET mode. Changing the lines that contained variables to be SHEET string formula lines resulted in something like this:

```
+First Name&" "&Last Name
+Street
Free Spirit, CA  90998
+"Dear "&Father&" and "&Mother&":"
```

While entering each of these formulas in automatic recalculation mode, the first record in the database was used to fill in these field names in the form letter. We could avoid that by using manual recalculation methods.

Although the form letter is completely set up, we have not provided the macro called Poor_Work that will print it. Having seen how we set up previous Print Settings sheets, this should be a useful exercise for you to undertake.

Summary

In this, the Third Movement of our Symphony orchestration, you have

Seen the skeleton of commands presented in the Second Movement come to life in an analysis of real-life applications situations

Learned how to "think integrated" and to deal with the necessity of prior planning on your macro applications

Taken a close look at a partially fleshed-out framework for a teacher's gradebook as an example of how a useful application would be designed, mapped, coded, and implemented

The remainder of the book is devoted to in-depth examinations of several full-blown, real-life applications. With the background you have just received in the first three movements of our exploration, and the review of Coda C, you should be now ready to make real music with Symphony's powerful macro language.

THE FOURTH MOVEMENT

Some Real-Life Teaching Examples

This, the final movement of our orchestration of Symphony's powerful Command Language, brings together much of what we have learned — and adds some new material as well. It provides four realistic applications that have been prepared to run under Symphony. All of them make varying use of SCL and macro coding techniques. All have some practical value. And all four of them provide opportunities for you to learn more about SCL macro programming techniques and to sharpen your skills.

The Purpose of These Examples

The primary reason we have included these macro applications and gone to great lengths to describe them is to teach you more about SCL programming by example. These applications do not purport to be either complete commercial products or examples of "elegant" or sophisticated program design. In some cases, we've deliberately done things less elegantly in order to do them more clearly.

Real commercial products designed to be sold to users of Symphony often involve *thousands* of lines of SCL macro code. They are sophisticated, interconnected, and difficult to program and to understand, but (we hope) not to *use*. None of the applications in this movement is nearly so complex as these commercially sold applications, but they differ primarily in degree of sophistication, not in types of programming obstacles and challenges presented.

Because of this, if you take the time to analyze each macro and application in this movement you will inevitably find your SCL programming skills to have increased noticeably as a result. If your goal is to develop your own useful applications — whether for personal use or commercial sale — you will find much here of value as you design and code your own Symphony applications.

The Applications in Brief

Four applications are included in this movement. One was designed, adapted, and programmed by the author. The others were designed and programmed by Mary Johnson, as indicated.

Professional Billing

Creating time sheets from which to prepare invoices for clients is the purpose of this moderately complex application. With extensive use of macros and file extraction capabilities, this application demonstrates one way that multiple files of information can be used in Symphony despite the software's inherent limitation of working only with data in a single worksheet stored entirely in your PC's memory. The macro was designed and coded by Mary Johnson.

Nonprofit Organization Fund-Raising

This macro enables a nonprofit organization to match volunteers and resources with individuals who need those resources. It also manages mailing lists and prepares personalized form letters to be sent to volunteers, clients, and contributors.

This application (one of the longer and more complex applications) is discussed from a different perspective than the others. It is viewed from the *design* standpoint, with less emphasis than usual on the contents of the macros and greater emphasis on how the application could be designed and implemented in a real-life situation. This macro was also designed and coded by Mary Johnson.

Personal Appointment Manager

This macro set enables you to keep track of appointments by making, rescheduling, and canceling them. It also permits you to keep the calendar from becoming cluttered with obsolete appointments and to display or print reports showing your appointments for any given day.

Designed in a highly modular and structured way, this application is described far more in terms of the macro contents than most of the applications in this movement. Given an application that is relatively easy to understand, we felt that spending more time on the contents of the macros that make up the application would have more value to you as you learn SCL.

Delivery Order

This macro is designed so that it actually meets all the current minimum reporting requirements of the U.S. government for contractors involved in cost-plus assignments. It helps track spending against budgeted and funded levels and keeps careful track of when the crucial "85% letter" is required to be sent.

One interesting aspect of this application that you'll find useful as a learning device is the degree to which the user is at times given total control of the worksheet (sometimes because Symphony forces such changes). A single-keystroke macro returns control to the main macro at a pre-selected point.

This macro was originally implemented in 1-2-3 for a government contractor by Ms. Johnson, who converted the macro and design to Symphony for this book.

Using the Macros

The chapters in this movement contain descriptions in varying degrees of detail of the programs and their set-up as Symphony applications. The macros themselves, however, are not necessarily described sequentially or completely. Complete, cell-by-cell listings of the macro applications are contained in Coda B of this book. To enter and use a macro, turn to the listing first and type the macro listing into your worksheet. Then a reading of the chapter will take on greater meaning.

When you decide to use one of the macros be sure that you have set up all the requisite areas of the worksheet and defined them as ranges. One way to double-check yourself on this is to position the cell pointer in an entirely empty region of the worksheet and use the Range Name Table routine to create a table of all known range names in the application. These required ranges are generally discussed in the description of each application and are listed after the macro listing in Coda B.

Starting a macro requires either that you set up the macro to automatically execute when the worksheet is loaded or that you explicitly invoke the macro itself. You do the latter by means of the User (F7) key followed by the starting macro's label.

On With the Symphony!

Enough intermission. Let us jump immediately into the first application.

Professional Time and Billing System

Job growth is rapidly increasing in the service industries which typically provide services that are billed on the basis of the time and type of service provided. The medical, dental, and legal professions are among the oldest and most widely recognized of the service industries. The application described here gives the service organization an easy way to keep track of the time and charges to be billed to its clients.

This application is a simple time-tracking and billing macro that demonstrates some easy but elegant ways to keep records using various SCL techniques. Certain techniques used for this macro are also utilized in the delivery order application described later in this movement.

The macro presented here is simple and easy to use. It can also be used as the basis for a more complex reporting and invoicing system. Some ideas for expanding on its capabilities will be presented later.

A Little Background

For the purposes of this macro, we will assume that we have been asked to set up a simple system to track the hours spent and charges billed by the hypothetical legal firm of Smith, Ramesey, LeVeque, and Jones. Each person in the firm was assigned one of four service levels: senior partner, junior partner, paralegal, and administration. Everyone used time sheets to log the amount of time spent each day working for a particular client, along with a brief description of the service performed. At the end of the day, the time sheets were turned over to an administrative assistant to be entered into the client time and billing records that were maintained as individual Symphony .wrk files. (The format for the records will be shown later in this discussion.) Once a month, or at the end of the case, invoices would be prepared using the information contained in the individual .wrk files.

With this application, we can set up a new client file, update an existing file, or print out an invoice. Using a menu-driven format enhances the day-to-day operation of the system. The beauty of the menu format, which SCL makes so easy to set up and use, is the speed with which new choices can be added to an application. This allows incremental expansion of applications without impacting those parts of an application that are already in use.

Approaching the Problem

The approach in building this application is to set up the Main menu, with four choices to begin: Add a new client, Update a client's file, prepare an Invoice, and Quit. Each client will have a .wrk file set up that uses his or her initials for the filename. For example, Sam D. Macgee would have his time and billing information saved in the file SDM.WRK. Of course, if there were more than one client with the initials SDM, some other identifier would have to be put in for the filename.

Taking advantage of the File Extract and Combine capabilities of the SHEET environment, the basic macro file for this application is set up with an area reserved for the manipulation of the data in each client's file. This area, or range, is assigned the name TSHEET. Within the boundaries of this range, the entire time and billing "file" for a client can be combined with the macro file, and appropriate updates can be made. A blank master time and billing "file" is used as a template to initiate a file for each new client.

Two basic factors determine the cost of the services performed for a client — the number of hours spent in performing the service and the class of service — so only two basic types of calculation are necessary to determine a client's total bill. By multiplying the number of hours spent by the rate associated with the class of service, a fee figure for each service performed is determined. At the end of a billing cycle, the totals for each service are added to give the grand total. Rather than requiring the administrative assistant to manually enter the rate with every service, the macro uses a rate table, which takes advantage of the string capabilities and the @VLOOKUP function of Symphony. Thus, the information concerning a particular service can be entered — the date of the service, a brief description, the number of hours spent, and a key letter as to the type of the service. The macro then looks up the rate and multiplies it by the number of hours spent to determine the costs associated with the particular service.

The Main Menu

As indicated earlier, the Main menu of this macro offers four choices: Add, Update, Invoice, and Quit. Using the convention of placing macros in one area of the worksheet, the following menu items were set up, starting with the label Main_Menu in location AA10. Try entering the various parts of the macro as it is presented, and you may find that you can use the macro itself to speed the development process. The first menu entry begins at location AB10 and looks like this:

```
Add
Add a client to the file
{ADD}
```

The next entry begins in location AC10:

```
Update
Update a client's file
{UPDATE}
```

The third entry begins in location AD10:

```
Invoice
Prepare invoices for clients
{MenuCall INVOICE}
```

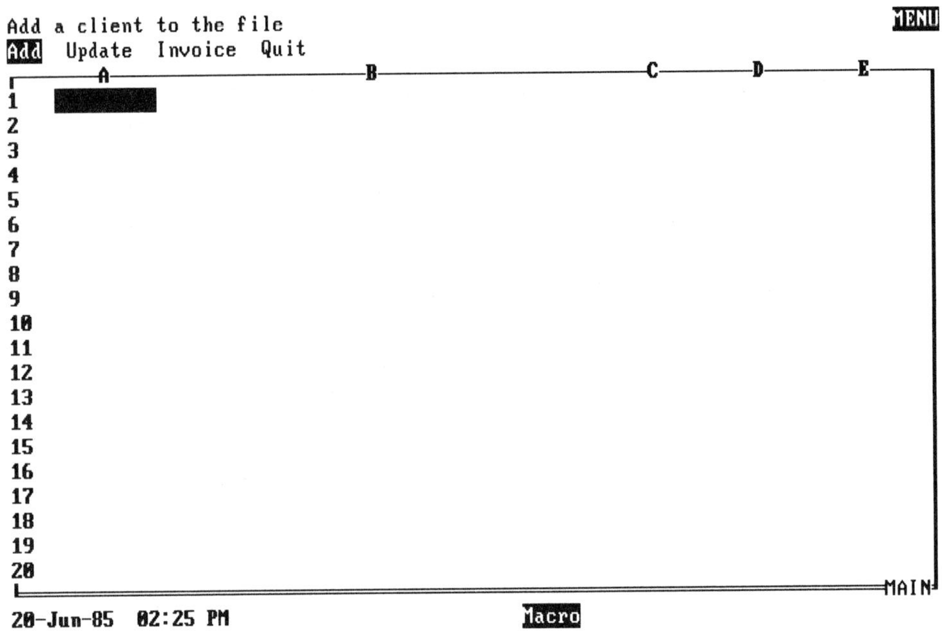

Figure 27
The Main Menu

The last entry in the Main menu begins in location AE10:

```
Quit
Return to Symphony
{S}e
```

Figure 27 shows you what the finished menu looks like.

The Save (\S) Macro

In addition to the Main menu, a very handy single-key macro (\S) is used in this application. The purpose of this macro is twofold: to clear out an area on the worksheet and save the information displayed in the area to a file. In developing this application, it was very easy to set up the initial macros on one worksheet. Then, after naming the range TSHEET, it was easy to use the File Extract and Save routine in this \S macro to save the work as the development progressed.

The macro itself is labeled in location AA15 and begins in location AB15:

```
{S}fxf{?}~TSHEET~
{right}~{m}cTSHEET~
{S}wuMAIN~
{MenuBranch Main_Menu}
```

The range TSHEET encompasses the area between A1 and E42 on the worksheet. This macro first calls the Services menu, then moves to the File menu and chooses the Extract option. For this macro, we want the area extracted to be saved with the Formula mode, so the Formula option is selected. The {?} allows us to specify to which file we would like to have the data in TSHEET stored. After giving the macro the filename, it continues with its processing and extracts the area TSHEET to the file.

Typically, the data are stored to an existing file, and when manually stepping through the procedure, Symphony will remind you that a file with the name given already exists. By including the {right}~ in the next step of the macro, we can circumvent this built-in protection. Whether this is a good idea will depend on the skill and attention level of the people who will be using this macro. To leave the protection in, the macro could be changed to have a {?}~ substituted for the {right}~. The next step in this line of the macro is to call the Menu function and erase the range TSHEET in the current worksheet. This is followed by {S}wuMAIN~, which is used to ensure that we are in the MAIN window before calling for the Main menu to be displayed.

The Master Client Invoice Template

The master client invoice template is stored as a file named TSMAS (for "Time Sheet MASter"). How it is set up and how it is loaded into the range TSHEET are the subjects of the next two sections.

The TSMAS Template

The TSMAS template fits into the area designated TSHEET in the main macro worksheet. The template contains a little more than two screens full of information. The length of this template can be adjusted to suit the estimated number of services that would be performed for the typical client in a given month. Figure 28 shows what the initial screen looks like when the TSMAS template is loaded into the TSHEET range.

```
A1: 'Time Sheet                                                      SHEET

       A                        B                        C         D         E
1   Time Sheet
2
3
4
5   Client:
6   Address:
7   City:
8
9                                                  <<Rate Chart>>
10
11                                            Rate       Service         Code
12                                            ====       =======         ====
13                                           20.00 Administration         a
14                                           50.00 Paralegal              p
15                                          100.00 Junior Partner         j
16                                          150.00 Senior Partner         s
17
18  =========================================================================
19  Date      Description                                Hours    Code    Bill Amt
20  ----      -----------                                -----    ----    --------
                                                                           MAIN
20-Jun-85  02:26 PM
```

Figure 28
First Screen of the TSMAS Template

There are really only three lines to be filled in. Cell B5 will contain the client's name; cell B6 will contain the street address, starting with an apostrophe because street addresses typically begin with numbers; and cell B7 will contain the city, state, and ZIP for the client. In the rate chart in the lower right-hand corner of the template, three columns of information list the rate, the service description, and the service code. This table is used a little farther down the template to compute the actual cost accrued. Figure 29 shows the remainder of the template.

The zeros in column E result from a calculation that is programmed in each cell in the E column in this part of the template, like this:

```
@VLOOKUP(Di,$KEY,-3)*Ci
```

where "i" stands for the row number. The absolute range, $KEY, is the area shown in Figure 28, from cell E13 to cell E17. The grand total, which includes the total number of hours billed and the total amount that the

```
A43:                                                              SHEET

┌─────A─────────────────B─────────────────C──────D──────E──────┐
24                                                        0.00
25                                                        0.00
26                                                        0.00
27                                                        0.00
28                                                        0.00
29                                                        0.00
30                                                        0.00
31                                                        0.00
32                                                        0.00
33                                                        0.00
34                                                        0.00
35                                                        0.00
36                                                        0.00
37                                                        0.00
38                                                        0.00
39                                                        0.00
40                                                        0.00
41                                        ---------------------------
42                            TOTALS:        0.0              0.00
43
└══════════════════════════════════════════════════════════════MAIN┘
20-Jun-85  02:26 PM
```

Figure 29
Lower Half of the TSMAS Template

client owes, is simply the result of column calculations making use of the @SUM function. They are

```
@SUM(C21..C40)
```

and

```
@SUM(E21..E40)
```

respectively. As you will see in the next section, as we fill in the blanks, the calculation of charges is done automatically.

The ADD Macro

After setting up the TSMAS template and naming the range TSHEET, the ADD macro can be constructed to allow us to add client files to the system. The ADD macro is entered into the area beginning in location AB20:

```
{home}
{S}fccnTSHEET~
rfTSMAS~
```

Stepping through the macro, we notice that the cursor is moved to the Home position, cell A1, before the Services menu is called up. This is done so that when the next line of the macro calls up the Services menu and File Combine, we have a clear space in the main worksheet and the underlying area of the worksheet is not destroyed. Following the File Combine option, the Copy and Named-Area choices are designated. The TSHEET area is identified as the named range to be incorporated.

The next line of the ADD macro continues the File Combine process by designating that the Read and Formula options are selected. This line means that the range TSHEET is read in from the file TSMAS and that the formulas rather than the values stored in the file are incorporated into the worksheet.

Once the TSMAS template has been loaded into the TSHEET range, we can begin to fill in the blanks.

Filling in the Blanks

As mentioned earlier, only three lines in the top part of this template, identified as client name, address, and city, need to be filled in. Figure 30 shows a sample of how a typical client file might look after a couple of entries.

When initiating a new client file, the TSMAS template is loaded, the appropriate data are entered in the billing area (more on this in a minute), and then the single-stroke Save macro (\S) is executed. When the filename is requested, the initials of the client are entered, and the macro then stores the client's file as a .wrk file.

Each day, a client's file can be updated by bringing up the main macro, calling the UPDATE macro, and adding the most recent date, services, and rate category. The only difference between the UPDATE and ADD macros is that the last line of the UPDATE macro reads:

```
rf{?}~
```

```
A23:                                                                  SHEET
┌──────A────────────────B─────────────────C──────D──────E──────┐
4
5   Client:  Miranda Johnson
6   Address: 6789 Bridgeway
7   City:    Sausalito, CA  94965
8
9                                          <<Rate Chart>>
10
11                                     Rate      Service         Code
12                                     ====      =======         ====
13                                    20.00 Administration        a
14                                    50.00 Paralegal             p
15                                   100.00 Junior Partner        j
16                                   150.00 Senior Partner        s
17
18  ======================================================================
19  Date     Description                         Hours    Code    Bill Amt
20  ----     -----------                         -----    ----    --------
21  Nov 4    Initial visit                         1.0 j            100.00
22  Nov 10   Review contracts                      0.5 p             25.00
23                                                                    0.00
└─────────────────────────────────────────────────────────────────MAIN┘
20-Jun-85  02:28 PM
```

Figure 30
A Typical Client File

This {?} allows us to enter or select from the menu the appropriate file to be updated.

Preparing an Invoice

When the end of the billing cycle rolls around, the main macro is loaded, and after typing in TIMESH to bring it up and running, we can select Invoice from the Main menu. This will bring us to the Invoice menu. There are three selections here: Single, Group, and Quit. The only difference between the Single and the Group printout macros is that the Group printout macro asks us after each invoice is printed if we would like to print another. The Single printout macro begins in location AB32:

```
{home}
{S}fccnTSHEET~
rf{?}~
{S}pasnuHEAD~qgll
```

```
snuADDR~qgl
snuBILL~qgpq
{m}eTSHEET~
{S}wuMAIN~
{MenuBranch Main_Menu}
```

After moving the cursor to Home to make sure that there is an area in which to combine the incoming file, the macro calls on the Services menu, using the same procedure as discussed in the ADD macro. At the {?}, we are expected to enter the name of the file that we wish to combine. It is brought into the TSHEET range, and the macro then moves on to the printing functions.

To facilitate the printing of the invoices, three Print Settings sheets are set up. Each is used to print a particular part of the invoice. The HEAD sheet prints out the range associated with the "letterhead" beginning at location AB54:

```
Smith, Ramesey, LeVeque, and Jones
345 Mount Diablo Drive
Pleasant Hill, CA  94523
(415) 555-4141
```

Of course, for your own application, you will put in your own name and return address.

After calling in the HEAD Settings sheet and printing the range called for, the macro causes two lines to be skipped (that is what the two l's are for in the fourth line of the macro) before going on to call for the next Print Settings sheet, ADDR. The range that the ADDR Settings sheet prints is the client's name, address, and city. This range is located in cells B4 to E8. After skipping another line, the next line of the macro calls in the last Print Settings sheet, BILL. The BILL Settings sheet prints out the BILL area, cell A18 to E42, and prints a footer on the bill identifying the firm and the date when the invoice was printed. Figures 31 through 33 show the Print Settings sheet, and Figure 34 shows what an invoice from this macro looks like.

As mentioned above, the Group print macro asks a question at the end of every printing cycle. The Group macro starts in location AB42:

```
{home}
{S}fccnTSHEET~
```

```
Use next settings sheet                                                    MENU
Use  Create  Delete  Previous  Next  Initial-Settings  Reset  Quit

 Page                          Source:       Range HEAD
   Length:      66             Destination: Printer
   Spacing:     1              Init-String:
   Number                      Margins          Other
     Print-Number: 1             Left:     4      Space Compression: No
     Start-Page:   1             Right:    76     Attributes:         Yes
     End-Page:     999           Top:      2      Format: As-Displayed
   Breaks:      Yes              Bottom:   2      Top-Labels:
   Wait:        No                                Left-Labels:
   Header:
   Footer:
                                              Print Settings: HEAD
```

Figure 31
HEAD Print Setting Sheet

```
Use next settings sheet                                                    MENU
Use  Create  Delete  Previous  Next  Initial-Settings  Reset  Quit

 Page                          Source:       Range ADDR
   Length:      66             Destination: Printer
   Spacing:     1              Init-String:
   Number                      Margins          Other
     Print-Number: 1             Left:     4      Space Compression: No
     Start-Page:   1             Right:    76     Attributes:         Yes
     End-Page:     999           Top:      2      Format: As-Displayed
   Breaks:      Yes              Bottom:   2      Top-Labels:
   Wait:        No                                Left-Labels:
   Header:
   Footer:
                                              Print Settings: ADDR
```

Figure 32
ADDR Print Settings Sheet

```
rf{?}~
{S}pasnuHEAD~qgll
snuADDR~qgl
snuBILL~qgpq
{m}eTSHEET~
{GetLabel "Are there more to be invoiced? (y or n), a1}~
{If a1="Y"#OR#a1="y"}{Branch loop1}
{S}wuMAIN~
{MenuBranch Main_Menu}
```

```
Use next settings sheet                                                    MENU
Use  Create  Delete  Previous  Next  Initial-Settings  Reset  Quit

 Page                         Source:      Range BILL
   Length:      66            Destination: Printer
   Spacing:     1             Init-String:
   Number                     Margins          Other
     Print-Number: 1            Left:     2      Space Compression: No
     Start-Page:   1            Right:    80     Attributes:        Yes
     End-Page:     999          Top:      2      Format: As-Displayed
   Breaks:      Yes             Bottom:   2      Top-Labels:
   Wait:        No                               Left-Labels:
   Header:
   Footer:      Smith, Ramesey, LeVeque, and Jones||@
                                                     Print Settings: BILL
```

Figure 33
BILL Print Settings Sheet

Loop1 is located adjacent to the line

```
{S}fccnTSHEET~
```

and if we select "yes", the macro returns to that location to continue asking for the file to be printed and whether there are more after printing out the invoice. This process continues until we respond with something other than a y or Y.

Variations

As mentioned earlier, variations on the theme can be accomplished with this macro. By learning how to move files into and out of each other, you can find new ways to combine information. For example, a macro that brings in the totals area from each client's file and uses the Add function rather than the Copy function could be used to produce a report of the productive hours and the revenue generated during a particular accounting period. Or you could take the information in each client's file, sort it as to the type of service provided, and do totals by service type during a given accounting period.

After thinking about this application for a while, you will probably come up with many variations of your own.

```
    Smith, Ramesey, LeVeque, and Jones
    345 Mount Diablo Drive
    Pleasant Hill, California  94523
    (415) 555-4141


    Miranda Johnson
    6789 Bridgeway
    Sausalito, CA  94965

==========================================================================
Date     Description                              Hours    Code    Bill Amt
----     -----------                              -----    ----    --------
Nov 4    Initial visit                              1.0 j            100.00
Nov 10   Review contracts                           0.5 p             25.00
                                                                       0.00
                                                                       0.00
                                                                       0.00
                                                                       0.00
                                                                       0.00
                                                                       0.00
                                                                       0.00
                                                                       0.00
                                                                       0.00
                                                                       0.00
                                                                       0.00
                                                                       0.00
                                                                       0.00
                                                                       0.00
                                                                       0.00
                                                                       0.00
                                                                       0.00
                                                                       0.00
                                        ---------------------------
                               TOTALS:     1.5                       125.00




Smith, Ramesey, LeVeque, and Jones                                  06/17/85
```

Figure 34
Sample Invoice

Nonprofit Organization

Although nonprofit organizations exist to satisfy a multitude of needs, they have many functions in common regardless of their purpose. The most common of these is fund-raising. Another common function, particularly among service-oriented nonprofit organizations, is that of matching resources (volunteers, housing, food, jobs, and so on) to clients' needs for those resources. The application presented here addresses these two key functions.

Before we go into detail, some background is in order. Fund-raising functions are crucial to the survival of any nonprofit organization. Integrated software applications can aid in improving the effectiveness of fund-raising campaigns by helping in the development of solicitation letters and other correspondence in a fast, economical way. It can help in several other areas as well. These include polling, targeting, and qualifying potential donors; establishing and analyzing scorecards to measure the effectiveness of a fund-raising approach; measuring the results of media purchases; and correlating data about target donor populations. Typically, such information is kept on index cards or in file folders. Extracting useful statistics to enhance fund-raising efforts becomes a time-consuming chore when done manually; as a consequence, it is frequently not done at all. The fund-raising portion of this Symphony application provides a good foundation for developing an effective fund-raising campaign. Enhancements you add may tailor it to your own uses, whether you are working with a small club, a political campaign, or some other organization that must rely on solicitations to raise revenue.

The other function of a nonprofit organization that will be addressed in this application is matching resources with clients. For the purposes of this macro, the resources will be volunteers for a tutoring program and the elementary school children who wish tutoring help. The organization referred to doesn't exist, and the names and addresses used are fictitious. With that out of the way, let's begin our scenario.

The Shady View Tutor Program

The Shady View Tutor Program is a program that brings adults and teenagers together with elementary school students to help the students master subjects such as reading, composition, math, history, geography, and science. It is a volunteer program funded by matching grants from a local trust fund and donations from the public. In administering the program, the director must be responsive to a board of directors and to various governmental agencies to assure that there is no discrimination in access to the tutoring program's services. To ease the director's workload, she has been fortunate enough to have a local computer consulting firm donate a computer, Symphony software, and the consulting time to develop SCL routines to assist in fund-raising and in matching volunteers with students.

What Do We Need?

One of the first things that the consultant did was to ask how many different functions the system was expected to perform. This helped the consultant determine how large the application would be. The director wanted the system to be easy enough to use so that unskilled volunteers could perform the clerical functions without knowing much about computers and knowing nothing at all about the Symphony program.

The director decided that the first priority was a database of donors so that a solicitation mailing could be sent. The next thing that was needed was some way of listing volunteers, and their skills and availability, as well as listing the children who needed the tutoring help.

After setting up the lists of volunteers and students, the director needed a way to match the volunteers and students that would be simple enough for the office volunteers to run without much training. This is where the Symphony software could really shine.

What Will This Look Like?

Like virtually all Symphony applications, this one would be menu driven. Five Main menu choices seemed to be necessary: Donors, Volunteers, Students, Reporting, and Quit. Under the Donors option the director would be able to add or delete donors, correct or update donor information, send correspondence, and return to the Main menu. Similar data-handling capabilities would be available under the Volunteers and Students options. In addition, the director would be able to match Volunteers and Students from either the Volunteers or the Students option. The Report menu was the area about which the director was least certain. The consultant said that this was not a problem, as Symphony was flexible enough to add menu items later if necessary. The director knew that she wanted to be able to print out masterlists of donors, volunteers, and students. The consultant

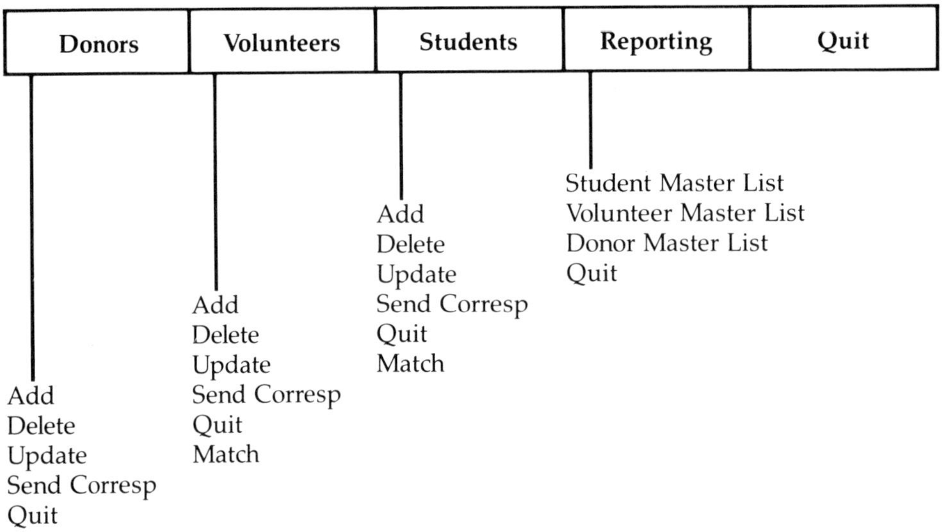

Figure 35
Main Menu for Nonprofit Application

said that this would mean four entries in the Reports menu: Students served, Volunteers, Donors, and Return to Main menu. Figure 35 shows how the Main menu is laid out.

Using this as a guide, the consultant set to work to build the Main menu macro. Using the Main menu layout, the consultant called the menus MAIN_MENU, DON_MENU, VOL_MENU, STU_MENU, and REPORT_MENU. The MAIN_MENU macro has five entries. The first, Donors, is started in location AA11:

```
Donors
Donor database
{MenuCall Don_Menu}
```

Next comes Volunteers, which begins in location AB11:

```
Volunteers
Volunteer database
{MenuCall Vol_Menu}
```

Next comes Students, which begins in location AC11:

```
Students
Student database
{MenuCall Stu_Menu}
```

Next comes Reports, which begins in location AD11:

```
Reports
Produce statistical reports
{MenuCall Report_Menu}
```

The last entry is Quit, which begins in location AE11:

```
Quit
Return to Symphony
{S}
```

Each entry, with the exception of the Quit option, calls additional submenus. Each of these menus will be described in further detail as it is encountered.

The consultant explained to the director that using a menu-driven application made it easy to add items. It would also shorten the amount of time before the Tutoring Program had something that office volunteers and the director could use to lighten their workload. As new macros were developed and checked out, they could then be integrated with the Main menu.

The consultant recommended a four-phase approach to implementing the system. Phase One would put the Donor database into shape and start generating funding for the project. Phase Two would establish the Volunteer and Student databases. Phase Three would match volunteers and students. Phase Four would provide ways to measure the effectiveness of both the funding and tutoring efforts. The remainder of this section will describe how the consultant set up the first three phases of the system.

Phase One: Funding the Program

The main goal of Phase One was to put the Tutoring Program on a sound financial footing. The way to do this was to attract donors to the program. This required establishing the Donor database and sending out mailings to attract donations.

The Donor Database

The first function that the consultant put together was a routine enabling the director to develop a mailing list and make a mass mailing to a list of suggested donors. Her present list had only names, addresses, phone numbers, and occupations. She wanted to set up the mailing list to avoid duplication of effort. If it could be made to serve as a mailing list as well as a database of other information, she wanted it to do so. She wanted some way to track the responses to the mailings and to do follow-up with such things as thank you letters and additional solicitations as time went on. She also wanted to set up the database so that as names of donors and potential donors were added, she could check on the sources of the names and use those sources to increase her effectiveness in attracting other donors. With this in mind, the consultant determined that each record in the Donor database should contain the following fields, with the indicated field lengths:

first name: 10
last name: 20
address: 30
city: 15
state: 2
zip code: 5
home phone: 10
occupation: 10
company: 30
company address: 30
company city: 15
company state: 2
company zip: 5
company phone: 10
total donated to date: 8
amount of last donation: 8

date of last donation: 8
solicitation type: 2
solicitation date: 8
thank you type: 2
thank you sent: 8
donor source: 2
referral numbers: 3

Although 23 fields looked like a lot of information, it provided a good basis for improving the odds of generating more donations for the Tutoring Program. The lengths of the various fields were set up to account for the various types of information they would contain. These field lengths were used to construct the Donor database and represented the column widths in the FORM window. The consultant used the method of entering the labels for each field in a vertical list starting in cell A251, and then let Symphony set aside the various ranges using DONOR as the FORM window name. These ranges included DONOR_DB (the database range), DONOR_CR (the criteria range), DONOR_EN (the entry range), and DONOR_DF (the definition range). Figure 36 shows the data entry form using the DONOR window (with most of the fields filled in).

After establishing the Donor database, the volunteers could enter the donor data. The initial information came from the mailing list that had been provided to the director, so there was little information in some of the fields, such as the solicitation date or the type of thank you sent. A chart of the codes used for the types of solicitation letters, thank you letters, and donor sources was printed up so that the volunteers wouldn't have to type out the full description each time an addition or change was made to the Donor database.

Here are the codes and their descriptions:

Solicitation letters:

in initial letter
sc second letter

Thank you letters:

ft first thank you letter
td thank you for $, more donors?

```
Editing Record 2 of 5                                                    FORM
Enter FIRST NAME

FIRSTNAME Farley____                      LASTNAME Smith______________
ADDRESS 876 Winnona___________________    CITY Will Valley____
STATE CA                                  ZIPCODE 94955
HOMEPHONE 4159987575                      OCCUPATION banker____
COMPANY Sells-Wargo___________________
COADDRESS 3 Market Plaza________________
COCITY San Francisco__                    COSTATE CA
COZIP 94011                               COPHONE 4159998558
$'STODATE 2500.00_                        LAST$AMT 2500.00_
DONATIONDATE 2-6-85__                     SOLICTYPE x_
SOLICDATE 1-5-85__                        THANKTYPE td
THXSENT ________                          DONSOURCE a1
#OFREFS 2__

DONOR                                                                   DONOR
19-Jun-85  03:18 PM                                       Calc
```

Figure 36
Donor Entry Form

Donor sources:

ml initial mailing list
rf referral from donor
a1 ad campaign #1
a2 ad campaign #2

The Donor Letters

After setting up the database, the consultant set up an area in the worksheet where the various donor solicitation and thank you letters could be inserted. For space considerations, we will include only two sample letters in this scenario. For your own implementation, you could include as many letters as you wish. The first letter to be set up was the initial solicitation letter; the second was the "thank you for your gift, do you have the names of other donors?" letter. The text of each one, as entered into the worksheet, is printed below. By now you should be familiar with the use of bracketed information. If you aren't, a refresher in the Third Movement may be in order.

The consultant set up the letters in DOC windows and then changed them to SHEET windows to enter the appropriate changes so that the letters could be used as reports drawing from the Donor database information to tailor each letter. By associating Settings sheets with each letter, it became easy for the consultant to develop the macro routines necessary to print out the letters.

Initial Solicitation Letter

This letter is the first one sent to the prospective donor. It sets a friendly tone by referring to the donor by first name. This technique, when employed with a well-worded letter, has been shown to increase the rate of response by several percent.

```
[FIRSTNAME] [LASTNAME]
[ADDRESS]
[CITY], [STATE] [ZIPCODE]

Dear [FIRSTNAME],

     I am taking the liberty of writing to you at this time to
ask your help in a new undertaking in this area.  You have
supported worthy causes, and I know that you will find the Shady
View Tutor Program deserving of your support.

     We are attempting to reach the elementary school population
of the Shady View School District with a program that will match
volunteer adults and teenagers with youngsters who need help in
the basic study areas of reading, composition, math, history,
geography, and science. The success of any program such as this
rests on the efforts of our dedicated volunteers, but we also
need other resources to make this program a real success.

     [FIRSTNAME], take a few moments to write a check to the
Shady View Tutor Program today and make the future bright for a
needy student tomorrow.  You will be glad that you did!
```

And don't forget, your donation is 100 percent tax deductible. Thank you from the volunteers and students of the Shady View Tutor Program.

Sincerely,

Ann Kurthy
Director

Thank You for Your Gift, Donors Names? Letter

The purpose of this letter is to solicit the names of additional donors after thanking the donor for the generous contribution. It uses references in the letter's text to the donor's first name, the date that the most recent donation was made, the amount of the donation, and the company with which the donor is affiliated. All these techniques for personalized references have been shown to improve the response in direct mailings.

[FIRSTNAME] [LASTNAME]
[ADDRESS]
[CITY], [STATE] [ZIPCODE]

Dear [FIRSTNAME],

Thank you very much for the generous donation that you made on [DONDATE]. The volunteers and students of the Shady View Tutor Program appreciate the interest that you have shown in our program. You can be sure that your [DONAMOUNT] will be put to good use.

May I at this time impose on your generosity again? We are trying to reach as many people as possible concerning this program. Do you know of anyone, perhaps at [COMPANY], or in your [CITY] neighborhood who might be interested in volunteering time or resources to this worthy cause? If you do, please jot down his or her name and address and forward it to us. Thank you

```
again, [FIRSTNAME], for your continued support of the Shady View
Tutor Program.

Sincerely,



Ann Kurthy
Director
```

The Donor Menu

After designing the database and the solicitation letters, the consultant developed the Donor menu and incorporated it into the Main menu macro structure. The entries for the Donor menu included Add Donors, Delete Donors, Update Donor information, Send Correspondence, and Return to the Main menu. The DOC_MENU macro for the Donor menu begins with the Add entry in location AA15:

```
Add
Add new donor
{AddDon}
```

The Delete entry begins in location AB15:

```
Delete
Delete a donor
{DelDon}
```

The Update entry allows the information stored for a particular donor to be changed, for example, when additional donations are made or when the address or phone number changes. The menu entry begins in location AC15:

```
Update
Update donor data
{UpDon}
```

The Send entry presents yet another menu so that the person using the macro can select the type of letter to be sent to the donor. The menu entry begins in location AD15:

```
Send
Send donor letters
{MenuCall Dlett_Menu}
```

The last entry of the Donor menu is the Quit option, and it will be the same for all of the submenus. The Donor menu begins in location AE15:

```
Quit
Return to Main Menu
{MenuBranch Main_Menu}
```

With that entry, only the Send correspondence menu remains to be developed for the donor part of the application.

The Send correspondence menu was set up to handle only the two letters that were to be sent initially. The consultant suggested that it was very simple to add the other letters to the menu. The Send menu entries shown here will illustrate how you might customize this application for yourself. The consultant called this menu the Dlett_Menu and set it up for three entries initially: Initial letter, Thanks/donor?, and Quit. The first entry begins in location AA19:

```
Initial
First solicitation
{Dinitial}
```

The second entry, Thanks, begins in location AB19:

```
Thanks
Thanks, donors names?
{Thankdonor}
```

The last entry, Quit, was set up to return the system to the Main menu. It begins in location AC19:

```
Quit
Return to Main Menu
{MenuBranch Main_Menu}
```

A note of caution here: because there was some desire on the part of the director for a second type of thank you letter, it was necessary in the second menu entry for a thank you letter to begin with some letter other than "T". If the menu had *not* been designed that way, the second letter could never be accessed by the user typing the first letter of the letter's name at the menu. Symphony, as you will recall, always finds the first word in a menu list that starts with the letter typed by the user as a command key.

The Donor Macros

The Donor menu and its submenu for sending letters needed macros to enable the selections. The following macros were developed to implement these menus:

AddDon — add donors to the database

DelDon — delete donors from the database

UpDon — update information about a donor

Dinitial — send the initial donor letter

Thankdonor — send a thank you letter and ask for the names of other potential donors

These macros will be described in detail in the following sections. Where you place macros in your implementation of this application is left up to you. We will indicate the location of our macros with the initial location of the label for the macro.

The Add Donor Macro

The Add Donor macro allows addition of donor names to the donor database. This is accomplished by accessing the Services menu and then moving to the Donor database. This macro is labeled AddDon at location AA50 and begins at location AB50:

```
{S}wuDONORS~{m}ci
```

This activates the DONOR window, then brings up the Database menu, selects Criteria, and then selects the Ignore option. This is done so that in case some selection criteria have been entered in the DONOR_CR range and haven't been flushed out, the data entry volunteer won't have a problem in entering data.

The Delete Donor Macro

The Delete Donor macro deletes names from the donor database. The label for this macro, DelDon, was put in location AA52; the first line of the macro begins at AB52. This macro accesses the Donor database, asks for the name that you want to delete, readjusts the database, clears the DONOR_CR range, and then returns to the Main menu. The macro commands look like this:

```
{S}wuDONORS~{m}ce{?}~{Insert}{esc}u{delete}{?}~{esc}
{blank a318..w318}
{S}wuMAIN~{Home}{MenuBranch Main_Menu}
```

The Update Donor Macro

The Update Donor macro provides ways of making changes to the Donor database entries. It checks first to see if a group of donors needs to be updated. If not, it requests the name of the donor who needs a modification, then goes to that donor in the database and allows the corrections to be entered. If a group of donors is to be updated, the macro branches to the Updgr macro. From there it searches for the donors who match the criteria selected so that corrections can be made. If there are no more corrections, the keystroke macro \C returns to the Main menu. The label for the Update macro, UpDon, is in location AA56, and the macro begins in location AB56:

```
{GetLabel "Do you want to update a group of donors? (y or n) ",a1}~
{if a1="y"#OR#a1="Y"}{branch Updgr}
{S}wuDONOR~{m}ce{?}~{Insert}{esc}u{?}~{Insert}{esc}
{blank a318..w318}{blank a1..a1}
{S}wuMAIN~{Home}{MenuBranch Main_Menu}
```

The macro that helps select the group of donors to be upgraded, Updgr, is labeled in location AA62 and begins in location AB62:

```
{S}wuDONOR~{m}ce{?}~{Insert}{esc}u{?}~{insert}
```

The last macro mentioned in this section is the \C macro. This macro is used to clear all the criteria areas for each of the three databases in this application and then return to the Main menu. It is labeled in location AA45 and begins in location AB45:

```
{blank a1..a1}{blank a318..w318}
{blank a565..w565}{blank a811..w811}
{S}wuMAIN~
{MenuBranch Main_Menu}
```

The Dinitial Macro

The Dinitial macro was designed to allow an initial solicitation letter to be sent to a person listed in the database. Rather than requiring a lot of extra work, it would pull the name and address information from the Donor database and personalize the letter. Since a limited number of volunteers help in the office, the director decided to send the initial solicitation letters out once a week. This meant that names could be added to the database as they came in, and then the Dinitial macro would be run weekly. It would review the Donor database, and any candidate donors who hadn't received the letter would have a letter prepared.

The actual macro is labeled Dinitial in location AA64, with the macro starting in AB64:

```
{S}wuDONOR~{m}ce{tab 17}IN~{insert}{esc}u{esc}
{S}pasnuDONINTIL~qgpq
{blank a318..w318}
{S}wuMAIN~{Home}{MenuBranch Main_Menu}
```

This macro accesses the Donor database, does a Criteria Edit, tabs to the entry in the DONOR form that lists the type of solicitation letter, and sets IN as the criterion that will be used. The macro then accesses the Services menu and moves to the Print selection. At this point, the Print Settings sheet, DONINTL, shown in Figure 37 is selected. The built-in Symphony Print routine goes to work, using the IN criterion and the DONINTL Database Settings sheet shown in Figure 38.

The Thankdonor Macro

Like the Dinitial macro, the Thankdonor macro was designed to allow a solicitation letter to be sent to a person listed in the database. In setting

```
Overall page settings                                                        MENU
Page  Source  Destination  Init-String  Margins  Other  Name  Quit

 Page                          Source:      Database DONINTL
   Length:      66             Destination: Printer
   Spacing:     1              Init-String:
   Number                      Margins         Other
     Print-Number: 1             Left:    4      Space Compression: No
     Start-Page:   1             Right:   76     Attributes:         Yes
     End-Page:     999           Top:     2      Format: As-Displayed
   Breaks:      Yes              Bottom:  2      Top-Labels:
   Wait:        No                               Left-Labels:
   Header:
   Footer:
                                            ===Print Settings: DONINTL
```

Figure 37
DONINTL Print Settings Sheet

```
Switch to next settings sheet                                                MENU
Use  Create  Delete  Previous  Next  Initial-Settings  Reset  Quit

Basic Ranges                           Report Ranges
  Database:      DONOR_DB                Main:          AA300..AH347
  Criterion:     DONOR_CR                Above:
  Output:                                Below:
Form Ranges                              Type           Single
  Entry:         DONOR_EN                  Entry list:
  Definition:    DONOR_DF                  Input cell:
Underscores:     Yes                   One-Record:      No
Sort-Keys
  1st-Key:               2nd-Key:                 3rd-Key:
    Order:                 Order:                   Order:
                                         ===Database Settings: DONINTL
```

Figure 38
DONINTL Database Settings Sheet

up this macro, the consultant used the copy capabilities of Symphony to copy the Dinitial macro into location AA69 and then made a few changes. The Thankdonor macro performed identically to the Dinitial macro with the following difference: any candidate donors who hadn't received the Thankdonor letter but who had made a contribution would have a letter prepared.

The actual macro is labeled Thankdonor in location AA69, with the macro starting in AB69:

```
{S}wuDONOR~{m}ce{tab 19}TD~{insert}{esc}u{esc}
{S}pasnuDONTHX~qgpq
```

```
Use next settings sheet                                                          MENU
Use  Create  Delete  Previous  Next  Initial-Settings  Reset  Quit

 Page                            Source:       Database DONTHX
   Length:       66              Destination:  Printer
   Spacing:      1               Init-String:
   Number                        Margins           Other
     Print-Number:  1              Left:     4       Space Compression:  No
     Start-Page:    1              Right:    76      Attributes:         Yes
     End-Page:      999            Top:      2       Format:  As-Displayed
   Breaks:       Yes               Bottom:   2       Top-Labels:
   Wait:         No                                  Left-Labels:
   Header:
   Footer:
                                                     Print Settings:  DONTHX
```

Figure 39
DONTHX Print Settings Sheet

```
Switch to next settings sheet                                                    MENU
Use  Create  Delete  Previous  Next  Initial-Settings  Reset  Quit

Basic Ranges                                Report Ranges
   Database:        DONOR_DB                  Main:          AJ300..AQ333
   Criterion:       DONOR_CR                  Above:
   Output:                                    Below:
Form Ranges                                   Type           Single
   Entry:           DONOR_EN                    Entry list:
   Definition:      DONOR_DF                    Input cell:
Underscores:        Yes                     One-Record:      No
Sort-Keys
   1st-Key:                 2nd-Key:                  3rd-Key:
     Order:                   Order:                    Order:
                                                  Database Settings:  DONTHX
```

Figure 40
DONTHX Database Settings Sheet

```
{blank a318..w318}
{S}wuMAIN~{Home}{MenuBranch Main_Menu}
```

This macro accesses the Donor database, does a Criteria Edit, tabs to the entry in the DONOR form that lists the type of thank you letter, and sets TD as the criterion that will be used. The macro then accesses the Services menu and moves to the Print selection. At this point, the Print Settings sheet, DONTHX, shown in Figure 39 is selected, and the built-in Symphony Print routine goes to work, using the TD criterion to select the letter's addressees. The DONTHX Print Settings sheet uses the DONTHX Database Settings sheet shown in Figure 40.

With this macro, the consultant had finished the work needed for Phase One. The staff overseeing the Shady View Tutoring Program could now maintain a list of prospective donors that was not only a mailing list but also a sophisticated database containing information that would be quite useful in the future solicitation of funds. They could also send personalized form letters asking for donations and acknowledging receipt of contributions. All these functions could be performed as simple menu-driven commands, thanks to the power of Symphony Command Language.

Phase Two: Attracting Volunteers and Students

The main goal of Phase Two was to build the Volunteer and Student databases. This was quite easy to do, once the type of information needed for each one was decided. Within the worksheet that the consultant set up, the Volunteer and Student databases were stored below the Donor database.

The Volunteer Database

The type of information that the director wanted was similar to that about the donors, except that she needed to be able to add the skills the volunteers possessed and the times when the volunteers would be available to help the students. The exact types of data included the following:

first name: 10
last name: 20
address: 30
city: 15
state: 2
zip code: 5
home phone: 10
occupation: 10
company: 30
company address: 30
company city: 15
company state: 2

company zip: 5
company phone: 10
subjects: 2
days available: 2
hours available: 4
thank you type: 2
thank you sent: 8
volunteer source: 2
referral numbers: 3

As with the Donor database, certain abbreviations for entries could be used. These, too, were printed out and distributed for ease of reference:

Subjects:

ma mathematics
re reading
co composition
hi history
ge geography
si science
sp spelling

Days of the week:

SU sunday
MO monday
TU tuesday
WE wednesday
TH thursday
FR friday
SA saturday

Hours of availability:

expressed in 24 hour time
e.g. 11:30 am 1130
3:30 pm 1530

```
Editing Record 2 of 4                                                    FORM
Enter FIRST NAME

VFNAME Ted_______                       VLNAME Bishop_____________
VADDRESS 67 Montgomery________________
VCITY San Francisco__                   VSTATE CA
VZIP 94123                              VHPHONE 4155559898
VOCCUPATION cartoonist
VCOMPANY Keep 'em Laffin______________
VCOADDRESS 67 Montgomery________________
VCOCITY San Francisco__                 VCOSTATE CA
VCOZIP 94123                            VCOPHONE 4155559898
VSUBJECTS sp                            VDAYS tu
VHOURS 1630                             VTHKTYPE  _
VTHXSENT  _______                       VSOURCE  _
VREF#  __

VOLUNTEER                                                          VOLUNTEER
19-Jun-85  03:26 PM                                          Calc
```

Figure 41
Volunteer Entry Form

Volunteer sources:

rf referral
a1 ad campaign #1
a2 ad campaign #2

Again, the consultant entered labels for each field in a vertical list, starting in cell A502, and let Symphony set aside the various ranges, using VOLUNTEER as the FORM window name. These ranges included VOLUNTEER_DB, VOLUNTEER_CR, VOLUNTEER_EN, and VOLUNTEER_DF. Figure 41 is an example of the data entry form using the VOLUNTEER window.

The Volunteer Letters

After setting up the Volunteer database, the consultant set up an area in the worksheet where the letters to Volunteers could be stored. This

```
Use next settings sheet                                                    MENU
Use  Create  Delete  Previous  Next  Initial-Settings  Reset  Quit

 Page                          Source:        Database VOLT1
   Length:      66             Destination: Printer
   Spacing:     1              Init-String:
   Number                      Margins          Other
     Print-Number: 1             Left:    4       Space Compression: No
     Start-Page:   1             Right:   76      Attributes:         Yes
     End-Page:     999           Top:     2       Format: As-Displayed
   Breaks:      Yes              Bottom:  2       Top-Labels:
   Wait:        No                                Left-Labels:
   Header:
   Footer:
                                               Print Settings: VOLT1
```

Figure 42
VOLT1 Print Settings Sheet

```
Switch to next settings sheet                                              MENU
Use  Create  Delete  Previous  Next  Initial-Settings  Reset  Quit

Basic Ranges                               Report Ranges
  Database:        VOLUNTEER_DB              Main:          AA560..AH600
  Criterion:       VOLUNTEER_CR              Above:
  Output:                                    Below:
Form Ranges                                  Type           Single
  Entry:           VOLUNTEER_EN                Entry list:
  Definition:      VOLUNTEER_DF                Input cell:
Underscores:       Yes                     One-Record:      No
Sort-Keys
  1st-Key:                2nd-Key:                   3rd-Key:
    Order:                  Order:                     Order:
                                            Database Settings: VOLT1
```

Figure 43
VOLT1 Database Settings Sheet

example will show you only one sample of the types of letters that could be used. The method for entering the letters into the worksheet is the same as that used for the Donor letters. By setting up a DOC window, the consultant could use the on-screen editing capabilities of Symphony; then she could change the window to SHEET format to enter in the appropriate changes to turn the letters into "reports" drawing on the VOLUNTEER database. Again, the consultant associated a Settings sheet, VOLT1 (see Figures 42 and 43), to the letter to help develop the macro routine necessary for printing out the letter.

The New Volunteer Letter

This letter is to be sent to new volunteers, after a list of matches to students is made. Its text and the bracketed information (to be used for tailoring the letter) follow:

```
[VFNAME] [VLNAME]
[VADDRESS]
[VCITY], [VSTATE]  [VZIP]

Dear [VFNAME],

     I am happy to welcome you to the Shady View Tutor Program.
You will find a list of names of students with whom we have been
able to match you.  After you have a chance to look this list
over, please give us a call at 333-4545.

     [VFNAME], we are really happy that you volunteered, and we
are sure that you will gain some real satisfaction from helping
the Shady View students.


Sincerely,



Ann Kurthy

Director
```

The Volunteer Menu

The Volunteer menu was very straightforward and, with the exception of the additional choice for matching students to volunteers, was laid out just like the Donor menu. The entries included Add Volunteers, Delete Volunteers, Update Volunteers, Send Correspondence, Match the Volunteer to the Students, and Return to the Main menu. The VOL_MENU macro begins with the Add entry in location AA23:

```
Add
Add a new volunteer
{AddVol}
```

The Delete entry begins in location AB23:

```
Delete
Delete a volunteer
{DelVol}
```

The Update entry allows the information stored for a particular volunteer to be changed, for example, when a schedule change is made or when the address or phone number changes. The menu entry begins at location AC23:

```
Update
Update volunteer data
{UpVol}
```

The Send entry presents yet another menu so that the person using the macro can select the type of letter to be sent to the volunteer. The menu entry begins in location AD23:

```
Send
Send volunteer letters
{MenuCall Vlet_Menu}
```

The Match entry in the Volunteer menu is used to request a match of a volunteer with the students in the Student database. This entry accesses another macro called MatchVS, starts in location AE23:

```
Match
Match volunteer to students
{MatchVS}
```

The last entry of the Volunteer menu is the Quit option; it begins in location AF23:

```
Quit
Return to Main Menu
{MenuBranch Main_Menu}
```

Following that entry, only one other menu had to be developed for the Volunteer part of the application, the Send Correspondence menu. That menu had two choices, Thanks and Quit. The Quit option looks like the one shown just previously and begins in location AB27. The Thanks option begins in location AA27:

```
Thanks
Thanks for volunteering
{Thankvol}
```

The Volunteer Macros

Using the power of Symphony, the consultant could set up the Volunteer macros by copying the Donor macros into the spaces below themselves and doing some minor editing. In the following discussion, the label location and name of the macro will be given, as well as the changes required in the Donor macro to make it work for the Volunteer database. The Match macro, which does not have a counterpart for the Donor database, will be discussed as part of the explanation of Phase Three. After moving and editing the Donor macros, the consultant handled the naming process by using the Range Name Label procedure suggested earlier in this book.

The Add Volunteer macro, AddVol, is labeled in cell AA74, and the only change made is to replace DONOR with VOLUNTEER. The Delete Volunteer macro, DelVol, is labeled in cell AA76, and two changes are made to replace DONOR with VOLUNTEER and to change the line.

```
{blank a318..w318}
```

to the line

```
{blank a565..w565}
```

The Update Volunteer macro, UpVol, substitutes the word *volunteers* for the word *donors*, VOLUNTEER for DONOR, and a565..w565 for a318..w318 in the Donor macro copied to location AA80. The companion macro, Upvgr, is based on the Updgr macro, with the substitution of VOLUNTEER for DONOR, and is labeled in location AA86.

The Send Correspondence macro, Thankvol, changes the Thankdonor macro by replacing DONOR with VOLUNTEER, {tab 19}TD with {tab 17}T1, DONTHX with VOLT1, and {blank a318..w318} with {blank a565..w565}. The Thankvol macro is labeled in location AA88.

The Student Database

After setting up the Volunteer database, the consultant went to work setting up the Student database. The information necessary for the Student database was similar to the other two. When actually setting up databases such as these three, the various copy commands in Symphony can save a significant amount of setup time. The data that the Student database contained included the following:

first name: 10
last name: 20
address: 30
city: 15
state: 2
zip code: 5
home phone: 10
responsible party first name: 10
responsible party last name: 20
responsible party phone: 10
school: 2
grade: 2
teacher: 15
subject: 2
days available: 2
hours available: 4
letter sent: 2

Because there were three schools in the Shady View School District, the only additional abbreviations that needed to be added to the abbreviations used for the Volunteer database were for the schools.

Schools:

sv Shady View Elementary
ns North Side Alternative
al Abraham Lincoln Elementary

```
Editing Record 4 of 4                                              FORM
Enter FIRST NAME

SFNAME Ricky_____
SLNAME Stubbs______________
SADDRESS 985 Seagull__________________
SCITY Will Valley____
SSTATE CA
SZIP 94955
SPHONE 4153334422
RPFNAME Richard___
RPLNAME Stubbs_____________
RPPHONE 4159993939
SCHOOL al
GRADE 4_
TEACHER Mrs. Brown_____
SSUBJECT ma
SDAY th
SHOUR 1530
SLETR __

STUDENT==================================================STUDENT
19-Jun-85  03:39 PM                                 Calc
```

Figure 44
Student Entry Form

Again the consultant entered the labels for each field in a vertical list, starting in cell A752, and let Symphony set aside the various ranges, using STUDENT as the FORM window name. These ranges included STUDENT_DB, STUDENT_CR, STUDENT_EN, and STUDENT_DF. Figure 44 shows the data entry form using the STUDENT window.

The Student Letters

As with the Donor and Volunteer databases, the consultant set up an area in the worksheet where the form letters to students could be stored. In this example, we will show you only one sample of the types of letters that could be used. The method for entering the letters into the worksheet is the same as that used for the donor and volunteer letters. By setting up a DOC window, the consultant could see the on-screen editing capabilities of Symphony and then change the window to SHEET format to enter in the appropriate changes to turn the letters into customized letters drawing on the Student database. Again the consultant associated a Settings sheet

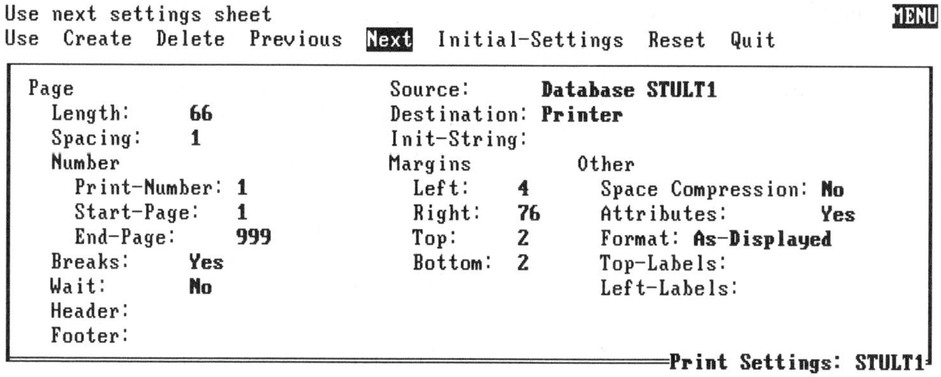

Figure 45
STULT1 Print Settings Sheet

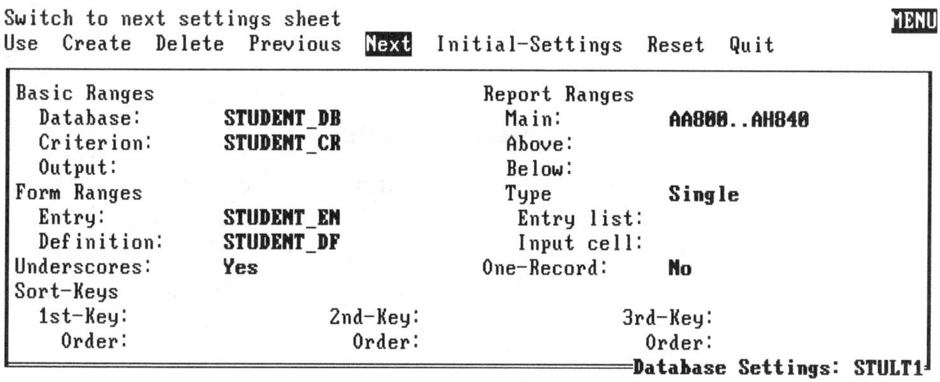

Figure 46
STULT1 Database Settings Sheet

(see Figures 45 and 46) to the letter to help develop the macro routine necessary for printing out the letter.

The New Student Letter

This letter is to be sent to new student participants after a list of matches to volunteers is made. Its text and the bracketed information (to be used for tailoring the letter) follow.

[RPFNAME] [RPLNAME]
[SADDRESS]
[SCITY], [SSTATE] [SZIP]

```
Dear [RPFNAME],

    I am happy to welcome your child to the Shady View Tutor
Program. You will find a list of names of tutors with whom we
have been able to match [SFNAME]. After you have a chance to
look this list over and talk about it with [SFNAME]'s teacher,
[TEACHER], and with [SFNAME], please give us a call at 333-4545.

    If you or [SNAME] have any questions, please give us a call.


Sincerely,


Ann Kurthy
Director
```

The Student Menu

The Student menu was also very straightforward and was laid out just like the Volunteers menu. The entries included Add Students, Delete Students, Update Students, Send Correspondence, Match the Student to the Volunteers, and Return to the Main menu. The STU_MENU macro begins with the Add entry in location AA31:

```
Add
Add a new student
{AddStu}
```

The Delete entry begins in location AB31:

```
Delete
Delete a student
{DelStu}
```

The Update entry allows the information stored for a particular student to be changed, for example, when a schedule change is made or when the address or phone number changes. The menu entry begins at location AC31:

```
Update
Update student data
{UpStu}
```

The Send entry presents yet another menu so that the person using the macro can select the type of letter to be sent to the student's family. The menu entry begins in location AD31:

```
Send
Send student letters
{MenuCall Slet_Menu}
```

The Match entry in the Student menu is used to request a match of a student with the volunteers in the Volunteer database. This entry accesses another macro called MatchSV, starts in location AE31:

```
Match
Match student to volunteers
{MatchSV}
```

The last entry of the Student menu is the Quit option; it begins in location AF31:

```
Quit
Return to Main Menu
{MenuBranch Main_Menu}
```

Only one other menu needed to be developed for the Student part of the application, the Send Correspondence menu. That menu had two choices, Initial and Quit. The Quit option looks like the one shown just previously and begins in location AB35. The Initial option begins in location AA35:

```
Initial
Welcome to the Program
{Sinitial}
```

The Student Macros

Using the Symphony magic one more time, the consultant set up the Student macros by copying the Volunteer macros into the space below themselves and doing some minor editing. As in the Volunteer discussion above, the label location and name of the macro will be given, and the changes required in the Volunteer macro to make it work for the Student database will also be shown. The Student Match macro will be discussed as part of the discussion of Phase Three. After moving and editing the Volunteer macros, the consultant handled the naming process by using the Range Name Label procedure.

The Add Student macro, AddStu, is labeled in cell AA104, and the only change made is to replace VOLUNTEER with STUDENT. The Delete Student macro, DelStu, is labeled in cell AA106, and the two changes that are made are to replace VOLUNTEER with STUDENT, and to change the line

```
{blank a318..w318}
```

with the line

```
{blank a811..w811}
```

The Update Student macro, UpStu, substitutes the word *students* for the word *volunteers*, STUDENT for VOLUNTEER, and a811..w811 for a565..w565 in the Volunteer macro copied to location AA110. The companion macro, Upsgr, is based on the Upvgr macro, with the substitution of STUDENT for VOLUNTEER, and is labeled in location AA116.

The correspondence macro, Sinitial, changes the Thankvol macro by replacing VOLUNTEER with STUDENT, {tab 17}T1 with {tab 16}S1, VOLT1 with STULT1, and {blank a565..w565} with {blank a811..w811}. The Sinitial macro is labeled in location AA118.

After completing the editing on these macros, the consultant finished the work necessary to complete Phase Two of the development of the application.

Phase Three: Matching Volunteers and Students

The goal of Phase Three was really the heart of the Shady View Tutoring Program — matching the students who had contacted the program for tutoring help with the volunteers who had responded. During Phase Three, the first few reports were designed as well. These reports were master lists of the Donors, Volunteers, and Students.

Matching Resources: Volunteers and Students

Within the structure of both the Student and Volunteer databases, the consultant set up three factors against which to match: the subject, the hour that the student or volunteer was available, and the day of the week that the student or the volunteer was available. Within the two macros set up to perform the matching function, the areas in the criteria ranges, STUDENT_CR and VOLUNTEER_CR, that contain this information are moved to the corresponding location in the opposite database's criteria range to make the matches. If there is no match, the error condition is handled, and the opportunity to change the matching criteria is provided.

This macro does not completely automate the matches. The person running the match must enter in the criteria for matching. Typically, this would be implemented by requesting a match right after the data concerning the student, or the volunteer, had been entered. Otherwise, the person running the matches would need to enter the name of the volunteer or the student to be matched, jot down the pertinent selection information (subject, time, day), and then enter it as called for in the matching macro.

Again, since the macros MatchVS and MatchSV are so similar, the complete listing for only one will be provided, with remarks as to which changes need to be made given in the text following. Both macros call another macro, reset, if an error condition occurs. This macro is labeled in location AA123:

```
{esc}{m}ce{?}~
{return}
```

The MatchVS macro is labeled in location AA93:

```
{S}wuVOLUNTEER~{m}ci
{m}ce{?}~{Insert}{esc}u
{type}s{m}rv0562..Q562~N811~
```

```
AJ800: +"Name: "&SFNAME&" "&SLNAME&""                                    SHEET

       AJ       AK       AL       AM       AN       AO       AP       AQ
800 Name: Sandy Ross
801 Address: 345 West King Dr.  Will City, CA  94960
802 Phone: 4153339999
803
804 Guardian: Fred Ross
805 Phone: 4153339999
806
807 Grade: 7
808 Teacher: Ms. Burks
809 School: ns
810 sv-Shady View Elem.  ns-North Side Alternative  al-A. Lincoln Elem.
811
812 Subject: sp         Day: mo            Hour: 1530
813 ma-math          re-reading      co-composition     hi-history
814 ge-geography     si-science      sp-spelling
815 ======================================================================
                                                                      MASV
18
19
20
                                                                      MAIN
19-Jun-85  03:41 PM
```

Figure 47
MASV Window

```
{type}f{S}wuSTUDENT~{m}ce{?}~{insert}{esc}u
{onerror reset}
{type}s{m}qeq
{S}pasnuMAV@S~qgpq
{blank a811..w811}{blank a565..w565}
{type}f{m}ci~
{S}wuMAIN~{Home}{MenuBranch Vol_Menu}
```

After entering the Volunteer database, the user enters the name of the volunteer to be matched. The part of the record that lists the subject, time, and day is then moved to the criteria area in the Student database. If there are no matches to the three criteria, the onerror macro calls the reset macro, which then resets the display and shows the user the three criteria.

The user can now delete some of the criteria to see about matching the volunteer with students who need a particular subject but don't match based on day or time. When matches are achieved, a printout of the matches is generated using the format shown in Figure 47. This makes use of the

```
Use next settings sheet                                                      MENU
Use  Create  Delete  Previous  Next  Initial-Settings  Reset  Quit

 Page                            Source:       Database MAV2S
   Length:     66                Destination: Printer
   Spacing:    1                 Init-String:
   Number                        Margins          Other
     Print-Number: 1               Left:     4      Space Compression: No
     Start-Page:   1               Right:    76     Attributes:          Yes
     End-Page:     999             Top:      2      Format: As-Displayed
   Breaks:     Yes                 Bottom:   2      Top-Labels:
   Wait:       No                                   Left-Labels:
   Header:
   Footer:
                                                   Print Settings: MAV2S
```

Figure 48
MAV2S Print Settings Sheet

```
Switch to next settings sheet                                                MENU
Use  Create  Delete  Previous  Next  Initial-Settings  Reset  Quit

Basic Ranges                              Report Ranges
  Database:        STUDENT_DB               Main:          AJ800..AQ815
  Criterion:       STUDENT_CR               Above:
  Output:          SV                       Below:
Form Ranges                                 Type           Single
  Entry:           STUDENT_EN                 Entry list:
  Definition:      STUDENT_DF                 Input cell:
Underscores:       Yes                    One-Record:      No
Sort-Keys
  1st-Key:                 2nd-Key:                  3rd-Key:
    Order:                   Order:                    Order:
                                                Database Settings: MAV2S
```

Figure 49
MAV2S Database Settings Sheet

Print Settings sheet MAV2S (Figure 48) and the Database Settings sheet MAV2S (Figure 49). The window used to format the list is named MASV and was set up as a DOC window and then changed to a SHEET window to enter the formulas to customize the list. This format is also used for the Student Master List discussed later in this movement.

Once the list is printed, criteria areas for both the Volunteer and Student databases are cleared, and the program returns to the Volunteer menu to see if there are any more Volunteer items to be done. This list can then be sent to the volunteer, along with the thank-you letter discussed earlier.

```
AA520: +"Name: "&VFNAME&" "&VLNAME&""                                SHEET

      AA      AB      AC      AD      AE      AF      AG      AH
520 Name: Sam Jones
521 Address: 765 Durant  Will Valley, CA  94955
522 Phone: 4159998877
523
524 Company: San Pablo High School
525 Phone: 4158886767
526
527 Subject: ma         Day: mo              Hour: 1530
528 ma-math          re-reading     co-composition     hi-history
529 ge-geography     si-science     sp-spelling
530
531 ======================================================================
532
533
534
535
                                                                    MAVS
18
19
20
                                                                    MAIN
19-Jun-85  03:43 PM
```

Figure 50
MAVS Window

The changes necessary to make this macro usable for matching in the other direction, that is, starting with a student rather than with a volunteer, are straightforward. The MatchVS macro is copied into location AA126 and renamed MatchSV. In the first line, STUDENT is substituted for VOLUNTEER. In the third line, O562..Q562 is replaced with N808..P808 and N811 is replaced with O565. In the next line, STUDENT replaces VOLUNTEER. In the seventh line, MAS2V replaces MAV2S, and in the last line, Stu_Menu replaces Vol_Menu.

The format that the list of volunteers who match the selected student takes is shown in Figure 50 and uses the window MAVS. This format is used for the Volunteer Master List, which is discussed in the "Reports" section below. Figures 51 and 52 illustrate the MAS2V Print Settings sheet and the MAS2V Database Settings sheet. With the changes, this macro functions in the same way as the MatchVS macro.

```
Use next settings sheet                                                    MENU
Use  Create  Delete  Previous  Next  Initial-Settings  Reset  Quit

 Page                           Source:      Database MAS2V
   Length:     66               Destination: Printer
   Spacing:    1                Init-String:
   Number                       Margins         Other
     Print-Number: 1              Left:    4      Space Compression: No
     Start-Page:   1              Right:   76     Attributes:        Yes
     End-Page:     999            Top:     2      Format: As-Displayed
   Breaks:     Yes                Bottom:  2      Top-Labels:
   Wait:       No                                 Left-Labels:
   Header:
   Footer:
                                              Print Settings: MAS2V
```

Figure 51
MAS2V Print Settings Sheet

```
Switch to next settings sheet                                              MENU
Use  Create  Delete  Previous  Next  Initial-Settings  Reset  Quit

Basic Ranges                            Report Ranges
  Database:       VOLUNTEER_DB            Main:          AA520..AH532
  Criterion:      VOLUNTEER_CR            Above:
  Output:         VS                      Below:
Form Ranges                               Type           Single
  Entry:          VOLUNTEER_EN              Entry list:
  Definition:     VOLUNTEER_DF              Input cell:
Underscores:      Yes                   One-Record:      No
Sort-Keys
  1st-Key:                2nd-Key:                 3rd-Key:
    Order:                  Order:                   Order:
                                              Database Settings: MAS2V
```

Figure 52
MAS2V Database Settings Sheet

The Reports

There are options for three reports in the Report menu: the Donor Master List, the Volunteer Master List, and the Student Master List. As the consultant explained to the director, the menu is expandable as the need for additional reports becomes apparent. Initially, these three reports will satisfy the needs of the program. The macros for these three reports are very similar. Each uses the appropriate Database and Print Settings

```
Use next settings sheet                                                  MENU
Use  Create  Delete  Previous  Next  Initial-Settings  Reset  Quit

 Page                           Source:      Database DONMAS
   Length:      66              Destination: Printer
   Spacing:     1               Init-String:
   Number                       Margins         Other
     Print-Number: 1              Left:    4      Space Compression: No
     Start-Page:   1              Right:   76     Attributes:          Yes
     End-Page:     999            Top:     10     Format: As-Displayed
   Breaks:      Yes               Bottom:  2      Top-Labels:
   Wait:        No                                Left-Labels:
   Header:      Shady View Tutor Program Donor Master List
   Footer:      Page #| |@
                                                 Print Settings: DONMAS
```

Figure 53
DONMAS Print Settings Sheet

```
Switch to next settings sheet                                            MENU
Use  Create  Delete  Previous  Next  Initial-Settings  Reset  Quit

Basic Ranges                          Report Ranges
  Database:     DONOR_DB                Main:         AA250..AH265
  Criterion:    DONOR_CR                Above:
  Output:                               Below:
Form Ranges                             Type          Single
  Entry:        DONOR_EN                  Entry list:
  Definition:   DONOR_DF                  Input cell:
Underscores:    Yes                   One-Record:     No
Sort-Keys
  1st-Key:                2nd-Key:                3rd-Key:
    Order:                  Order:                  Order:
                                              Database Settings: DONMAS
```

Figure 54
DONMAS Database Settings Sheet

sheets and runs through the standard printing routine. The Donor Master List macro is labeled in location AA 145 as DonList:

```
{S}wuDONOR~{m}ci
{S}pasnuDONMAS~qgpq
{S}wuMAIN~{Home}{MenuBranch Main_Menu}
```

This macro uses the DONMAS Print Settings and DONMAS Database Settings sheets (Figure 53 and 54) and produces a report that looks like Figure 55.

```
Shady View Tutor Program Donor Master List


Name: Fred Schwartz
Address: 987 Ryan  Will Valley, CA  94955

Phone: 4159987766

Company: Easy Way Movers
Address: 54 Commercial  San Rafael, CA  94945

Total Donations to Date:  $500.00
Last Donation: $500.00
Number of Refs:  0

Donor Source:  rf

======================================================================

Name: Farley Smith
Address: 876 Winnona  Will Valley, CA  94955

Phone: 4159987575

Company: Sells-Wargo
Address: 3 Market Plaza  San Francisco, CA  94011

Total Donations to Date:  $2500.00
Last Donation: $2500.00
Number of Refs:  2

Donor Source:  al

======================================================================

Name: Shiela Cruller
Address: 987 Dumbarton  Will Valley, CA  94955

Phone: 4158883333

Company: Shady Realty
Address: 4 Main Street  Will Valley, CA  94956

Total Donations to Date:  $0
Last Donation: $0
Number of Refs:  0

Donor Source:  rf

======================================================================


Page 1                                                          06/17/85
```

Figure 55
Sample Donor Master List

```
Use next settings sheet                                                          MENU
Use  Create  Delete  Previous  Next  Initial-Settings  Reset  Quit
┌─────────────────────────────────────────────────────────────────────────────────┐
│ Page                             Source:       Database MAS2V                    │
│   Length:     66                 Destination:  Printer                           │
│   Spacing:    1                  Init-String:                                    │
│   Number                         Margins          Other                          │
│     Print-Number: 1                Left:     4      Space Compression: No        │
│     Start-Page:   1                Right:    76     Attributes:        Yes       │
│     End-Page:     999              Top:      7      Format: As-Displayed         │
│   Breaks:     Yes                  Bottom:   2      Top-Labels:                  │
│   Wait:       No                                    Left-Labels:                 │
│   Header:     Shady View Tutor Program Volunteer Master List                     │
│   Footer:     Page #: |@                                                         │
└══════════════════════════════════════════════════════Print Settings: VOLMAS══════┘
```

Figure 56
VOLMAS Print Settings Sheet

The Volunteer Master List macro is labeled VolMaslst in location AA141:

```
{S}wuVOLUNTEER~{m}ci
{S}pasnuVOLMAS~qgpq
{S}wuMAIN~{Home}{MenuBranch Main_Menu}
```

This macro uses the VOLMAS Print Settings sheet (Figure 56) and the MAS2V Database Settings sheet used for matching a student to volunteers. A sample page of the Volunteer Master List is shown in Figure 57.

The Student Master List macro, StuServ, is labeled in location AA137:

```
{S}wuSTUDENT~{m}ci
{S}pasnuSTUMAS~qgpq
{S}wuMAIN~{Home}{MenuBranch Main_Menu}
```

This macro uses the STUMAS Print Settings sheet (Figure 58) and the MAV2S Database Settings sheet used for matching a volunteer to students. A sample page of the Student Master List is shown in Figure 59.

```
Shady View Tutor Program Volunteer Master List


Name: Sam Jones
Address: 765 Durant  Will Valley, CA  94955
Phone: 4159998877

Company: San Pablo High School
Phone: 4158886767

Subject: ma         Day: mo            Hour: 1530
ma-math         re-reading     co-composition     hi-history
ge-geography    si-science     sp-spelling

=======================================================================

Name: Ted Bishop
Address: 67 Montgomery  San Francisco, CA  94123
Phone: 4155559898

Company: Keep 'em Laffin
Phone: 4155559898

Subject: sp         Day: tu            Hour: 1630
ma-math         re-reading     co-composition     hi-history
ge-geography    si-science     sp-spelling

=======================================================================

Name: Peter Paul
Address: 43 Sweetooth Dr  Will City, CA  94956
Phone: 4156668888

Company: Choco-lot's
Phone: 4156667700

Subject: si         Day: th            Hour: 1630
ma-math         re-reading     co-composition     hi-history
ge-geography    si-science     sp-spelling

=======================================================================

Name: Ami Semple
Address: 938 Rockwood Court  Will Valley, CA  94955
Phone: 4159993324

Company: Starrunner Films
Phone: 4153459999

Subject: hi         Day: th            Hour: 1630
ma-math         re-reading     co-composition     hi-history
ge-geography    si-science     sp-spelling

=======================================================================


Page 1                                                        06/17/85
```

Figure 57
Sample Volunteer Master List

```
Use next settings sheet                                                   MENU
Use  Create  Delete  Previous  Next  Initial-Settings  Reset  Quit
┌────────────────────────────────────────────────────────────────────────────┐
│ Page                        Source:      Database MAV2S                     │
│   Length:     66            Destination: Printer                           │
│   Spacing:    1             Init-String:                                   │
│   Number                    Margins         Other                          │
│     Print-Number: 1           Left:    4      Space Compression: No        │
│     Start-Page:   1           Right:   76     Attributes:          Yes     │
│     End-Page:     999         Top:     10     Format: As-Displayed         │
│   Breaks:     Yes             Bottom:  2      Top-Labels:                  │
│   Wait:       No                              Left-Labels:                 │
│   Header:     Shady View Tutor Program Student Master List                 │
│   Footer:     Page #: |@                                                   │
└══════════════════════════════════════════════Print Settings: STUMAS═══════┘
```

Figure 58
STUMAS Print Settings Sheet

Where to from Here?

With the three databases as a foundation, the Shady View Tutor Program is off to a good start. Director Kurthy told the consultant about the interest shown by the local Boy Scouts and Girl Scouts in using just such a system for sustaining membership drives and for matching volunteers with troops and packs in the area.

By expanding on the reporting that can be extracted from the databases, the Shady View Tutoring Program (or any other organization using such a system) could measure the effectiveness of its ad campaign, for example, by counting the number of donors recruited by each ad. The best sources of volunteers could be determined in a similar fashion. As time went on, profiles of the amount of money donated by donors from each type of ad, or perhaps each type of occupation, could also be determined. A profile of volunteers showing occupation, residence, and other useful criteria for more successfully recruiting additional volunteers could also be developed. The possibilities for extracting data are extensive. And they are all based on setting up a well thought out database to begin with, coupled with the power of Symphony Command Language and the time to develop a useful set of macros.

```
Shady View Tutor Program Student Master List


Name: Sandy Ross
Address: 345 West King Dr.  Will City, CA  94960
Phone: 4153339999

Guardian: Fred Ross
Phone: 4153339999

Grade: 7
Teacher: Ms. Burks
School: ns
sv-Shady View Elem.  ns-North Side Alternative  al-A. Lincoln Elem.

Subject: sp         Day: mo              Hour: 1530
ma-math          re-reading     co-composition     hi-history
ge-geography     si-science     sp-spelling
=======================================================================
Name: George Booker
Address: 765 Main Street  Will City, CA  94956
Phone: 4156660000

Guardian: Ralph Worthington
Phone: 4156660000

Grade: 8
Teacher: Mr. Jenkins
School: al
sv-Shady View Elem.  ns-North Side Alternative  al-A. Lincoln Elem.

Subject: sp         Day: mo              Hour: 1630
ma-math          re-reading     co-composition     hi-history
ge-geography     si-science     sp-spelling
=======================================================================
Name: J.J. Johnson
Address: 45 Creekside Lane  Will Valley, CA  94955
Phone: 4152234545

Guardian: Herman Jones
Phone: 4152234545

Grade: 6
Teacher: Mr. Firkins
School: ns
sv-Shady View Elem.  ns-North Side Alternative  al-A. Lincoln Elem.

Subject: ma         Day: tu              Hour: 1530
ma-math          re-reading     co-composition     hi-history
ge-geography     si-science     sp-spelling
=======================================================================


Page 1                                                        06/17/85
```

Figure 59
Sample Student Master List

Personal Appointment Manager

This application is designed to permit you to keep track of appointments in the free-form way in which most of us handle that assignment. It is completely menu-driven and makes extensive use of SCL macro programming language and techniques.

Besides allowing you to *make* appointments, this macro also permits you to reschedule an appointment by changing its date and/or time, cancel an appointment, clear old appointments from your calendar, and get a list of a particular day's scheduled activities. It does all this within the confines of a SHEET environment. Only by using SCL macros can we implement such a relatively complex task without access to Symphony's FORM environment, with its additional operational complications.

An Overview of the Application

We have named our main macro for this application APPT and have stored the macros themselves beginning at cell address AA1. With appropriate spacing, the macros occupy the range AA1..AG99.

Starting the macro by pressing [F7] and typing APPT[↵] results in the screen shown in Figure 60 being displayed. The Main menu displayed across the top describes the first-level options available to the user of this application. The screen instructions are stored in a predetermined location (in this case, beginning in location A1). Setting the width of column A to be 80 characters enables us to create pleasant-looking and easy-to-follow instruction and title screens like that shown here. We use this technique in three places in this application, and it shows up in other applications in the Fourth Movement as well.

Note that the Main menu lists the following options: Add Appointments, Change Appointment, Purge Old Dates, Report, and the traditional Quit. We will briefly discuss how each option works and will then examine the macro code and Symphony environments of which each is composed.

Add Appointments

If you choose the Add Appointments option from the Main menu, you'll be asked to:

```
Enter date as 08-Aug-84
```

```
Creates new appointment                                                MENU
Add Appointments  Change Appointment  Purge Old Dates  Report  Quit

1                    Personal Calendar/Appointment Manager
2                          Lotus Symphony Application
3
4                                by Dan Shafer
5
6                      (c)1985, The Waite Group, Inc.
7
8
9   This application permits you to keep track of appointments, add and
10  reschedule appointments, and obtain reports showing your schedule for
11  certain dates.  Used in conjunction with your computer's built-in date
12  and time functions -- whether with a clock board or your manual entry
13  of this information -- the system can be asked to inform you of all
14  appointments for the day that fall AFTER the time you are running the
15  program.
16
17
18
19
20
                                                                     MAIN
26-Jun-85  05:51 PM                         Macro
```

Figure 60
Opening Screen of APPT Macro

The sample date is provided to indicate the format you should use to enter a date. Actually, whichever format your Symphony system is set to use for dates is acceptable. Since the macros at the core of this application make extensive use of the built-in @DATEVALUE function, this date must be entered in a usable format.

When you have given Symphony the date for which you wish to schedule an appointment, the program checks the range we call CAL (for CALendar) to see if that date already exists. If you already have at least one appointment on file for that date, the program simply creates a new entry for that date above the first one it finds and then allows you to enter the time and a description of the appointment. A sample entry screen for an appointment being entered on June 17, 1985, is shown in Figure 61. The program automatically created the 17-Jun-85 entry in which it has now positioned the cursor.

After you've added an appointment, the system automatically updates the file on the disk and then returns to the Main menu.

```
Enter time of appointment                                        SHEET

┌─────────B─────────C──────────────────D──────────────────────────────┐
200 12-MAY-85      2030     Meeting of finance committee at church
201 13-May-85      1115     Leave for San Francisco - public service meeting
202 13-May-85      1930     Huntington's for dinner
203 13-May-85      1430     Meet with attorneys re: lawsuit
204 14-May-85      1930     Anniversary dinner with Carolyn
205 14-May-85      0900     Breakfast with Mr. Okimoto re: Japanese markets
206 06-Jun-85      1100     Lunch in Berkeley with corporate suitors
207 17-Jun-85      ██████
208 17-Jun-85      0600     All day: trial begins in Davis
209 25-Dec-85      0900     Leave for Hawaii with wife
210
211
212
213
214
215
216
217
218
219
└═══════════════════════════════════════════════════════════════MAIN┘
26-Jun-85  04:16 PM                        Macro
```

Figure 61
Entry Screen Showing Appointment Being Added

If the date you indicate for your appointment doesn't already exist in your calendar, the program will ask if you wish to add the date, as shown in Figure 62. This is a new menu with a Yes-No-Quit range of selections.

Assuming that the date you entered was intentional, you'll want to choose the "Yes" option, which you can do by pressing Y or ↵. The system then adds the date to the bottom of the CAL range and asks you to enter the time and a description for the appointment. It then automatically updates the disk file and returns again to the Main menu.

Change Appointment

From the Main menu, selecting the Change Appointment option will result in a new submenu, shown in Figure 63, being displayed. You can do three things from this menu: reschedule an appointment, cancel an appointment, or Quit and return to the Main menu.

If you choose either of the first two options, you'll be asked to enter the date of the appointment you wish to change. The program will then

```
Add this date to calendar                                                MENU
Yes  No
┌──────────B──────────C──────────────────────D──────────────────────────────┐
200 12-MAY-85       2030      Meeting of finance committee at church
201 13-May-85       1115      Leave for San Francisco - public service meeting
202 13-May-85       1930      Huntington's for dinner
203 13-May-85       1430      Meet with attorneys re: lawsuit
204 14-May-85       1930      Anniversary dinner with Carolyn
205 14-May-85       0900      Breakfast with Mr. Okimoto re: Japanese markets
206 06-Jun-85       1100      Lunch in Berkeley with corporate suitors
207 17-Jun-85       0600      Leave for Davis
208 17-Jun-85                 All day: trial begins in Davis
209 25-Dec-85       0900      Leave for Hawaii with wife
210
211
212
213
214
215
216
217
218
219
└──────────────────────────────────────────────────────────────────────MAIN┘
26-Jun-85  04:22 PM                                              Macro
```

Figure 62
Do You Want to Add a Date?

```
Move an appointment                                                      MENU
Reschedule  Cancel  Quit
┌─────────────────────────────────A─────────────────────────────────────────┐
1               Personal Calendar/Appointment Manager
2                   Lotus Symphony Application
3
4                           by Dan Shafer
5
6                   (c)1985, The Waite Group, Inc.
7
8
9  This application permits you to keep track of appointments, add and
10 reschedule appointments, and obtain reports showing your schedule for
11 certain dates.  Used in conjunction with your computer's built-in date
12 and time functions -- whether with a clock board or your manual entry
13 of this information -- the system can be asked to inform you of all
14 appointments for the day that fall AFTER the time you are running the
15 program.
16
17
18
19
20
└──────────────────────────────────────────────────────────────────────MAIN┘
03-Jul-85  01:05 PM                                              Macro
```

Figure 63
Change Appointment Menu

```
Cancel this appointment                                                      MENU
Yes  No  Quit
       B              C                                D
200 12-MAY-85      2030     Meeting of finance committee at church
201 13-May-85      1115     Leave for San Francisco - public service meeting
202 13-May-85      1930     Huntington's for dinner
203 13-May-85      1430     Meet with attorneys re: lawsuit
204 14-May-85      1930     Anniversary dinner with Carolyn
205 14-May-85      0900     Breakfast with Mr. Okimoto re: Japanese markets
206 06-Jun-85      1100     Lunch in Berkeley with corporate suitors
207 17-Jun-85      0600     Leave for Davis
208 17-Jun-85               All day: trial begins in Davis
209 25-Dec-85      0900     Leave for Hawaii with wife
210 16-Nov-85      1120     Plane leaves for Boston conference
211
212
213
214
215
216
217
218
219
                                                                            MAIN
03-Jul-85  01:06 PM                         Macro
```

Figure 64
Cancellation Submenu Display

look through your CAL range to find the first appointment with that date. (If it cannot find such a date, a message appears indicating that the date is invalid.) Assuming that it finds an appointment with that date, the system displays another submenu (see Figure 64) asking if you want to cancel (or reschedule) the appointment to which the cell pointer is now pointing, look for the next appointment for the same date, or cancel the operation and return to the Main menu.

Answering "N" or "Q" to this submenu selection has the same effect whether you are canceling or rescheduling appointments. An "N" tells the computer: "You're on the right track, but this isn't the one I want to work with. Please find the next one for this date." A "Q" means: "I decided not to change any appointment. Take me back to the Main menu, please." What happens when you answer "Y" depends on whether you are canceling or rescheduling appointments.

```
New date=                                                              MENU

   B              C                    D
200 12-MAY-85      2030     Meeting of finance committee at church
201 13-May-85      1115     Leave for San Francisco - public service meeting
202 13-May-85      1930     Huntington's for dinner
203 13-May-85      1430     Meet with attorneys re: lawsuit
204 14-May-85      1930     Anniversary dinner with Carolyn
205 14-May-85      0900     Breakfast with Mr. Okimoto re: Japanese markets
206 06-Jun-85      1100     Lunch in Berkeley with corporate suitors
207 17-Jun-85      0600     Leave for Davis
208 17-Jun-85               All day: trial begins in Davis
209 25-Dec-85      0900     Leave for Hawaii with wife
210 16-Nov-85      1120     Plane leaves for Boston conference
211
212
213
214
215
216
217
218
219
                                                                       MAIN
05-Jul-85   11:06 AM                    Macro
```

Figure 65
Rescheduling an Appointment

Canceling Appointments

If you are canceling appointments and answer "Y" to the submenu, the indicated appointment will be removed from the CAL range, all appointments below it will be moved up one position, and the disk will be automatically updated.

No further intervention on your part is required. You will be automatically returned to the Main menu for your next instruction.

Rescheduling Appointments

Rescheduling an appointment is a simple matter of changing its date and/or time. The application simply positions the cell pointer over the date cell and asks you to enter a new date, as shown in Figure 65. You must enter a date, even if it is the same. Then the cell pointer moves to the time cell and asks for a new time. Once again, you must enter a time, even if it is unchanged.

```
Enter purge date...                                              SHEET

                         PURGE CALENDAR INSTRUCTIONS

This routine clears all appointments from your calendar that fall before
a specific date.  You may either enter a date in the usual format (e.g.,
08-Aug-84) or simply type T (and press RETURN) to mean you want
to remove all calendar items that are older than today's date.

The purge process can take a few moments and is IRREVERSIBLE.  Be sure
it's what you want to do before you call for it.

You may now enter the date the system should use as the purge date.

                                                                   MAIN
03-Jul-85  01:08 PM                         Macro
```

Figure 66
Purge Old Dates Instructional Display

Once you've given the system the new date and time for the appointment, it automatically updates the disk file and returns you to the Main menu.

Purging Old Dates

There are two ways to ensure that your calendar stays current (assuming that you want it to do so), without a lot of old appointments cluttering it up. The first is to cancel appointments as they happen; the second is to use the system's handy Purge Old Dates function.

Using the Purge Old Dates option, you can have the system automatically delete any appointment that falls before a date you supply. When you run this option, a new display screen of instructions (see Figure 66) is provided so that you can understand both the process and the importance of being sure of your ground before purging dates from the calendar.

Notice that one option available on this selection is the ability to enter "T" to mean "today" instead of a date in the usual format. Thus if you

```
A41:                                                              SHEET
                                   A
41
42        Please wait while I search your calendar for the date you've
43              requested.  A new menu will appear when I'm done.
44
45
46
47
48
49
50
51
52
53
54
55
56
57
58
59
60
                                                                  MAIN
03-Jul-85  01:11 PM
```

Figure 67
Report Instructional Display

want to purge all old dates from your calendar, choose Purge Old Dates and enter "T" for the date.

The system automatically performs the disk file update when the purge process is complete (which is, of course, why you must be sure that you're purging the dates you want to purge before you order the system to proceed!).

Reports

In the application's present design, you can get only one report: a listing of all of the appointments for a given date. Once again you can enter either "T" to mean "today" or a date in the usual format.

When you ask for the Report option, a screen of instructions such as that shown in Figure 67 appears. You are asked to enter the date for which you would like to see your appointments. After entering the date, or "T" for today, the message shown in Figure 67 is displayed.

```
Display Appointments                                                      MENU
Display  Print  Quit
            B         C                                  D
200 12-MAY-85      2030    Meeting of finance committee at church
201 13-May-85      1115    Leave for San Francisco - public service meeting
202 13-May-85      1930    Huntington's for dinner
203 13-May-85      1430    Meet with attorneys re: lawsuit
204 14-May-85      1930    Anniversary dinner with Carolyn
205 14-May-85      0900    Breakfast with Mr. Okimoto re: Japanese markets
206 06-Jun-85      1100    Lunch in Berkeley with corporate suitors
207 17-Jun-85      0600    Leave for Davis
208 17-Jun-85              All day: trial begins in Davis
209 25-Dec-85      0900    Leave for Hawaii with wife
210 16-Nov-85      1120    Plane leaves for Boston conference
211
212
213
214
215
216
217
218
219
                                                                          MAIN
03-Jul-85  01:11 PM                           Macro
```

Figure 68
Report Submenu

Once the system has located all the relevant appointments, regardless of where they are found in your CAL range, it will position the cell pointer at the bottom of that range and ask if you want to see the report on the screen (Display) or as a printed report (Print) or if you want to Quit and return to the Main menu. This submenu is shown in Figure 68.

Figure 69 shows what a typical display might look like for a single day's schedule. Note that the appointments are not sorted by time (a process that in Symphony would require use of the FORM environment). Since we typically have only a few appointments in a day, that should not pose a serious problem.

The APPT Macros

Now that you understand how to *operate* the appointment application, let's look at how the macros that control it are designed. In the process we'll uncover some interesting aspects of macro programming.

```
Pres RETURN to Continue                                                          SHEET

    B              C                    D
300
301 13-May-85      1115     Leave for San Francisco - public service meeting
302 13-May-85      1930     Huntington's for dinner
303 13-May-85      1430     Meet with attorneys re: lawsuit
304
305
306
307
308
309
310
311
312
313
314
315
316
317
318
319
                                                                                  MAIN
03-Jul-85  01:12 PM                                  Macro
```

Figure 69
Single Day's Schedule

Startup Macro

The first macro stored in our worksheet is called APPT. This is the macro we execute to get the application started. It contains only one line:

```
{BLANK TEMP}{GOTO}A1~{MENUCALL MAINMENU}
```

This macro erases anything that might presently be stored in an area we call TEMP (which in our case is a range covering cell addresses B1..C21 — essentially one "page" of cells). Since this area is used extensively by the program to store temporary values during execution, it must be blank at the start of each run of the application.

After clearing that temporary storage area, the macro positions the cell pointer at cell A1, a process that we have already explained results in a displayed title screen and some basic instructions about the program.

Finally, the menu MAINMENU is displayed.

MAINMENU Macro

The macro labeled MAINMENU is the point at which all the action in the program originates and to which it returns after executing one of the subtasks it manages. In keeping with good modular, top-down program design, all of the Main menu choices execute calls to routines. The only exception to this rule is the Quit option, which performs its usual exit from Symphony by means of the following sequence:

```
{S}EY~
```

The menu macro for the Add Appointments portion looks like this:

```
Add Appointments
Creates new appointment
{ADD}
```

The Change Appointment option differs slightly in that it calls a submenu, as you can see from this listing of its contents:

```
Change Appointment
Reschedule or Cancel
{MENUCALL MODMENU}
```

The Purge Old Dates option calls a routine called {PURGE}, and the Report option executes a routine labeled {TICKLER}. (We used the name "TICKLER" because what we have created is a tickler file of future dates for you to be reminded about.)

Let's look at the {ADD}, {PURGE}, and {TICKLER} macros as well as the {MODMENU} menu and its associated segments in greater detail.

The {ADD} Macro Collection

The {ADD} macro looks like this:

```
            {GETLABEL Enter date as 08-Aug-84 ,B1}~
            {LET C1,@DATEVALUE(B1)}
            {LET B2,0}~{GOTO}CAL~
LOOP1       {IF @DATEVALUE(@INDEX(CAL,0,+B2)))=C1}{BRANCH ENTRY}
            {IF @CELLPOINTER(``TYPE")="b"}{BRANCH ADD_DATE}
            {DOWN}{LET B2,B2+1}~{BRANCH LOOP1}
```

It includes two other macros, which will be discussed shortly: ENTRY and ADD_DATE.

The first line of the {ADD} macro is a GETLABEL command that asks the user to enter the date of the appointment to be added, supplies an example of the format, and stores the answer in cell B1, which is the upper left corner of our TEMP range. The next line converts the date that has just been entered into a serial number (see *Symphony Reference Manual*, Chapter 13, for a detailed discussion of date formats and the @DATEVALUE function). It stores the result in cell C1 for later use. This permits us to compare the dates stored in the CAL range against the date the user is seeking.

Next, our {ADD} macro places a zero in cell B2 and then moves the cell pointer to the CAL range.

These first three steps are repeated frequently during other portions of the application, so you should be sure that you understand their operation now.

An important thing to note about the named range CAL is that you must set aside and name this range before you run this macro. If you refer to the list of named ranges in Coda B, you will find that we set aside B200 to D264 for CAL. It also helps when setting your calendar up initially to enter one date into B200..D200 manually. This gives your macro values with which to operate.

The @INDEX Function in a Scanning Loop

The next three lines of the {ADD} SCL macro comprise a loop with two conditional expressions and a "scanning" process. The first line of this loop, labeled LOOP1, checks the @DATEVALUE of the first entry in the CAL range against the contents of cell C1.

To do this, we use Symphony's @INDEX function. The expression

```
@INDEX(CAL,0,+B2)
```

tells Symphony to look at the zero-th column, in the row number contained in cell address B2. This is a method of *indirect cell addressing*, which you'll find quite useful as you develop your own SCL macros. It is worth spending a moment to explain.

The first row and column of a range such as CAL are referred to as the zero-th row and the zero-th column. Thus in Figure 70, the expression

```
@INDEX(CAL,0,0)
```

```
B200: '12-MAY-85                                                        SHEET

        B              C                          D
200 12-MAY-85       2030      Meeting of finance committee at church
201 13-May-85       1115      Leave for San Francisco - public service meeting
202 13-May-85       1930      Huntington's for dinner
203 13-May-85       1430      Meet with attorneys re: lawsuit
204 14-May-85       1930      Anniversary dinner with Carolyn
205 14-May-85       0900      Breakfast with Mr. Okimoto re: Japanese markets
206 06-Jun-85       1100      Lunch in Berkeley with corporate suitors
207 17-Jun-85       0600      Leave for Davis
208 17-Jun-85                 All day: trial begins in Davis
209 25-Dec-85       0900      Leave for Hawaii with wife
210 16-Nov-85       1120      Plane leaves for Boston conference
211
212
213
214
215
216
217
218
219
                                                                        MAIN
03-Jul-85  01:13 PM
```

Figure 70
CAL Range for @INDEX Retrieval

yields the result "12-May-85".

The first value after the @INDEX function — in our example the range CAL — is the name or cell addresses of a range where the data is to be looked up. The next value is the column to be searched, and the next is the row to be used. Looking again at Figure 70, using the expression

```
@INDEX(CAL,0,2)
```

yields the result "13-May-85", and the expression

```
@INDEX(CAL,0,4)
```

will produce the result "14-May-85". The @INDEX function, then, allows us to scan a range of data looking for something specific, a row or column at a time.

Returning to the example macro we are discussing, we check the particular row in column 0 (the date column) of the CAL range to see if its contents match those in cell C1. Remember that C1 contains the @DATE-VALUE of the date for which we are searching. If we find a match, the macro calls for a branch to a routine called ENTRY, which we will examine shortly.

If the entry being looked at does not match what we are searching for, the next statement is carried out. This statement uses the built-in Symphony function @CELLPOINTER to determine the type of data contained in the cell in question. If the type is "b", then the cell is blank. Because of the way we've set up the CAL range and handled deletions and changes to it, a blank cell indicates the end of the values stored in the range. When Symphony encounters a blank cell, it concludes that it must have been given a date that doesn't yet exist in the CAL range. In response, it branches to a routine called ADD_DATE, which we will discuss shortly.

If the cell being pointed to at the moment is neither a match nor a blank cell, the final line of the {ADD} macro is executed. This line moves the cell pointer down one cell to look at the next cell in sequence, adds one count to the value in cell B2, and returns to the line labeled LOOP1, where the checking process is repeated.

By incrementing the contents of cell B2 each time we scan through another line of the CAL range, we will eventually look at all the cells unless we find a match.

{ENTRY} Macro

The {ENTRY} macro looks like this:

```
        {M}IR~
        {PANELOFF}{DOWN}{M}C~{UP}~{UP}{RIGHT}
ENTRY2  +"{GETLABEL Enter time of appointment
        ,C"&@STRING(B2+200,0)&"}{RIGHT}"
        +"{GETLABEL Description ==> ,D"&@STRING(B2+200,0)&"}"
        {S}FS~Y
        {GOTO}A1~{MENUBRANCH MAINMENU}
```

Except for some fairly intricate string arithmetic, this macro should be easy to follow. The first line opens a row at the location where the date for which we have been looking has been found. The next line, after turning off the control panel so that the screen display won't confuse the user, copies the date from the entry where it was found into the date field of the newly created appointment row.

The next two lines use string arithmetic to handle indirect cell addressing. We often have the *address* (or part of the address, usually a row number) of a cell stored in a location, but we don't necessarily know in advance which address we'll want to access until we have carried out some other tasks. What we need is a way of branching to a cell location without knowing in advance what that location will be. String arithmetic is the only workable solution to this problem that will operate correctly in all situations.

We start a string arithmetic line with a plus sign so that Symphony will know it is not a label but a formula. In the example lines shown, the next material must be entered into the formula line exactly as it is furnished, so we put this information inside double quotation marks. (Single quotation marks won't do, by the way.)

Now we come to a place where we need an @ function to complete the string manipulation process. In this case, we use the @STRING function to convert the value stored in cell address B2 — plus an arbitrary 200, which is there because of where we place the CAL range in our application — into a string with no decimal places. The decimal places are defined by the second argument in the parentheses after the @STRING function is coded; usually, we will use zero there.

When cell B2 contains a zero, as it does when the program starts, this arithmetic will put the following command line in place in the macro:

```
{GETLABEL Enter time of appointment ,B200}{RIGHT}
```

In fact, if you code such a string arithmetic line in a macro, you may be surprised to see that as you press [↵] to indicate to Symphony that the line is ready for entry into the SHEET, Symphony actually performs the calculation on the @STRING and stores the line above in the macro. Yet if you look at the contents of this cell on the control panel, you will see that the formula as it was originally entered is still stored there.

The remainder of the {ENTRY} macro is easy to follow, so no further explanation will be offered.

{ADD_DATE} Macro

The macro we've labeled ADD_DATE offers an example of using a submenu inside a macro to continue the friendly, menu-driven approach to program design that we decided was important to the program's usefulness. Its contents are as follows:

```
{BEEP 3}
{MENUCALL DATEMENU}
```

The DATEMENU, on the other hand, looks like this:

```
Yes                                 No
Add this date to calendar           Date entered in error
+"{GOTO}B"&@STRING(B2+200,0)&"~"    {APPT}
{M}cb1~~
{RIGHT}{BRANCH ENTRY2}
```

Note the use of string arithmetic for indirect cell addressing in the third line of the menu macro. This line moves the cell pointer to the end of the CAL range, and the next line copies the contents of cell B1 to this new location. The last line of the Yes portion of the macro moves the cell pointer into the time column and then branches to ENTRY2, a special location inside the {ENTRY} macro. This location avoids doing certain tasks that we want to do only when adding an appointment through the normal menu process.

The No option demonstrates a different way to return to the beginning of the macro execution. Normally this application will use a construction like this:

```
{GOTO}A1~{MENUBRANCH MAINMENU}
```

to return to the beginning of the macro. This line is clearer for people who need to understand our code, but it is obviously not nearly as efficient as the single-entry macro call.

Changing Appointments: {MODMENU} Macros

As we have indicated, the Change Appointment option from the Main menu of the Appointment application immediately calls a submenu, MODMENU. This menu is a modularly designed portion of the program, with each menu option except Quit simply invoking a call to another macro. The

Quit option executes the familiar {MENUCALL MAINMENU} command. The other two options on the menu look like this:

```
Reschedule                    Cancel
Move an appointment           Cancel an appointment
{RESKED}                      {CANCEL}
```

Let us now look at the {RESKED} and {CANCEL} macros, each of which invokes yet another menu during the course of its execution.

{RESKED} Macro

Here is a complete listing of the macro {RESKED}. Much of it is familiar, so we will explain only new material in the discussion that follows its listing.

```
         {GETLABEL Enter date as 08-Aug-84 ,b1}~
         {LET C1,@DATEVALUE(B1)}
         {LET B2,0}~{GOTO}CAL~
LOOP3    {IF @DATEVALUE(@INDEX(CAL,0,+B2)))}{MENUBRANCH
         MOVEMENU}
         {IF @CELLPOINTER("TYPE")="b"}{BRANCH BAD_DATE}
         {DOWN}{LET B2,B2+1}~{BRANCH LOOP3}
```

There are two key differences between this macro and other macros we've seen that handle calendar management. First, when the program finds a date that matches the date entered by the user and whose @DATE-VALUE is stored in cell C1, it calls another menu, MOVEMENU, instead of branching to a macro routine. Second, when it reaches the end of the calendar area, as signified by its encountering a blank cell, it branches to a routine that informs the user that the date he is trying to reschedule doesn't exist.

{MOVEMENU} Macro

The MOVEMENU macro represents an effective way of handling Yes-No input from users in our SCL applications. The part of the menu that handles rescheduling looks like this:

```
Yes
Reschedule this appointment
```

```
+"{GETLABEL New date= ,B"&@STRING(B2+200,0)&"}"
+"{RIGHT}{GETLABEL New Time= ,C"&@STRING(B2+200,0)&"}"
{S}FS~Y
{GOTO}A1~{MENUBRANCH MAINMENU}
```

Note again the use of string arithmetic to create an executable string formula containing indirect cell references. Again, cell B2's contents — increased by 200 to position the cell pointer within the CAL range that starts at B200 — provide the row number for the new entries. The last lines update the file and return to the Main menu.

The segment of the MOVEMENU that looks for the next occurrence of the requested date, if the one last found is not the one to be rescheduled, looks like this:

```
{DOWN}{LET B2,B2+1}~{BRANCH LOOP3}
```

This line is identical to the last line of the RESKED macro itself. Another way of handling this task would be to give that last line a label and then simply code a branch to that label here. We chose the method shown because it is cleaner and easier to read. But the alternative approach would be slightly more memory efficient.

{BAD_DATE} Macro

The macro called BAD_DATE, which is also used by the CANCEL macro discussed in the next section, simply informs users of their mistake, waits for them to indicate that they've read the message, and then returns to the Main menu with nothing in the CAL range affected. It looks like this:

```
{BEEP}
{GETLABEL No such date.  Try again.  Press RETURN,TEMP}
{GOTO}A1~{MENUBRANCH MAINMENU}
```

There is nothing mysterious here. Such a macro is one for which we find frequent need in designing Symphony applications.

{CANCEL} Macro

The macro that handles cancellation of an appointment is virtually identical to the {RESKED} macro we have just examined. It is located in the range AA37..AD47 in the application listing in Appendix B and is not reproduced here in its entirety. It calls a menu called {KILLMENU}, which looks like this:

```
Yes                       No
Cancel this appointment   Look for next one
{M}DR~{S}FS~Y             {DOWN}{LET B2,B2+1}~{BRANCH LOOP2}
{GOTO}A1~{MENUBRANCH MAINMENU}
```

The Quit option, not shown here, is identical to the other Quit selections we've examined.

The cancellation of an appointment is handled by simply deleting the row on which it occurs. We can do this without interfering with the application only because we mapped out the use of the worksheet in advance (as we suggested you do in the Third Movement of our orchestration of Symphony). The one-line macro here carries out some very powerful processes: deleting a row and updating the file, all with a very small number of one-letter commands. It is a good example of the power — and the danger — of SCL!

Purging Old Dates: {PURGE} Macros

The next Main menu function we will examine is the Purge Old Dates option. In some ways, this set of macros is similar to those that manage making, rescheduling, and canceling appointments. However, it introduces a peculiarity or two of its own, and so we will examine it in some detail.

Stored in the range AA67..AB75 of our worksheet (see Appendix B), the main PURGE macro looks like this:

```
        {GOTO}A22~
        {GETLABEL Enter purge date... ,B1}
        {IF B1="T"#OR#B1="t"}LET C1,@INT(@NOW))}~{BRANCH LOOPP}
        {LET C1,@DATEVALUE(B1)}~
LOOPP   {LET B2,1}~{GOTO}CAL~{DOWN}
LOOP4   {LET C2,@DATEVALUE(@INDEX(CAL,0,+B2))}~
        {IF C2=0}{BRANCH DONE}
        {IF C2<C1}{M}DR~{BRANCH LOOP4}
LOOP5   {DOWN}{LET B2,B2+1}{BRANCH LOOP4}
```

The first line of this macro moves the cell pointer to cell A22. The instructions for the use of the PURGE macro shown in Figure 66 are stored in this area.

The {GETLABEL} command in the second line allows the user to enter the purge date to be used. The third line then checks to see if a "t" has been entered, meaning that the user wants to use today's date as the purge date. Note that we check for both an uppercase "T" and a lowercase "t"; either will result in the IF expression evaluating to a true condition. It is important to remember to check for both (or all) possible occurrences of user input when performing this kind of input evaluation.

If the user enters a "T" or a "t", the program places the integer value of the current date and time (@NOW) into cell C1. The integer value is the date, while the decimal portion (which we ignore here) contains the time serial number. We must then branch *around* the next line, which stores in cell C1 the @DATEVALUE of the date entered when that date is *not* today.

The three lines of code at the label LOOP4 require a brief explanation. The first stores at cell C2 the @DATEVALUE of the cell being looked at. The next line checks to see if this value is zero. We do this because of an idiosyncrasy in Symphony. As rows are deleted in a worksheet, cells below those being deleted occasionally take on types other than blank, even though they appear to be blank. Thus our usual method for checking for the end of the CAL range — checking for @CELLPOINTER("TYPE") = "b" — doesn't work in this situation. The method used here will work in every case where the cell being looked at contains anything that does not evaluate to a valid date.

{DONE} Macro

When we *do* encounter the end of the CAL range in the PURGE process, we call the macro {DONE}. This macro looks like this, and its functions should be quite familiar:

```
{S}FS~Y{GOTO}A1~{MENUBRANCH MAINMENU}
```

If you modify this application, consider using a call to {DONE} each time you want to update the file and return to the Main menu. Again, we have chosen not to do this here because we are more interested in providing you with a good education in macro programming than in elegant technique.

Reports: The {TICKLER} Macro Set

The last set of macros that make up the Appointment application is collected under the label {TICKLER}. The primary macro here looks like this:

```
        {GETLABEL Enter date as 08-Aug-84 or T for Today ,B1}~
        {IF +B1="T"#OR#B1="t"}{LET C1,@INT(@NOW)}~{BRANCH LOOPT}
        {LET C1,@DATEVALUE(B1}{GOTO}A41~
LOOPT   {LET B2,0}~{LET B3,0}~{BLANK
        REPORT_RANGE}{PANELOFF}{WINDOWSOFF}{GOTO}CAL~
LOOP6   {IF @DATEVALUE(@INDEX(CAL,0,+B2)))=C1}{REPORTIT}
        {IF
        @CELLPOINTER(``TYPE"="b"}{PANELON}{WINDOWSON}{MENUBRANCH
        REPTMENU}
        {DOWN}{LET B2,B2+1}~{BRANCH LOOP6}
```

Other than using panel and window display commands to make the screen activity less obtrusive to the user, this segment of code is very much like several others we've discussed. We will not discuss it further here.

{REPORTIT} Macro

The macro labeled {REPORTIT} is at the effective core of the {TICKLER} macro set. It looks like this:

```
{LET B3,B3+1}~
{M}C{TAB}{RIGHT 2}~
+"B"&@STRING(B3+300,0)&"}"
{RETURN}
```

We use cell B3 — which is in the range we defined early as the TEMP area for holding transient values — to keep track of how many lines of information the report contains and to point correctly to the cells into which data for the report are to be placed. The first thing that we do is increment its contents by 1.

The next line defines data in the first three cells (B, C and D) in the row on which the cell pointer is positioned to be copied. The following line defines the destination address for the move in response to Symphony's query. None of this action is visible to the user, since we have turned windows off during this process. If you want to see why we did that, delete the {WINDOWSOFF} command from the macro {TICKLER} above and run the application!

Building the report's contents in another area of the worksheet is an excellent technique, particularly when the report will be relatively short (ideally, 21 lines or less). It leaves the original data undisturbed and moves only the data for the report to another area for access.

The Menu {REPTMENU}

When the end of the CAL range is reached during this report-building process, the program displays a menu with three choices: Display, Print, and Quit. Quit does its usual return to cell A1 and branch to the Main menu, so we won't reproduce it here.

Display Appointments Macro

The Display Appointments option is simplicity itself:

```
{GOTO}REPORT_RANGE~
{GETLABEL Press RETURN to continue,TEMP}
{GOTO}A1~{MENUBRANCH MAINMENU}
```

Having placed the data for the report in the range defined by the name REPORT_RANGE — in our case, B300..D364 — to display it for our users, we need only move to the top of the range and wait for them to indicate that they've finished looking at the calendar. (You could even do this automatically and then ask if they want to print the report, but our approach is more in keeping with the menu-driven, top-down design method we've been using.)

Printing the Day's Schedule

If users choose the Print option from the menu called REPTMENU, the program branches to location PRINT1. There the macro looks like this:

```
{S}PSOF~SRREPORT_RANGE~QGPQ
{GOTO}A1~{MENUBRANCH MAINMENU}
```

The first line of this macro calls the {Services} menu, asks for the Print Settings Other Format sequence, and then enters a ↵ to select As-Displayed format for the report. It then calls the Source Range option and types in the name of the range — REPORT_RANGE — followed by a ↵.

Finally, it quits from the Settings area; chooses the Go option, which prints the report; and then calls for a Page Advance before quitting the Print option. The second line is familiar by now.

What's Next?

This Appointment application, while quite useful as a tool, lacks some features we might like to see in a full-scale product. For example, we'd probably like our report of appointments to be sorted by times. And we might want to be able to look at an appointment by searching for a keyword in the description. This change would require the use of the Symphony FORM environment to define a database range and sort fields. Having done that, selecting the sort options could be done without leaving the SHEET environment.

Certainly we'd want to be able to print a report for a range of days — say, a whole week — rather than one day at a time. This would be relatively straightforward. We would simply ask the user for a beginning date and store that in one location in the TEMP area (which is big enough to accommodate a great many dates!), then ask for an ending date for the appointment report. Finally, we would check each date as it is encountered against the beginning and ending dates by using the logical #AND# connector to be sure that it is both later than the earliest date and earlier than the latest date.

We might also want to be able to have multiple calendars, one for each attorney, accountant, or consultant in our office. There are a number of ways of accomplishing this. One method is shown in the government delivery order and professional billing applications in this movement and involves File Extract methods of copying and combining information from other files into the current worksheet.

Government Delivery Order

The application presented in this section is designed to enable companies managing "cost-plus-fee" contracts issued by the United States government to comply with major report requirements. At the time it was written, it complied with all known federal rules regarding such reports.

Operational Overview

The main macro in this application is called TRACK. To start the macro's execution, press the User ([F7]) key and then type the word *TRACK* (case doesn't matter here). When you do so, you will see a screen like that shown in Figure 71.

In addition to the traditional Quit function, there are three choices on this Main menu: Update, Print, and Graphs. The first two are handled to varying degrees and at various points by SCL macros that are listed in Coda B and discussed in this section. The Graphs option is handled partially this way as well, but if you wish to print a graph, the application simply describes the process and then leaves it to you to carry it out. This is because Symphony uses a separate program, PrintGraph, to handle the production of printed graphs. Macro or programming control is impractical for this step in any Symphony application design.

Update Functions

If you choose the Update option from the Main menu, you will be presented with a submenu like that shown in Figure 72. This menu asks you to Start a new delivery order, Update an existing delivery order file, or Quit.

The system provides a standard format for entering, storing and reporting information to the government if you choose to start a new delivery order file from this menu. The blank form for the main data area is shown in Figure 73.

You should notice two things about this blank form. First, some information has been filled in for you. The dates for the project are set up to be from October 1, 1985, to September 30, 1986. This is the standard U.S. Government fiscal year as of this writing. You will, of course, modify these dates to reflect the actual dates covered by your contract. Second, you are no longer operating under macro control; the word *Macro* is no longer visible at the bottom of the display, and the top of the display indicates that you are at the menu level of Symphony. This application was intentionally designed this way. Rather than predetermining which data you will put into this blank form in which order, you use the form as much as possible in a way that closely matches your present method of tracking this information.

Now that you are "on your own", however, you must know what to do when you've finished creating a new delivery order or updating an existing one. In either case, use the [Alt] key, held down simultaneously with the S (for "Save") key. The S can be upper-or lowercase. When you

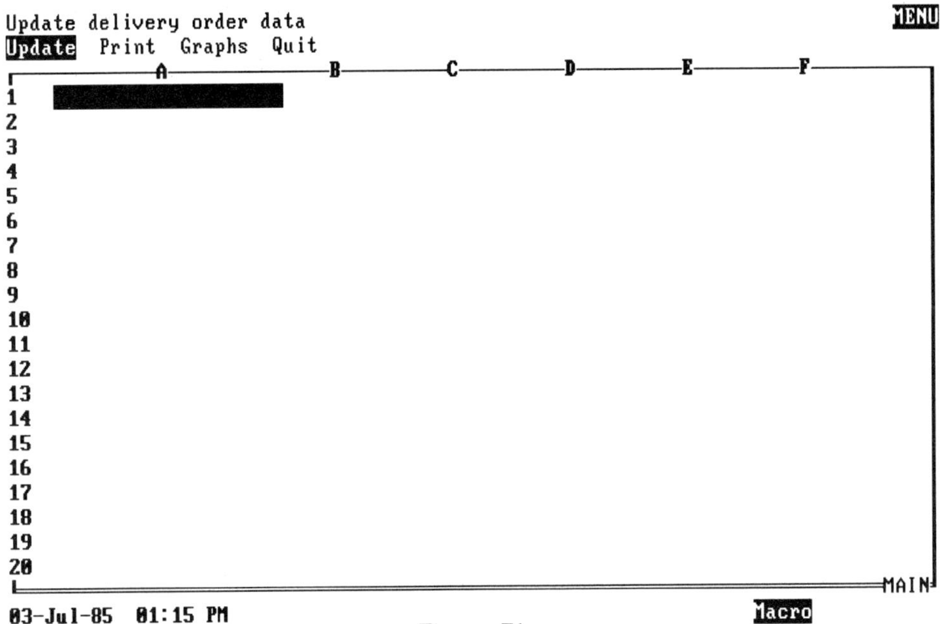

Figure 71
Opening Screen for TRACK Macro

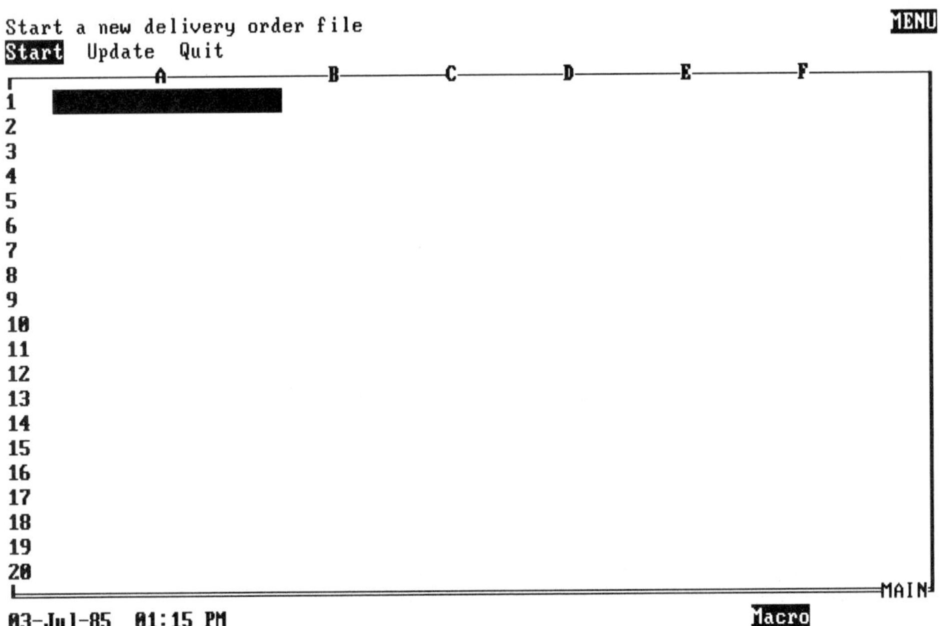

Figure 72
Update Menu Choices

have done this, you will be returned to the Main menu of the application, where you can choose to update or obtain information.

If you choose Update from the menu in Figure 71, you will be asked to choose the name of the delivery order file to be updated. It will then be loaded, and you will once again be outside macro control for the data-updating process.

An explanation of the data areas to be updated and some indication of the information to be placed in those areas will be presented soon. First, let's look at each of the other options on the Main menu.

Printing Reports

When selected, the Print option from the Main menu will present you with a submenu like that shown in Figure 74. There are two main options available: Task and Group. The former prints reports about a single file of information, while the latter permits the efficient printing of reports on any number of tasks without the necessity of returning to the Main menu and getting back to this level by menu selections. Since most companies with government contracts divide tasks into delivery order groups, this approach is quite realistic.

Operationally, the only difference between the two menu choices is that when the Task option is selected and the reports for one delivery order are run, control is returned to the Main menu; however, when the Group option is selected, users are asked after each report has run whether they wish to print additional reports. This process continues until the user answers "No" to the question about more reports, at which point control is passed back to the Main menu.

The reports produced for a sample delivery order are shown in Figures 75 and 76. Both pages of this report are automatically produced in the formats shown without any user intervention once the file has been selected.

Producing Graphs

If you choose the Graphs option from the Main menu, you will be presented with a submenu like that shown in Figure 77.

As a rule, you will first update information about a given delivery order so that you can produce a current graph. When you choose the Update option from the Graphs menu, you will be asked for the name of the delivery order file to be graphed. It will then be loaded, and after a few moments and some screen activity, you will see a display like that shown in Figure 78. Notice that there are two windows present; a new one called GRAFVU has been created at the bottom of the display area.

```
Modify current window or use another window                                MENU
Window  File  Print  Configuration  Application  Settings  New  Exit
            A              B         C         D         E         F
1   Delivery Order
2           as-of DATE: 01-Oct-85 WEEKS EXP:         0       Fee
3   DELIVERY ORDER NO:  MDJ-xxx   85% letter             per hour:    $1.25
4           START DATE: 01-Oct-85    sent:         ERR
5             END DATE: 30-Sep-86                            G&A
6     est END OF FUNDS: 30-Sep-86 WEEKS REM:        52     per $:     $0.05
7
8                           WEEKS     HOURS   LABOR $     ODC $     FEE $
9           AUTH/ALLOC:        52                                       0
10
11              FUNDED:        52                                       0
12
13            EXPENDED:         0                                       0
14
15
16
17
18
19
20
                                                                         MAIN
03-Jul-85  01:16 PM
```

Figure 73
Blank Form for Main Data Area

```
Print a report for one delivery order only                                 MENU
Task  Group  Quit
            A              B         C         D         E         F
1
2
3
4
5
6
7
8
9
10
11
12
13
14
15
16
17
18
19
20
                                                                         MAIN
14-May-85  01:23 AM                                              Macro
```

Figure 74
Print Menu Choices

DELIVERY ORDER NO.: MDJ-001 As of: 01-Nov-85
Start: 01-Oct-85 End: 31-Mar-86 End/fund: 31-Mar-86

	WEEKS	HOURS	LABOR $	ODC $	FEE $	TOTAL $
AUTH/ALLOC:	25	3000	60000	15000	3750	82500
FUNDED:	25	3000	60000	15000	3750	82500
EXPENDED:	4	160	5000	6000	200	13000
OBLIG(total):	4	200	5000	6900	250	13945
REMAINING:	21	2800	55000	8100	3500	68555
OBLIG/AUTH:	18%	7%	8%	46%	7%	17%
OBLIG/FUNDED:	18%	7%	8%	46%	7%	17%

	HOURS	DOLLARS
100% of funded at current rate	09-Jan-87	02-Apr-86
85% of funded at current rate	31-Oct-86	05-Mar-86
85% of funded at planned rate	26-Feb-86	26-Feb-86
	----------	----------

85% letter due: 27-Jan-86 sent: ERR

==

Figure 75
First Page of Report

LABOR CAT HOURS:	AUTH	ALLOC	EXPEND	REM	PER WEEK
400 PROJECT MGR	50	50	10	40	2
401 ADMIN SPEC	50	50	10	40	2
402 MGT SYS SPEC	50	50	8	42	2
403 SECRETARY	600	600	35	565	26
404 SR ENGR				0	0
405 ENGR	900	900	68	832	39
406 SYS ENGR SPEC				0	0
407 TECH WRITER	300	300	2	298	14
408 TECH DATA ENGR				0	0
409 DRAFTER	150	150	2	148	7
410 SR ANALYST				0	0
411 COMP SYS ANAL	450	450	3	447	21
412 COMP PROGR				0	0
413 COMP S/W SPEC				0	0
414 SYS MGT SPEC				0	0
415 SYS REQ ENGR	450	450	2	448	21
416 COMP OPER				0	0
417 SR COMP OPER				0	0
897 SUBCON/CONSULT				0	0
898 CONTRACT TYPIST				0	0
899 INTER-DIVISION				0	0
	--------	--------	--------	--------	--------
	3000	3000	140	2860	133

OBLIGATIONS: totals	40	900	50	945
	hours	ODC $	FEE $	TOT $w/G&A
1 PO# 123	40	550	50	
2 terminal rental		350	0	
3			0	
4			0	
5			0	
6			0	
7			0	
8			0	
9			0	
10			0	

Delivery Order MDJ-001 Manhour and Obligations Report

Figure 76
Second Page of Report

```
Update data for a project's graph                                    MENU
Update  Print  Quit
┌──────────A──────────B────────C────────D────────E────────F─────────┐
1
2
3
4
5
6
7
8
9
10
11
12
13
14
15
16
17
18
19
20
└══════════════════════════════════════════════════════════════MAIN┘
15-Jul-85  10:09 AM                                          Macro
```

Figure 77
Graphs Menu Choices

```
I41: 'GRAPH AREA                                                   SHEET

┌────────B────────C────────D────────E────────F────────G────────H──────┐
1
2   15-Nov-85 WEEKS EXP:        6       Fee
3   MDJ-001   85% letter             per hour:     $1.25
4   01-Oct-85    sent:        ERR
5   31-Mar-86                           G&A
6   31-Mar-86 WEEKS REM:       19      per $:      $0.05
7
8        WEEKS     HOURS   LABOR $     ODC $     FEE $   TOTAL $
9           25      3000     60000     15000      3750     82500
10
11          25      3000     60000     15000      3750     82500
12
13           6       160      5000      6000       200     13000
┌──────────────────────────────────────────────────────────────────────┐
 GRAPH AREA                   MDJ-001 Delivery Order Status
                              DOLLARS
              WEEKS     ALLOC    FUNDED     OBLIG       85%     ALLOC
                  0         0     82500         0     70125         0
                  4     13200     82500      9000     70125       480
                  5     16500     82500     13000     70125       600
└═════════════════════════════════════════════════════════════GRAFVU┘
05-Jul-85  11:13 AM
```

Figure 78
Update Screen from Graphs Menu

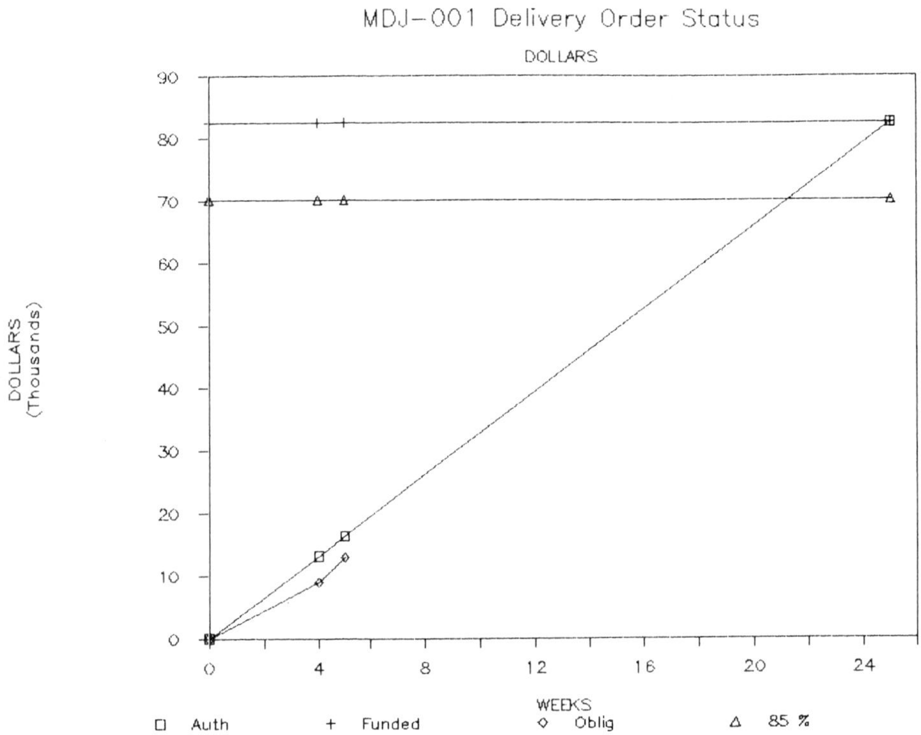

Figure 79
Dollar Status Graph

We will discuss the data to be provided here in a few moments. For now, assume that the data have been brought up to date and that you are ready for the graphs to be produced. Two single-keystroke macros permit the graphs to be previewed on your screen (assuming that your system has graphics display capability, of course). Pressing the [Alt] and D keys simultaneously permits you to preview the graph that shows the *dollars* status of the project (see Figure 79). This graph compares dollars authorized and funded against actual expenditures plus obligations (more on that subject in a moment). The critical 85 percent level is also shown as a separate line. Similarly, a graph of labor hours expended compared to authorized and funded levels can be produced (see Figure 80) by using the [Alt] and H keys together.

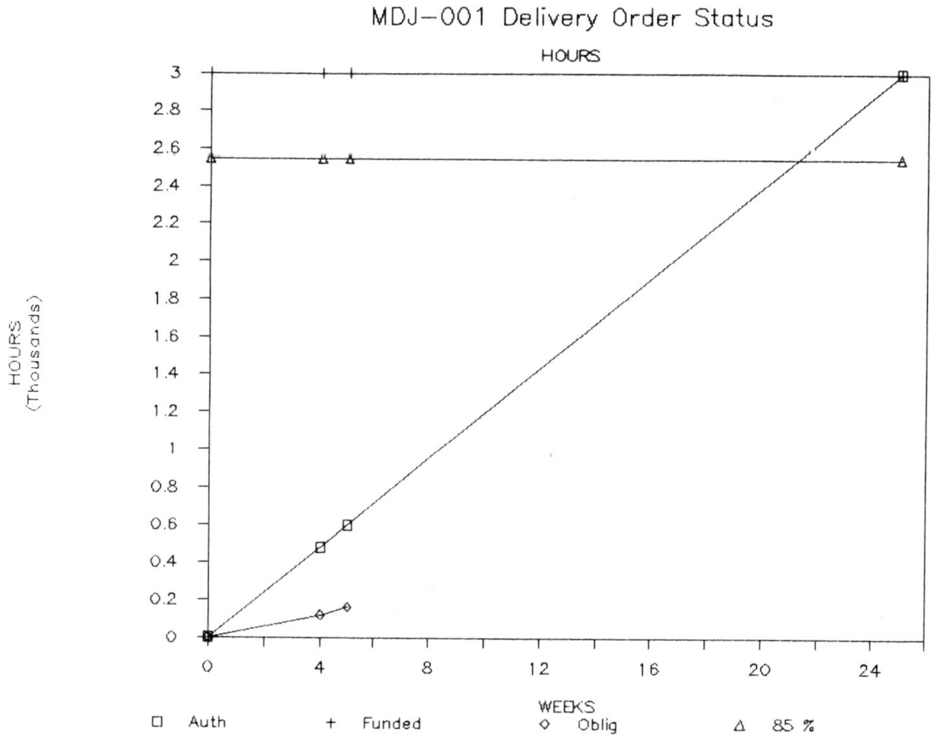

Figure 80
Hours Status Graph

If you choose to *print* graphs, you will be shown a screen of instructions (see Figure 81) designed to remind you of the procedure. From there, you will be returned to the usual menu screen and will be on your own.

Explanation of Data Required for Updates

The next few paragraphs will provide basic information about the data needed to perform updates and to produce meaningful reports and graphs using this application. Please note that this is *not* intended to be a course

```
AA200: 'To print out the graphs that this program creates requires the PrinSHEET

      AA         AB         AC         AD         AE         AF         AG
200 To print out the graphs that this program creates requires the PrintGraph
201 diskette.
202
203 1.  Follow the instructions on the PrintGraph disk.  Run the PrintGraph
204 program after you have finished updating all your project files.
205
206 2.  Make very sure that you have saved all your work before proceeding
207 with the printing of the graphs.
208
209 3.  After pressing the RETURN key when you are ready to continue, wait
210 for the screen menu to appear.  When it does, press E for exit.  If
211 you have saved your work and are ready to continue, press Y, and
212 then choose the PrintGraph option.  Follow the instructions from there.
213
214
215
216
217
218
219
                                                                     INST
03-Jul-85  02:25 PM                         Macro
```

Figure 81
Graph Printing Instructions

in government contract management. However, we can and will provide you with some idea of the data to be entered in this application and the meaning of the reports and graphs produced by it. If you plan to use this application in a real-life government contract situation, ensure that the regulations under which the contract was issued are being complied with by this report's capabilities.

Dollar and Schedule Data

Whether updating an existing report or creating a new one, there are two areas of data storage with which you will be concerned. One holds information about dollar expenditures and commitments made, while the other contains data about labor hours expended and obligated. Virtually all government contracts require that you notify the agency involved 30 days *before* you anticipate having used up 85 percent of the money *or* staff hours authorized and funded for the project. Therefore, this application is designed not only to keep track of those two aspects of the project but to do so separately so that the 85 percent rule can be easily monitored.

When updating a report, the first screen you see will look something like that shown in Figure 82 (though the numbers will of course be different).

If you are setting up a new project, you will usually enter data into the following areas of the blank form:

```
as-of DATE
DELIVERY ORDER NO.
START DATE
END DATE
est END OF FUNDS
Fee per Hour
G&A per $
```

The expression G&A stands for "General and Administrative" costs. The Fee per Hour and G&A per $ expressions may be different depending on the type of contract. For example, G&A might be calculated using a labor hour basis rather than a dollar basis. Change your calculations within the work sheet to accommodate this. That is why the program is not under total macro control.

You will also fill in the rows labeled AUTH/ALLOC and FUNDED in the table across the bottom of the area. (The column headed ODC $ stands for "Other Direct Costs".) In the process, you should *skip* entries under WEEKS and FEE $; these columns are calculated by the program. You must, however, enter a total. Because of the way such reporting is handled, factors beyond those reported here frequently affect those totals, so the program cannot accommodate that calculation.

If, on the other hand, this is an update to an existing delivery order file, you will usually complete the following fields:

```
as-of DATE
HOURS EXPENDED
LABOR $ EXPENDED
ODC $ EXPENDED
TOTAL $ EXPENDED
```

All other fields are usually either unchanged or calculated by the program.

```
A1: 'Delivery Order                                                                  SHEET

          A                B              C              D              E              F
1   Delivery Order
2          as-of DATE:  15-Nov-85 WEEKS EXP:          6           Fee
3   DELIVERY ORDER NO:  MDJ-001    85% letter                  per hour:      $1.25
4          START DATE:  01-Oct-85      sent:            ERR
5            END DATE:  31-Mar-86                                  G&A
6     est END OF FUNDS: 31-Mar-86 WEEKS REM:           19       per $:        $0.05
7
8                           WEEKS       HOURS       LABOR $       ODC $        FEE $
9          AUTH/ALLOC:         25        3000        60000        15000         3750
10
11             FUNDED:         25        3000        60000        15000         3750
12
13           EXPENDED:          6         160         5000         6000          200
14
15
16
17
18
19
20
                                                                                  MAIN
05-Jul-85   11:14 AM
```

```
G1:                                                                                SHEET

          B              C              D              E              F              G            H
1
2   15-Nov-85 WEEKS EXP:            6           Fee
3   MDJ-001    85% letter                    per hour:      $1.25
4   01-Oct-85      sent:          ERR
5   31-Mar-86                                    G&A
6   31-Mar-86 WEEKS REM:           19         per $:        $0.05
7
8       WEEKS       HOURS      LABOR $       ODC $        FEE $      TOTAL $
9          25        3000       60000        15000         3750        82500
10
11         25        3000       60000        15000         3750        82500
12
13          6         160        5000         6000          200        13000
14
15
16
17
18
19
20
                                                                                  MAIN
05-Jul-85   11:15 AM
```

Figure 82
Sample Form Showing Dollar Data Fields

A21: "LABOR CAT HOURS: SHEET

	A	B	C	D	E	F
21	LABOR CAT HOURS:	AUTH	ALLOC	EXPEND	REM	PER WEEK
22						
23	400 PROJECT MGR	50	50	10	40	2
24	401 ADMIN SPEC	50	50	10	40	2
25	402 MGT SYS SPEC	50	50	8	42	2
26	403 SECRETARY	600	600	35	565	29
27	404 SR ENGR				0	0
28	405 ENGR	900	900	68	832	43
29	406 SYS ENGR SPEC				0	0
30	407 TECH WRITER	300	300	2	298	15
31	408 TECH DATA ENGR				0	0
32	409 DRAFTER	150	150	2	148	8
33	410 SR ANALYST				0	0
34	411 COMP SYS ANAL	450	450	3	447	23
35	412 COMP PROGR				0	0
36	413 COMP S/W SPEC				0	0
37	414 SYS MGT SPEC				0	0
38	415 SYS REQ ENGR	450	450	2	448	23
39	416 COMP OPER				0	0
40	417 SR COMP OPER				0	0

MAIN

03-Jul-85 02:27 PM

Figure 83
Sample Form Showing Labor Data Fields

Labor Data

When you have finished entering and updating all the information in the dollars portion of the file, you should press [Home] and then [PgDn]. You will now be in the labor area of the report, where hours and labor costs are recorded for later use and analysis. A sample labor data area is shown in Figure 83.

When setting up a new delivery order, you will usually be entering the labor category and the hours authorized (AUTH) and allocated (ALLOC). During progress updates, you will usually (though not always) leave these fields unchanged while updating the total hours expended. From this information, the system will calculate the total remaining hours available for the delivery order in each labor category and will then determine how many hours during each remaining week can be expended on this category without exceeding the authorized level. Though not visible in Figure 82, this section of the form also calculates totals for all the labor data fields.

Saving Updated Information

After entering updated information in either or both of the hours and labor areas of the worksheet, be sure to save your work by invoking the single-keystroke Save macro with the [Alt]-S key combination. You will have to give the system the name of the file to be used.

> Caution! Do *not* use the filename MAS. This file is used to store a blank copy of the data areas to be used as a starting blank form when you want to add a delivery order to the system.

Graph Data

From the Update option on the Graphs menu, you will be taken to a window called GRAFVU, as shown earlier (see Figure 77). To produce accurate, current graphs, you will be required to update some information in this window manually.

The procedure for updating this window is somewhat complex and is handled largely manually, although two single-keystroke macros have been designed to assist you. The following procedure indicates the process to be used:

1. Position the cell pointer so that it is on top of the week number previous to which your project is funded. Almost always, this will be the last of the weeks listed. Occasionally, when a project is partially funded, there will be two weeks listed at the lower end of the graphing range: the week to which the project is funded and the week at which the project is scheduled to end.
2. Use the [Alt]-A (for "Adjust") key combination. After a few moments, a new screen will show a space for the new week to be inserted above the point where you were located when you called this macro.
3. Position the cursor on the line that contains the information from last week, one line up from where the blank line is.
4. Press the [Alt] key and the C (think of this as meaning "clear" or "copy") simultaneously to invoke another single-keystroke macro. This means bring down information from the line above, and then erase those cells that will contain the new information.
5. Enter the week number that corresponds to the figure shown at cell address B13 in the window above. Notice how the figures in the allocated column automatically recalculate.

6. Move the cell pointer to the fourth column, OBLIG, and enter the figure from the window above at cell address G13.
7. Move the cell pointer to the eighth column, which is the *labor* obligation column (also labeled OBLIG), and enter the number found in the window above at cell address C13.

You have now updated all the graphics information for this report run. At this point, you may preview either the dollar or hours graph (using the single-keystroke macros [Alt]-D or [Alt]-H, respectively) or print the graphs as described above. In any case, save the data ([Alt]-S macro) before you exit the program or load a new delivery order file.

The 85 Percent "Magic"

A key aspect of this application is its continual monitoring of the 85 percent level. As we have pointed out, most government contracts require that the contractor notify the agency with which the contract has been negotiated when it is 30 days from expending 85 percent of *either* the money or labor hours allocated by the contract. There can be stiff penalties for forgetting to make this notification. In recent months, an increased emphasis on proper reporting procedures has grown out of widely publicized bidding irregularities, particularly in Department of Defense contracts.

The first page of the standard report produced by this application (see Figure 75) clearly indicates the presently calculated date on which the 85 percent letter must be sent. This date is determined automatically by the system and will change as the project status is updated.

The Application Macros

So much for the question of how the application *works*. Now let's turn our attention to the macros and formulas that constitute the application.

As with most applications in this book, the menu is displayed by invoking the macro, whether by User key ([F7]) or automatically. This menu is called Main_Menu. A return from a submenu or macro will execute the key sequence [Esc][Esc][Esc]S. The result of this sequence is that the Services menu appears, and control is returned to the user outside the macro.

Main_Menu Macro

The macro called Main_Menu displays a menu consisting exclusively of menu calls to other menus. The Update selection calls the DO_Menu, the Print option calls on the Pri_Menu, and the Graphs selection brings into play the Grap_Menu.

DO_Menu Macro

Like the Main_Menu macro, the DO_Menu macro simply calls on other macros depending on which command is executed by the user. Selecting the option to Start a new delivery order file executes a macro called {StNew}, while the Update option invokes a macro called {DelOrd}.

The Quit option offers the usual return to the Main_Menu but leaves the user where he is in the worksheet, thus simplifying debugging.

{StNew} Macro

This macro looks like this:

```
{Home}
{S}fccnWOOSH~
rfMAS~
```

The second line is the most interesting in this small but mighty macro. It brings up the Services menu and then invokes the File Combine Named-Range command sequence. In response to a request for the range name, it enters WOOSH and adds a ↵. This permits you to have as many different delivery order files as you want (up to some practical limit). As you'll see later, using File Combine and erasures judiciously, you can create and use many different delivery order files.

A file called MAS — the one where the blank form is stored — is retrieved by the last line of the macro. Control is then passed to the user, who ends up in the Services menu because of the Esc Esc Esc S sequence described earlier.

{DelOrd} Macro

When an existing file is to be updated, the macro labeled {DelOrd} (for "Delivery Order") is called upon. This macro is identical to the {StNew} macro except that the last line, rather than loading a predetermined filename, asks the user to enter the filename. That last line looks like this:

```
rf{?}~
```

The \S Macro

As we said earlier, when you finish updating the hours, labor, or graph data area of the delivery order file, you should save your work using the [Alt]-S command. The macro invoked by this key sequence looks like this:

```
{S}fxf{?}~WOOSH~
{RIGHT}~{M}EWOOSH~
{S}WUMAIN~
{MENUBRANCH MAINMENU}
```

The first line is another method by which multiple files can be handled in Symphony. This time, instead of a File Combine, we use a File eXtract to pull the data (all in the area known as WOOSH) we wish to save. The {?} indicates that you will be asked for a file name. If this is a new file, give it a meaningful name. If you are saving a file that you have been updating, be careful that you save it under the correct name. By keeping a back-up file, and updating it every time you make changes to your files, you will lose only one week's data if you do make a mistake here.

The second line of the macro erases the range labeled WOOSH. Line 3 sends us back to using the MAIN window, and the fourth line branches to the Main menu.

Print Macros

The printing process for reports begins when the Main menu is invoked and the Print option is selected. The Pri_Menu is called into play at that point. It offers the user the choice of printing one task or a group of tasks. The former uses a routine called {PriTsk} and the latter a routine labeled {PriGrp}.

{PriTsk} Macro

The macro labeled {PriTsk} looks like this:

```
{home}
{S}fccnWOOSH~
rf{?}~
{S}pasnuTSKSUM~QGP
snuMANHR~QG11
snuOBLIG~qgpq
{M}eWOOSH~
```

```
Maintain a catalog of Print settings sheets                              MENU
Page  Source  Destination  Init-String  Margins  Other  Name  Quit
 Page                          Source:       Range I1..O29
   Length:      66             Destination: Printer
   Spacing:     1              Init-String: \015
   Number                      Margins       Other
     Print-Number: 1             Left:    4    Space Compression: No
     Start-Page:   1             Right:   84   Attributes:        Yes
     End-Page:     999           Top:     2    Format: As-Displayed
   Breaks:      Yes              Bottom:  2    Top-Labels:
   Wait:        No                             Left-Labels:
   Header:
   Footer:
                                          Print Settings: TSKSUM
```

Figure 84
TSKSUM Print Settings Sheet

```
{S}wuMAIN~
{MenuBranch Main_Menu}
```

There is nothing new here except for the contents of lines 4, 5, and 6 of the macro, all of which include the program segment:

```
snu
```

which means, in the Print function, "Settings Name Use" (that is, use a named Settings sheet). We have predefined three such sheets for use with the application.

Figure 84 shows the Print Settings sheet named TSKSUM. Figure 85 shows MANHR, and Figure 86 shows OBLIG. Note the differences and similarities among these sheets. Setting up such a sheet during macro establishment is an efficient way to handle report requirements where more than one "standard" form or format is involved.

{PriGrp} Macro

The macro that prints a group of tasks is, not surprisingly, nearly identical to the {PriTsk} macro just discussed. The only difference is that after the WOOSH area is erased, this macro includes a new set of lines that look like this:

```
{GETLABEL "Are there any more tasks to be printed out? (y or n)
``,a1}~
```

```
Use next settings sheet                                                   MENU
Use  Create  Delete  Previous  Next  Initial-Settings  Reset  Quit

 Page                          Source:      Range A61..F75
   Length:      66             Destination: Printer
   Spacing:     1              Init-String:
   Number                      Margins          Other
     Print-Number: 1             Left:    4       Space Compression: No
     Start-Page:   1             Right:   80      Attributes:        Yes
     End-Page:     999           Top:     2       Format: As-Displayed
   Breaks:      Yes              Bottom:  2       Top-Labels:
   Wait:        No                                Left-Labels:
   Header:
   Footer:
                                                    Print Settings: OBLIG
```

Figure 85
MANHR Print Settings Sheet

```
Use next settings sheet                                                   MENU
Use  Create  Delete  Previous  Next  Initial-Settings  Reset  Quit

 Page                          Source:      Range A21..F45
   Length:      66             Destination: Printer
   Spacing:     1              Init-String: \018
   Number                      Margins          Other
     Print-Number: 1             Left:    4       Space Compression: No
     Start-Page:   1             Right:   80      Attributes:        Yes
     End-Page:     999           Top:     2       Format: As-Displayed
   Breaks:      Yes              Bottom:  2       Top-Labels:
   Wait:        No                                Left-Labels:
   Header:
   Footer:
                                                    Print Settings: MANHR
```

Figure 86
OBLIG Print Settings Sheet

```
{IF A1="Y"#OR#A1="y"}{BRANCH AA47}
{BLANK A1}
{S}WUMAIN~
{MENUBRANCH MAIN_MENU}
```

This routine simply asks the user for a yes or no response and, if the answer is "yes", branches to AA47, where the File Combine command is called in to ask for a filename again.

The Graphs Menu

The graphics routines begin with a menu called Grap_Menu. If the user chooses the Update function, the macro named {UpGraph} is called; if the Print option is selected, the macro labeled {PriInst} is called. The Quit option, as usual, returns the user to the Main menu.

{UpGraph} Macro

The {UpGraph} macro looks like this:

```
{home}
{S}fccnWOOSH~
RF{?}~{RIGHT 6}
{S}WUGRAFVU~{ESC}
```

This macro calls for another File Combine to bring in the appropriate file. The {?} indicates that you will be asked for the file name. Following that file retrieval, the macro positions the cell pointer six columns to the right of where it had been. The last line of the macro then makes the window called GRAFVU the active window and moves back to the Services menu.

{PriInst} Macro

As previously indicated, printing a graph is not easily done within Symphony. A special program, PrintGraph, is required. Macro control of this program is not yet feasible. Therefore, if the user wishes to print a graph, the macro simply opens a new window called INST, waits for the user to press the [↵] key, and then uses the MAIN window.

Single-Keystroke Graphics Macros

Four single-keystroke macros are associated with the Graphs function in this application.

The first is the macro which looks like this:

```
{M}M.{RIGHT 8}~{DOWN}~
{DOWN}~
```

This macro opens a blank line immediately above the row on which the cell pointer is positioned when the user presses [Alt]-A. It does this by moving the row down one position. The range for the move is specified by pointing. One edge of the move range is fixed by the period (.) following the M. The other edge is fixed by {Right 8}.

The second single-keystroke macro in the graphics area of the application is the \C macro, which copies certain information into the blank area for use by the person performing an update. The macro looks like this:

```
{M}C{RIGHT 8}~{DOWN}~
{DOWN}{M}E~
{RIGHT 3}{M}E~
{RIGHT 4}{M}E~
{LEFT 7}
```

The macro's first line invokes the Symphony Copy command, which asks for the range to be copied. An eight-column row of data is chosen. The following several lines move the cursor to the positions where the material is to be copied to so that Symphony will know what to do with the data being copied.

The two remaining single-keystroke macros are used to preview the Dollars (\d) and Hours (\h) graphs on the screen. They are essentially the same, so we will show you the \d macro (look up the \h macro in Coda B at cell address Z81 if you wish to see it).

```
{HOME}{S}WUMAIN~{HOME}
{M}G1NUDOLLARS~QP{?}~
```

The essence of this macro is in the second line which calls the {Menu} command to use the 1st-Settings sheet. The name of the sheet is asked for, and the word *DOLLARS* is typed, followed by a ↵. Then the Preview (P) command is called, and the system is set up with the general entry command {?} to wait for the user to press the ↵ key.

Figure 87 shows the DOLLARS Graph Settings sheet, and Figure 88 shows the HOURS Graph Settings sheet invoked by the \h single-keystroke macro.

What's Next?

Although this application is nearly a complete stand-alone package as provided, it could be made even more efficient. Here are some suggestions.

```
Maintain catalog of Graph settings sheets                                        MENU
Switch  Type  Range  Hue  Format  Data-Labels  Legend  Cancel  Name  Quit

    Type:      XY

 Range                Hue  Format  Data-Labels          Legend

 X GWEEKS              1
 A GALLOC              2  Both                          Auth
 B GFUND               3  Both                          Funded
 C GOBLIG              4  Both                          Oblig
 D GATEF               5  Both                          85 %
 E                     6  Both
 F                     7  Both
                                          Graph 1st-Settings: DOLLARS
```

Figure 87
DOLLARS Graph Settings Sheet

```
Maintain catalog of Graph settings sheets                                        MENU
Switch  Type  Range  Hue  Format  Data-Labels  Legend  Cancel  Name  Quit

    Type:      XY

 Range                Hue  Format  Data-Labels          Legend

 X GWEEKS              1
 A GHALL               2  Both                          Auth
 B GHFUND              3  Both                          Funded
 C GHOBL               4  Both                          Oblig
 D GHATEF              5  Both                          85 %
 E                     6  Both
 F                     7  Both
                                            Graph 1st-Settings: HOURS
```

Figure 88
HOURS Graph Settings Sheet

One obvious suggestion is to write the 85 percent letter using a DOC window and then set it up to handle the merging of data in from the report areas so that the letter is automatically generated. For an example of how to do this, look at the form letters generated by the nonprofit fund-raising application discussed earlier.

Your specific use for this package may be sufficiently clear and precise that leaving the user in control outside the macro during data entry makes no sense. Instead, you may wish to predetermine the order of the data to be entered and position the cell pointer at each cell, prompt for the input, and move on. See the personal appointment application discussed earlier for some examples of how to handle this particular issue.

CODA A

Alphabetical Table of SCL Commands

The table below provides a quick reference to the commands available in the Symphony Command Language. The following notes apply to its contents.

1. Arguments are required for the command to function properly unless enclosed in square brackets, in which case they are optional.
2. In the EXAMPLES column, material enclosed in square brackets is explanatory information that would *not* be coded in the macro itself.
3. Examples provided do not, for purposes of space and readability, conform to the normal format rules for macros. For example, blank lines between macros are omitted when displaying a group of macros.

Table 5
Alphabetical Table of SCL Commands

NAME	*ARGUMENTS*	*DESCRIPTION*	*EXAMPLES*
{BEEP}	[tone]	Sounds computer's "bell", to alert user.	SOUND {BEEP3} [Produces a short chirping sound]
{BLANK}	location	Erases contents cell in the **location** range.	{BLANK A1} {GETLABEL "Enter your user number:",A1}
		Using BLANK leaves the format of numeric display and protection settings unchanged.	[Erases contents of cell A1, prints request for user number, writes response into A1.]
		BLANK differs from the SHEET Erase command in that it can be used in an active window that is not a SHEET window.	{BLANK PROSPECT-MOVE} [Erases contents of the range named PROSPECT-MOVE.]
		BLANK can be used during data entry and when typing a command.	
{BRANCH}	location	Sends macro operation to the new **location**.	PEOPLE C.C. Riley {IF OFFICER= "Yes"} {BRANCH FIRST}

Command	Description	Example
	Differs from subroutine calls in that the program will not return to the current location except by use of another {BRANCH} command.	SECOND Employee{QUIT} FIRST Officer {QUIT} [The PEOPLE macro branches to SECOND and enters Employee or to FIRST and enters Officer depending upon value of the contents of the cell named OFFICER.]
{BREAKON}	Cancels the {BREAKOFF} command. "Enables" use of the BREAK key to interrupt execution of a macro.	PEOPLE {BREAKOFF} {MENUCALL END} END QUIT Exit macro program {BREAKON} {QUIT}
{BREAKOFF}	"Disables" the BREAK key. Forbids use of the BREAK key to interrupt execution of a macro. Used in some applications to force users to stay under macro control. {BREAKOFF} is in effect until canceled by {BREAKON}.	[The PEOPLE program turns off the BREAK key with a {BREAKOFF} command. Running END from the menu will cause the {BREAKON} command to restore normal operation to the BREAK key.]

NAME	ARGUMENTS	DESCRIPTION	EXAMPLES
		When {BREAKOFF} is used in a macro, care must be taken to include a {BREAKON} command when terminating the macro, or subsequent attempts to use the BREAK key will be frustrated.	
{CONTENTS}	dest'ion location, source-location, [width-number], [format-number]	Stores a label in one cell that represents a number in a second cell. In other words, it displays a string value in one cell standing for the numeric contents of the other cell. {CONTENTS} carries out two kinds of functions: 1. It looks at the **source-location**. {CONTENTS} retrieves the contents of the cell. It begins with the upper left corner cell when a range has been specified.	{CONTENTS A10,B10} [Places the contents of cell B10 as a label into the cell A10.] {CONTENTS A10,B10,16} [Places the contents of cell B10 as a number into cell A10, using a width of 16 regardless of the correct width setting of cell A10.]

2. {CONTENTS} stores the retrieved information at the **destination-location.**

-In the case of numbers, {CONTENTS} displays the numbers in **destination-location** cell according to that cell's current column width and numeric format. The optional **width-number** argument may be specified with the command to override the destination cell's settings, if desired.

-In the case of strings, {CONTENTS} creates left-aligned labels in the **destination-location** cells.

{CONTENTS} permits specifying **width-number** with no corresponding **format-number**, though **format-numbers** must have corresponding **width-numbers**.

NAME	ARGUMENTS	DESCRIPTION	EXAMPLES
		See Table 2-1 for the codes for {CONTENTS} Statement Formats Numbers.	
{DEFINE}	cell:type1 [cell2:type2 celln:typen]	Specified locations values for use in a subroutine. {DEFINE} specifies any large or small number of pairs of cells and corresponding types. **Location** may be either a cell or a range. In the case of ranges, the value of the argument is stored in the upper lefthand cell of the range. **Type** may be either **:value** or **:string**. {DEFINE} stores entries as labels by default. Entries may be declared as numbers by use of the **value** type declaration. The number of arguments in the {DEFINE} statement must match the number	{SUBR5 50*5,units} {DEFINE X1,X2} [The subroutine carries out the math called for in the argument and stores the resulting number, "250", in cell X1 and stores the string, "units", in cell X2. Note that the program will default to storing both of these as labels.]

		in the subroutine call statement. A mismatch will produce the error message "Too many arguments in DEFINE" or "Missing argument in DEFINE."	
{FOR}	counter-location, stop-number, start-number, step-number, starting-location	Repeats a series of steps a specified number of times. **counter-location** identifies the current value of the counter; **start-number** assigns a value to the first counter in the series; **stop-number** assigns the final counter value for ending the series; **step-number** specifies the amount by which to increment the counter for each repetition. **starting-location** specifies where in the program the repetition will begin.	COUNTER 1 TOTAL 5 TEST {GETNUMBER "How many columns to format:" ,TOTAL}~ {FOR COUNTER, 1, TOTAL, 1, ROUTINE} {LEFT TOTAL-1} ROUTINE {menu}WS15~ {menu}FC2 {down}{down} {down}{down} {right} {RETURN} [The program gets a value for the **stop-number** from the user and assigns it to TOTAL. In our example, the value was "5", which will cause the program to repeat the ROUTINE five times, creating five columns.]

NAME	ARGUMENTS	DESCRIPTION	EXAMPLES	
{GET}	location	Holds program operation until receiving a single keystroke — which it saves in memory in the upper left corner of **location**.	TEST	(D)aily or (M)onthly reports {GET CHOICE} {IF CHOICE="d" #OR#CHOICE="D"} {BRANCH DAY-RPT} {IF CHOICE="m" #OR#CHOICE="M"} {BRANCH MONTH-RPT} {BEEP} {BRANCH TEST}
		The command {GET} does not display a control panel prompt. Use {GETLABEL} or {GETNUMBER} for situations demanding such a prompt.		
		Note that in cases where more than one of Symphony's special commands are mapped to the same keyboard key, {GET} will be able to use only one of the names. For example, <EDIT> might always be used by {GET}, rather than <JUSTIFY>.	CHOICE	d
			DAY-RPT	{right} {quit}
			MONTH-RPT	{down} {quit}
			[The program asks for a single keystroke choice, "D" or "M" — which it then uses to branch to an appropriate routine.]	
{GETLABEL}	prompt-string, location	Holds program operation until receiving a character	TEST	{GETLABEL "Type your first name...",FIRST}

string — which it saves in memory as a label entry in the upper left corner of the **location** cell. (Similar to {GET} function above.)	{GETLABEL "Now type your last name...",LAST} {LET FULL,FIRST&" "&LAST}
The first argument, a prompt string, must be included. It will be displayed in the control panel area. If a prompt is needed or desired, use a set of quotation marks with nothing between them.	FIRST Leslie SECOND Parrish FULL Leslie Parrish [The program asks the user the first and last names — which it stores in the cells labeled FIRST and LAST. It combines the two and shows the result in the cell location called FULL.]
The prompt string should be enclosed in quotation marks if it includes the argument separator character (usually a comma).	
{GETLABEL} will accept a maximum string of 80 characters in length.	
The string entry must be terminated by the user with a <CARRIAGE RETURN>.	

NAME	ARGUMENTS	DESCRIPTION	EXAMPLES	
{GETNUMBER}	prompt-string, location	Holds program operation until receiving a number — which it saves in memory as a number entry in the upper left corner of **location**. (Similar to {GET} function above.)	TEST	{GETNUMBER "How old are you?", AGE}~ {IF AGE<100} {WRONG} {INDICATE " OK "}
		Symphony uses its upper left corner cell when a range is specified as a **location**.	WRONG	{BEEP} {INDICATE WHAT?} {GETNUMBER "I really don't believe you...",AGE} {IF AGE<100} {BRANCH WRONG} {RETURN}
		The **prompt-string** argument must be included in the macro statement. The minimum length of the number that can be entered will depend upon the length of the prompt string. The combined lengths of the two may not exceed 80 characters.	AGE	
			[The program requests the age of the user and evaluates the number to determine if it is less than 100.]	
		prompt-string may include an argument separator. This is usually a comma. The argument separator		

Command	Arguments	Description	Example
		must be enclosed in quotation marks unless the entire prompt string is so enclosed.	
{HANDSHAKE}	send-string, receive-string, timeout-value, capture-location	Exchanges a single line of information with another computer. {HANDSHAKE} transmits **send-string** as a log-on to a second computer and looks for **receive-string** as a response from the other computer. This is the means by which Symphony verifies that it has established communication with the other computer. Type **send-string** and **receive-string** arguments in double quotes directly into {HANDSHAKE}. Formulas and cell addresses will not work. Nonprinting characters are expressed as arguments for {HANDSHAKE} by using	TEST {MENU}scrCAP~q {HANDSHAKE "FINSTAT KODAK\013",OK, 10} {QUIT} [The program TEST will write data captured from the other computer to the **capture-location** named CAP on the Communications Settings sheet. The other computer is looking for the string FINSTAT KODAK, followed by a RETURN (coded as \013). If the data are found, the other computer responds "OK". After ten seconds with no **receive-string**, {HANDSHAKE} will timeout and Symphony will continue program execution in the cell below the one where the command is located.

NAME	ARGUMENTS	DESCRIPTION	EXAMPLES
		a backslash followed by the appropriate ASCII code.	
		When a **receive-string** is received within the time specified by the argument **timeout-value**, program execution passes to the cell below the {HANDSHAKE} command; otherwise, a timeout causes program execution to continue in the same cell, just past the {HANDSHAKE} command.	
		Information is captured by {HANDSHAKE} in the specified **capture-location**. The information is stored in the **capture-location** cell line by line in exactly the way the lines are received from the other computer.	
{IF}		Evaluates a **logical expression** and, conditioned on that expression, branches	{IF NAME_OFFICER= "SMITH"} {BRANCH LIST_1} {BRANCH LIST_2}

		to another part of the program.	
		Binary (i.e. either/or) choices are made by {IF}. Any numeric or string expression can be either TRUE or FALSE.	[If the string stored in the cell labeled NAME_OFFICER is "SMITH", then the IF expression is TRUE and the program will cause control to be passed to a location labeled LIST_1 by means of the {BRANCH} command. Any other name stored in that location causes the IF expression to be FALSE, resulting in the next line of the macro being executed. Control is then passed to a location labeled LIST_2.]
		{IF} employs IF/THEN/ELSE logic. If TRUE, Symphony continues program execution in the cell. In these cases, the contents of the cell beyond the {IF} command is a THEN clause. If FALSE, program execution moves to the next cell in the program. The contents of this cell form an ELSE clause.	
		A FALSE statement in Symphony has a value of zero. Any value not zero is regarded as TRUE.	
{INDICATE}	string	Displays a **string** as a mode indicator highlighted in the upper right corner.	{INDICATE Office} [Displays highlighted "Office" in upper right corner.]

NAME	ARGUMENTS	DESCRIPTION	EXAMPLES
		Symphony gives the {INDICATE} command priority over indicators automatically included by the system.	{INDICATE " Page 1 "} [Displays highlighted "Page 1" centered in upper right corner.] {INDICATE ""} [Turns off mode indicator.]
		A mode indicator created by {INDICATE} will be displayed even when the mode changes. Indicators created by {INDICATE} can only be changed by a subsequent {INDICATE} command.	
		Mode indicators created by {INDICATE} may be turned off by using {INDICATE} with no **string** argument.	
		Type {INDICATE} with a blank **string** argument to competely remove the mode indicator from the control panel.	
		{INDICATE} centers the **string** in the upper right corner	

		when a **string** argument is enclosed in double quotes, including some blank spaces.	
{LET}	location, number [:type] or location, string [:type]	Stores a label or number entry at **location**. The argument **location**, **number** indicates a number label; **location, string** indicates a label. The information is stored in the upper left corner cell.	{Let A33,10*15:string} [Executing this line will store the label "10*15" in cell A33.]
		When {LET} is used without a type argument, Symphony tries to create either a label or number entry at **location** by evaluating the number or string argument. If it fails in this, Symphony creates a label entry that contains the characters supplied in the argument with no evaluation.	{LET A33, + "Dear, "&L22: value} [Executing this line will store the label "Dear, Frank" (assuming the value of cell L22 to be "Frank") in cell A33.]

NAME	ARGUMENTS	DESCRIPTION	EXAMPLES
{LOOK}	location	Checks to see if the user has typed a character since execution of the macro began. When the first character is typed, Symphony stores the character at **location**. The {LOOK} command allows the macro to continue to function. A keystroke will be stored in the system's keyboard buffer and then passed to Symphony, which, because of [LOOK], will then interrupt program execution. The {LOOK} command is used to interrupt macro operation. It is suitable for situations where you want a program to continue running until you want to get its attention.	TEST {LOOK SCREEN} {IF SCREEN=""} {BRANCH START} {GETLABEL "Now what do you want?",STORE} [The program keeps looping until a key is pressed on the keyboard. Whatever is typed is stored in the range SCREEN.]

Command	Argument	Description	Example
{MENUBRANCH}	menu-location	Permits selection of a menu item and makes appropriate branch.	TEST {MENUBRANCH MENU-1} {GOTO}F15
{MENUCALL}	menu-location	Permits selection of a menu item and makes appropriate subroutine call. Symphony permits choice from among eight menu items. {MENUBRANCH} and {MENUCALL} commands will operate even in PANELOFF mode. Menu lists must not be separated by empty cells. The final menu item must be followed by moving the highlight and pressing RETURN. Each menu item should begin with a different character. Menu items will be selected by the first letters of the items.	MENU-1 Add / Add an entry / {BRANCH {ADD Edit / Edit entries / {BRANCH EDIT} Quit / End / {QUIT} [The above shows three menu items in MENU-1. Each has two lines of code that will be executed when the particular choice is run.]

NAME	ARGUMENTS	DESCRIPTION	EXAMPLES	
		{MENUBRANCH} and {MENUCALL} do not distinguish between upper- and lowercase characters. {MENUBRANCH} and {MENUCALL} are used somewhat interchangeably. They differ in what Symphony does when the menu-driven execution ends. {MENUBRANCH} requires explicit instruction. {MENUCALL} requires only that a {RETURN} be coded for execution to return to the point where the menu was invoked.		
{ONERROR}	branch-location, [message-location]	When a Symphony error occurs, program control branches to **branch-location**; when a **message-location** argument is used, the error message will be stored in the cell specified in the argument.	TEST	{ONERROR OOPS,ERRMSG} {SERVICES} fcceivDATA~
			OOPS	{GOTO} MESSAGE-CELL~ The following error has occurred: {DOWN} {MENU}cERRMSG~~ {Down 2}

Command	Description	Example
	Only one {ONERROR} can be used at a time. Each {ONERROR} command may be used only once. Include an {ONERROR} command in the **branch-location** routine in order to continue trapping errors. {ONERROR} commands take effect when the <BREAK> key is pushed.	Replace data disk. Press any key when ready.~ {BRANCH TEST} [The program brings data from a file, using the File Combine command. The {ONERROR} statement keeps the program running if no disk is in the drive.]
{PANELOFF}	Stops updating of the control panel. Use {PANELOFF} only during execution of Symphony commands that sometimes cause confusing, meaningless activity on video display. Remember to execute {PANELON} to restore the display to its normal condition. If normal display is interrupted by an error in {PANELOFF} mode, difficulty could result.	TEST {PANELOFF} {SERVICES}fccn ONE~ivSOURCE~ {DOWN10} {SERVICES}fccn TWO~ivSOURCE~ {DOWN10} {SERVICES}fccn THREE~iv SOURCE~ {DOWN10} {SERVICES}fccn FOUR~ivSOURCE~ {DOWN10} {PANELON} [The program retrieves data worksheet file called SOURCE. Four different ranges in the worksheet are accessed by four File Combine

NAME	ARGUMENTS	DESCRIPTION	EXAMPLES
			commands. {PANELOFF} suppresses the display of filenames and range names that would otherwise keep appearing during program execution.]
{PANELON}		Turns off {PANELOFF} command. Restores normal functions to control panel.	
{PHONE}	phone number-string	Dials a telephone number. {PHONE} bypasses the use of a COMM window in dialing a phone number. Phone numbers prestored in Symphony may be accessed by the {PHONE} command. Information cannot be captured, however, without using a COMM window.	CALL {PHONE PNUMBER} [The cell named PNUMBER is in the Value column of the DEFINITION range.]

		{PHONE} can be used by a macro created in a FORM window.	
		The **phone number-string** argument can be a string-value formula or a cell address.	
		The command uses the same telephone codes that are used in the COMM Phone Call command: T specifies touch phone and P specifies pulse phone.	
		Commas will pause dialing.	
		When a connection is established, program execution continues in the cell below the {PHONE} statement. Failure to establish the connection causes program execution to continue in the same cell.	
{PUT}	range, column-	Stores an expression at a specific	{PUT A1..C5,0,2,Here}

NAME	*ARGUMENTS*	*DESCRIPTION*	*EXAMPLES*
	number, row-number, location	**column-number**, and **row-number** in a **range**. {PUT} creates numbers and labels in specific cells. {PUT} differs from {LET} only in that it stores information at a specific location and not merely in a specified cell. An error condition results from the attempt to specify a cell rather than a range. When assigning values to the arguments, remember that the measures for row and column all include a zero-th position. A "1" is really the second position.	[Places the word "Here" in cell A3.]
{QUIT}		Ends execution of a macro. {QUIT} brings macro execution to a complete halt — not	TEST Quit Save work and exit {QUIT}

		just a subroutine in which it might happen to be used.	
{RECALC}	location	Carries out row-by-row recalculation of formulas in a specific **location**.	{RECALC A1..D1}
{RECALCCOL}	location	Carries out column-by-column recalculation of formulas in a specific **location**. Used to carry out partial recalculations of a larger worksheet. When a formula will be used to calculate material in cells above and to the right of its position, use {RECALC}. For data below and to the left of the formula, use {RECALCCOL}. Appropriate for use with {LET} and {GETNUMBER} — which normally would waste time in a large worksheet in performing	

NAME	ARGUMENTS	DESCRIPTION	EXAMPLES
		calculations after each data entry. Be careful of the potential effect of partial recalculation upon formulas that are not included in the {RECALC} or {RECALCCOL} functions. A general recalculation should be performed at the end of a macro routine that uses {RECALC} or {RECALCCOL}.	
{RETURN}		Returns program control to the location being used before program execution was passed to a subroutine. {RETURN} is used with **routine-name** to return to the calling routine. {RETURN} is not required when a subroutine ends	SAVE {GETLABEL "Do you want to save your changes? (Y/N):",Input} {IF (INPUT="N") #OR#(INPUT= "n")} {RETURN} {SERVICES}FS~Y [The program responds to the user's answer to the request "Do you want to save your changes?" either by saving the changes or

Command	Argument	Description	Example
		with a blank cell. In that case, program control returns automatically to the point where the **routine-name** was called.	by exiting to the calling routine.]
{WAIT}	time-serial-number	Causes the program to wait until **time-serial-number**. The program will not accept any keyboard input until the specified time is reached and program execution continues. Running the {WAIT} command causes Symphony to display a WAIT indicator in the upper right corner. {WAIT} can be interrupted by the BREAK key.	TIME {WINDOWS}{WAIT @NOW-@TIME (0,0,10)} {BEEP}{BRANCH TIME} [The program changes from window to window with intervening ten-second intervals and beeps.]
{WINDOWSOFF}		Freezes the display screen. {WINDOWSOFF} does not affect the control panel.	

NAME	ARGUMENTS	DESCRIPTION	EXAMPLES	
		{WINDOWSOFF} permits processing data without irrelevant, confusing messages flashing across the screen.		
{WINDOWSON}		Turns off the {WINDOWSOFF} command. Use of {WINDOWSOFF} and {WINDOWSON} permits "clean" program design, such as altering windows and then displaying the reconfigured windows after the alterations are complete. {WINDOWSOFF} and {WINDOWSON} do the same things for Symphony windows as {PANELOFF} and {PANELON} do for the control panel.	TEST [The program hides the display of the windows, configures windows 1, 2, and 3, and then displays them. Note the window isolate command in the third line.]	{WINDOWSOFF} {SERVICES}wul~ {SERVICES}wi {SERVICES}wu2~ {SERVICES}wu3~ {WINDOWSON}
{?}		Pauses program execution to give temporary keyboard control to the user.	TEST	{goto}a9~ Type an entry here~ {?}

Program execution following a {?} command will continue when the RETURN key is pressed. The {?} command is used for implementing interactive macros. In this respect it is an alternate command to {GET}, {GETLABEL}, {GETNUMBER}, {LOOK}, {MENUBRANCH}, and {MENUCALL}.	~{edit}***{home} {right}***~ [The program moves the pointer to cell A9 and displays the message "Type an entry here". When the user finishes typing the entry and presses RETURN, the program adds preceding and following asterisks to the message.]

For a description of the twelve additional commands that Symphony 1.1 puts at your disposal, read Coda C where you learn how to {OPEN}, {CLOSE}, {READ} and {WRITE} to files, and how to use {DISPATCH} and {RESTART} in macro processing.

CODA B

Listings

Here are listings, in formula format, of the major macros found in the third movement and the fourth movement. Only those cells which contain information are printed out under this option. A list of named ranges is also provided following each of the macros from the fourth movement.

GRADEBOOK

This is the formula format listing for the GRADEBOOK application developed in the third movement. As mentioned there, this is an incomplete macro. There are menu items here that are not implemented.

```
AA1: 'Macro to be used by a teacher to
AA2: 'maintain class lists, mailing lists, etc.,
AA3: 'calculate grades on a curve basis or enter
AA4: 'letter grades and print various reports.
AA5: '(C) 1985, The Waite Group
AA6: 'Macro by Dan Shafer
AA8: 'GRADES
AB8: '{MenuCall Main_Menu}
AB9: '{ESC}{ESC}{ESC}{S}
AA11: 'Student
AB11: 'Grades
```

```
AC11:  'Reports
AD11:  'Quit
AA12:  'Work with student files
AB12:  'Enter grades, calculate curve
AC12:  'Produce lists, notices
AD12:  'Return to Symphony
AA13:  '{MenuCall Stu_Menu}
AB13:  '{MenuCall Grade_Menu}
AC13:  '{MenuCall Report_Menu}
AD13:  '{S}
AA15:  'Add
AB15:  'Change
AC15:  'Drop
AD15:  'Quit
AA16:  'Enter New Student
AB16:  'Correct Student Information
AC16:  'Delete a Student
AD16:  'Return to Gradebook Menu
AA17:  '{AddStu}
AB17:  '{FixStu}
AC17:  '{DropStu}
AD17:  '{MenuBranch Main_Menu}
AA19:  'Enter
AB19:  'Modify
AC19:  'Curve
AD19:  'Quit
AA20:  'Enter Grades
AB20:  'Correct a Student's Grade
AC20:  'Calculate Curve for Assignment
AD20:  'Return to Gradebook Menu
AA21:  '{AddGrades}
AB21:  '{FixGrades}
AC21:  '{CalcGrades}
AD21:  '{MenuBranch Main_Menu}
AA23:  'Class_List
AB23:  'Mailing_List
AC23:  'Grade_Report
AD23:  'Poor_Work
AE23:  'Quit
AA24:  'Print a Class List
AB24:  'Print a Mailing List
AC24:  'Print Grade Reports
AD24:  'Send Poor Work Notices
AE24:  'Return to Gradebook Menu
AA25:  '{Class_List}
AB25:  '{Mail_List}
AC25:  '{Grade_Report}
AD25:  '{Poor_Work}
AE25:  '{MenuBranch Main_Menu}
AA28:  'DropStu
AB28:  '{S}wuSTUDENTS~{m}ce{?}~{Insert}{PgUp}{Delete}{Get a1}
AB29:  '{S}wuMAIN~{Home}{MenuBranch Main_Menu}
AB47:  'AddGrades
AC47:  '{GetNumber "Exam Number (1-5): ",a1}~
AC48:  '{if a1<1#or#a1>5}{beep 100}{addgrades}
AC49:  '{S}wuBOOK~
AC50:  '{if a1=1}{goto}b104~{getscores}
```

```
AC51: '{if a1=2}{goto}c104~{getscores}
AC52: '{if a1=3}{goto}d104~{getscores}
AC53: '{if a1=4}{goto}e104~{getscores}
AC54: '{if a1=5}{goto}f104~{getscores}
AB56: 'GetScores
AC56: '{for a2,1,40,1,input1}
AC57: '{S}wuMAIN~{home}{menubranch main_menu}
AB59: '
AC59: '
AB60: 'Input1
AC60: '{?}~{Down}
AB62: 'FixGrades
AC62: '{GetNumber "Which Exam? ",a1}~
AC63: '{GetLabel "Which Student (Last Name)? ",a2}~
AC64: '{goto}a3~+@vlookup(a2,a104..a143,0)~
AC65: '{S}wuBOOK~{Home}
AC66: '{Down +a3+3}{right a1}
AC67: '{?}~
AC68: '{GetLabel "More grade changes? ",a101}~
AC69: '{if a101="y"#OR#a101="Y"'}{S}wuMAIN~{home}{fixgrades}
AC70: '{blank a1..a3}{blank a101}{menubranch main_menu}
AA72: 'Class_List
AB72: '{PanelOff}{WindowsOff}{S}pssrA293..C296~
AB73: 'ota292..c292~qgpq{S}wuMAIN~
AB74: '{PanelOn}{WindowsOn}{menubranch main_menu}
AA76: 'AddStu
AB76: '{S}wuSTUDENTS~{ESC}
AA79: '\e
AB79: '{S}wuMAIN~{Goto}BOOK~{?}~{Home}
AB80: '{MenuBranch Main_Menu}
```

PROFESSIONAL TIME AND BILLING SYSTEM

This set of listings provides the main macros for the PROFESSIONAL TIME AND BILLING SYSTEM developed in the fourth movement. The first listing is of the macro itself. The second listing is of the invoice and data area which would be saved initially as the master format. The third listing is of the named ranges and their locations for this application.

PROFESSIONAL TIME AND BILLING MACRO

```
AA1: 'This macro is a time tracking and billing macro
AA2: 'suitable for use in an organization that bills
AA3: 'by time and type of service.
AA4: '(C) 1985, The Waite Group
AA5: 'Macro by Mary Johnson
AA7: 'TIMESH
AB7: '{MenuCall Main_Menu}
AB8: '{esc}{esc}{esc}{S}
AA10: 'Main_Menu
AB10: 'Add
AC10: 'Update
AD10: 'Invoice
```

```
AE10: 'Quit
AB11: 'Add a client to the file
AC11: 'Update a client's file
AD11: 'Prepare invoices for clients
AE11: 'Return to Symphony
AB12: '{ADD}
AC12: '{UPDATE}
AD12: '{MenuCall INVOICE}
AE12: '{S}e
AA15: '\S
AB15: '{S}fxf{?}~TSHEET~
AB16: '{right}~{m}eTSHEET~
AB17: '{S}wuMAIN~
AB18: '{MenuBranch Main_MENU}
AA20: 'ADD
AB20: '{home}
AB21: '{S}fccnTSHEET~
AB22: 'rfTSMAS~
AA24: 'UPDATE
AB24: '{home}
AB25: '{S}fccnTSHEET~
AB26: 'rf{?}~
AA28: 'INVOICE
AB28: 'Single
AC28: 'Group
AD28: 'Quit
AB29: 'Print out one client invoice
AC29: 'Print out invoices for several clients
AD29: 'Return to the Main Menu
AB30: '{SINGLE}
AC30: '{GROUP}
AD30: '{MenuBranch Main_Menu}
AA32: 'SINGLE
AB32: '{home}
AB33: '{S}fccnTSHEET~
AB34: 'rf{?}~
AB35: '{S}pasnuHEAD~qgll
AB36: 'snuADDR~qgl
AB37: 'snuBILL~qgpq
AB38: '{m}eTSHEET~
AB39: '{S}wuMAIN~
AB40: '{MenuBranch Main_Menu}
AA42: 'GROUP
AB42: '{home}
AA43: 'loop1
AB43: '{S}fccnTSHEET~
AB44: 'rf{?}~
AB45: '{S}pasnuHEAD~qgll
AB46: 'snuADDR~qgl
AB47: 'snuBILL~qgpq
AB48: '{m}eTSHEET~
AB49: '{GetLabel "Are there more to be invoiced? (y or n), a1}~
AB50: '{If a1="Y"#OR#a1="y"}{Branch loop1}
AB51: '{S}wuMAIN~
AB52: '{MenuBranch Main_Menu}
AA54: 'HEAD
AB54: 'Smith, Ramesey, LeVeque, and Jones
```

```
AB55: '345 Mount Diablo Drive
AB56: 'Pleasant Hill, California  94523
AB57: '(415) 555-4141
AA60: 'ADD
AB60: 'AB20
AA61: 'ADDR
AB61: 'B4..E8
AA62: 'BILL
AB62: 'A18..E42
AA63: 'GROUP
AB63: 'AB42
AA64: 'HEAD
AB64: 'AB54..AB57
AA65: 'INVOICE
AB65: 'AB28
AA66: 'KEY
AB66: 'E13..E17
AA67: 'LOOP1
AB67: 'AB43
AA68: 'MAIN_MENU
AB68: 'AB10
AA69: 'SINGLE
AB69: 'AB32
AA70: 'TIMESH
AB70: 'AB7
AA71: 'TSHEET
AB71: 'A1..E42
AA72: 'UPDATE
AB72: 'AB24
AA73: '\S
AB73: 'AB15
```

PROFESSIONAL TIME AND BILLING MASTER

```
A1: 'Time Sheet
A5: 'Client:
A6: 'Address:
A7: 'City:
C9: '<<Rate Chart>>
B11: "Rate
C11: "     Service
E11: 'Code
B12: "====
C12: "     =======
E12: '====
B13: (F2) 20
C13: 'Administration
E13: 'a
B14: (F2) 50
C14: 'Paralegal
E14: 'p
B15: (F2) 100
C15: 'Junior Partner
E15: 'j
B16: (F2) 150
C16: 'Senior Partner
```

```
E16: 's
A18:
'=============================================================
A19: 'Date
B19: 'Description
C19: ^Hours
D19: ^Code
E19: ^ Bill Amt
A20: '----
B20: '-----------
C20: ^-----
D20: ^----
E20: ^ --------
E21: (F2) @VLOOKUP(D21,$KEY,-3)*C21
E22: (F2) @VLOOKUP(D22,$KEY,-3)*C22
E23: (F2) @VLOOKUP(D23,$KEY,-3)*C23
E24: (F2) @VLOOKUP(D24,$KEY,-3)*C24
E25: (F2) @VLOOKUP(D25,$KEY,-3)*C25
E26: (F2) @VLOOKUP(D26,$KEY,-3)*C26
E27: (F2) @VLOOKUP(D27,$KEY,-3)*C27
E28: (F2) @VLOOKUP(D28,$KEY,-3)*C28
E29: (F2) @VLOOKUP(D29,$KEY,-3)*C29
E30: (F2) @VLOOKUP(D30,$KEY,-3)*C30
E31: (F2) @VLOOKUP(D31,$KEY,-3)*C31
E32: (F2) @VLOOKUP(D32,$KEY,-3)*C32
E33: (F2) @VLOOKUP(D33,$KEY,-3)*C33
E34: (F2) @VLOOKUP(D34,$KEY,-3)*C34
E35: (F2) @VLOOKUP(D35,$KEY,-3)*C35
E36: (F2) @VLOOKUP(D36,$KEY,-3)*C36
E37: (F2) @VLOOKUP(D37,$KEY,-3)*C37
E38: (F2) @VLOOKUP(D38,$KEY,-3)*C38
E39: (F2) @VLOOKUP(D39,$KEY,-3)*C39
E40: (F2) @VLOOKUP(D40,$KEY,-3)*C40
C41: (F1) '---------------------------
B42: "TOTALS:
C42: (F1) @SUM(C21..C40)
E42: (F2) @SUM(E21..E40)
```

PROFESSIONAL TIME AND BILLING NAMED RANGES

```
ADD       AB20
ADDR      B4..E8
BILL      A18..E42
HEAD      AB54..AE57
INVOICE   AB28
KEY       E13..E17
LOOP1     AB43
MAIN_MENU AB10
SINGLE    AB32
TIMESH    AB7
TSHEET    A1..E42
UPDATE    AB24
\S        AB15
```

PERSONAL APPOINTMENT MANAGER

This set of listings provides the macro listing for the PERSONAL APPOINTMENT MANAGER developed in the fourth movement. In addition to the macro, the named ranges are listed.

PERSONAL APPOINTMENT MANAGER MACRO

```
AA1:  'APPT
AB1:  '{BLANK TEMP}{GOTO}A1~{MENUCALL MAINMENU}
AA3:  'MAINMENU
AB3:  'Add Appointments
AC3:  'Change Appointment
AD3:  'Purge Old Dates
AE3:  'Report
AF3:  'Quit
AB4:  'Creates new appointment
AC4:  'Reschedule or Cancel
AD4:  'Delete obsolete data
AE4:  'Print calendar reminders
AF4:  'Exit Symphony
AB5:  '{ADD}
AC5:  '{MENUCALL MODMENU}
AD5:  '{PURGE}
AE5:  '{TICKLER}
AF5:  '{S}EY~
AA8:  'MODMENU
AB8:  'Reschedule
AC8:  'Cancel
AD8:  'Quit
AB9:  'Move an appointment
AC9:  'Cancel an Appointment
AD9:  'Return to Appointment Menu
AB10:  '{RESKED}
AC10:  '{CANCEL}
AD10:  '{MENUCALL MAINMENU}
AA12:  'ADD
AB12:  '{GETLABEL Enter date as 08-Aug-84 ,b1}~
AB13:  '{LET C1,@DATEVALUE(B1)}
AB14:  '{LET B2,0}~{GOTO}CAL~
AA15:  'LOOP1
AB15:  '{IF (@DATEVALUE(@INDEX(CAL,0,+B2)))=C1}{BRANCH ENTRY}
AB16:  '{IF @CELLPOINTER(``TYPE")="b"}{BRANCH ADD_DATE}
AB17:  '{DOWN}{LET B2,B2+1}~{BRANCH LOOP1}
AA20:  'ENTRY
AB20:  '{M}IR~
AB21:  '{PANELOFF}{DOWN}{M}C~{UP}~{UP}{RIGHT}
AA22:  'entry2
AB22:  +"{GETLABEL Enter time of appointment
       ,C"&@STRING(B2+200,0)&"}{RIGHT}"
AB23:  +"{GETLABEL Description==> ,D"&@STRING(B2+200,0)&"}"
AB24:  '{S}FS~Y
AB25:  '{GOTO}A1~{MENUBRANCH MAINMENU}
AA28:  'ADD_DATE
AB28:  '{BEEP 3}
```

```
AB29: '{MENUCALL DATEMENU}
AA31: 'DATEMENU
AB31: 'Yes
AC31: 'No
AB32: 'Add this date to calendar
AC32: 'Date entered in error
AB33: +"{GOTO}B"&@STRING(B2+200,0)&"~"
AC33: '{APPT}
AB34: '{M}cb1~~
AB35: '{right}{branch entry2}
AA37: 'CANCEL
AB37: '{GETLABEL Enter date as 08-Aug-84 ,b1}~
AB38: '{LET C1,@DATEVALUE(B1)}
AB39: '{LET B2,0}~{GOTO}CAL~
AA40: 'LOOP2
AB40: '{IF (@DATEVALUE(@INDEX(CAL,0,+B2)))=C1}{MENUBRANCH
      KILLMENU}
AB41: '{IF @CELLPOINTER(``TYPE")="b"}{BRANCH BAD_DATE}
AB42: '{DOWN}{LET B2,B2+1}~{BRANCH LOOP2}
AA44: 'KILLMENU
AB44: 'Yes
AC44: 'No
AD44: 'Quit
AB45: 'Cancel this appointment
AC45: 'Look for next one
AD45: 'Go back to main menu
AB46: '{M}DR~{S}FS~Y
AC46: '{DOWN}{LET B2,B2+1}~{BRANCH LOOP2}
AD46: '{GOTO}A1~{MENUBRANCH MAINMENU}
AB47: '{GOTO}A1~{MENUBRANCH MAINMENU}
AA49: 'BAD_DATE
AB49: '{BEEP}
AB50: '{GETLABEL No such date.  Try again. Press RETURN,TEMP}
AB51: '{GOTO}A1~{MENUBRANCH MAINMENU}
AA53: 'RESKED
AB53: '{GETLABEL Enter date as 08-Aug-84 ,b1}~
AB54: '{LET C1,@DATEVALUE(B1)}
AB55: '{LET B2,0}~{GOTO}CAL~
AA56: 'LOOP3
AB56: '{IF (@DATEVALUE(@INDEX(CAL,0,+B2)))=C1}{MENUBRANCH
      MOVEMENU}
AB57: '{IF @CELLPOINTER("TYPE")="b"}{BRANCH BAD_DATE}
AB58: '{DOWN}{LET B2,B2+1}~{BRANCH LOOP3}
AA60: 'MOVEMENU
AB60: 'Yes
AC60: 'No
AD60: 'Quit
AB61: 'Reschedule this appointment
AC61: 'Look for next one
AD61: 'Go back to main menu
AB62: +"{GETLABEL New date= ,B"&@STRING(B2+200,0)&"}"
AC62: '{DOWN}{LET B2,B2+1}~{BRANCH LOOP3}
AD62: '{GOTO}A1~{MENUBRANCH MAINMENU}
AB63: +"{RIGHT}{GETLABEL New Time= ,C"&@STRING(B2+200,0)&"}"
AB64: '{S}FS~Y
AB65: '{GOTO}A1~{MENUBRANCH MAINMENU}
AA67: 'PURGE
```

```
AB67: '{GOTO}A22~
AB68: '{GETLABEL Enter purge date... ,B1}
AB69: '{IF B1="T"#OR#B1="t"}{LET C1,@INT(@NOW))}~{BRANCH LOOPP}
AB70: '{LET C1,@DATEVALUE(B1)}
AA71: 'LOOPP
AB71: '{LET B2,1}~{GOTO}CAL~{DOWN}
AA72: 'LOOP4
AB72: '{LET C2,@DATEVALUE(@INDEX(CAL,0,+B2))}~
AB73: '{IF C2=0}{BRANCH DONE}
AB74: '{IF C2<C1}{M}DR~{BRANCH LOOP4}
AA75: 'LOOP5
AB75: '{DOWN}{LET B2,B2+1}{BRANCH LOOP4}
AA77: 'DONE
AB77: '{S}FS~Y{GOTO}A1~{MENUBRANCH MAINMENU}
AA79: 'TICKLER
AB79: '{GETLABEL Enter date as 08-Aug-84 or T for Today ,b1}~
AB80: '{IF +B1="T"#OR#B1="t"}{LET C1,@INT(@NOW)}~{BRANCH LOOPT}
AB81: '{LET C1,@DATEVALUE(B1)}{GOTO}A41~
AA82: 'LOOPT
AB82: '{LET B2,0}~{LET B3,0}~{BLANK
      REPORT_RANGE}{PANELOFF}{WINDOWSOFF}{GOTO}CAL~
AA83: 'LOOP6
AB83: '{IF (@DATEVALUE(@INDEX(CAL,0,+B2)))=C1}{REPORTIT}
AB84: '{IF
      @CELLPOINTER(``TYPE")="b"}{PANELON}{WINDOWSON}{MENUBRANCH
      REPTMENU}
AB85: '{DOWN}{LET B2,B2+1}~{BRANCH LOOP6}
AA87: 'REPORTIT
AB87: '{LET B3,B3+1}~
AB88: '{M}C{TAB}{RIGHT 2}~
AB89: +"B"&@STRING(B3+300,0)&"~"
AB90: '{RETURN}
AA92: 'REPTMENU
AB92: 'Display
AC92: 'Print
AD92: 'Quit
AB93: 'Display Appointments
AC93: 'Print Appointments
AD93: 'Return to Main Menu
AB94: '{INDICATE}{GOTO}REPORT_RANGE~
AC94: '{INDICATE}{BRANCH PRINT1}
AD94: '{INDICATE}{GOTO}A1~{MENUBRANCH MAINMENU}
AB95: '{GETLABEL Press RETURN to Continue ,temp}
AB96: '{GOTO}A1~{MENUBRANCH MAINMENU}
AA98: 'PRINT1
AB98: '{S}PSOF~SRREPORT_RANGE~QGPQ
AB99: '{GOTO}A1~{MENUBRANCH MAINMENU}
```

PERSONAL APPOINTMENT MANAGER NAMED RANGES

```
ADD        AB12
ADD_DATE   AB28
APPT       AB1
BAD_DATE   AB49
CAL        B200..D264
CANCEL     AB37
```

```
DATEMENU  AB31
DONE      AB76
ENTRY     AB20
ENTRY2    AB22
KILLMENU  AB44
LOOP1     AB15
LOOP2     AB40
LOOP3     AB56
LOOP4     AB72
LOOP5     AB75
LOOP6     AB83
LOOPT     AB82
MAINMENU  AB3
MODMENU   AB8
MOVEMENU  AB60
PRINT1    AB98
PURGE     AB67
REPORTIT  AB87
REPORT
  _RANGE  B300..D364
REPTMENU  AB92
RESKED    AB53
TEMP      B1..C21
TICKLER   AB79
\Z        AB37
```

NONPROFIT ORGANIZATION

This set of listings provides the main macros for the NONPROFIT ORGANIZATION developed in the Fourth Movement. You will see that there are a large number of named ranges on the list of ranges which is also included.

NONPROFIT ORGANIZATION MACRO

```
AA1: 'This is a macro for organizations that solicit funds
AA2: 'and match parameters from several data bases.
AA3: '(C) 1985, The Waite Group
AA4: 'Macros by Mary Johnson
AA7: 'NOPRO
AB7: '{MenuCall Main_Menu}
AB8: '{ESC}{ESC}{ESC}{S}
AA11: 'Donors
AB11: 'Volunteers
AC11: 'Students
AD11: 'Reports
AE11: 'Quit
AA12: 'Donor database
AB12: 'Volunteer database
AC12: 'Student database
AD12: 'Produce statistical reports
AE12: 'Return to Symphony
AA13: '{MenuCall Don_Menu}
```

```
AB13: '{MenuCall Vol_Menu}
AC13: '{MenuCall Stu_Menu}
AD13: '{MenuCall Report_Menu}
AE13: '{S}
AA15: 'Add
AB15: 'Delete
AC15: 'Update
AD15: 'Send
AE15: 'Quit
AA16: 'Add a new donor
AB16: 'Delete a donor
AC16: 'Update donor data
AD16: 'Send donor letters
AE16: 'Return to Main Menu
AA17: '{AddDon}
AB17: '{DelDon}
AC17: '{UpDon}
AD17: '{MenuCall Dlett_Menu}
AE17: '{MenuBranch Main_menu}
AA19: 'Initial
AB19: 'Thanks
AC19: 'Quit
AA20: 'First solicitation
AB20: 'Thanks, donors names?
AC20: 'Return to Main Menu
AA21: '{Dinitial}
AB21: '{Thankdonor}
AC21: '{MenuBranch Main_menu}
AA23: 'Add
AB23: 'Delete
AC23: 'Update
AD23: 'Send
AE23: 'Match
AF23: 'Quit
AA24: 'Add a new volunteer
AB24: 'Delete a volunteer
AC24: 'Update volunteer data
AD24: 'Send volunteer letters
AE24: 'Match volunteer with students
AF24: 'Return to Main Menu
AA25: '{AddVol}
AB25: '{DelVol}
AC25: '{UpVol}
AD25: '{MenuCall Vlet_Menu}
AE25: '{MatchVS}
AF25: '{MenuBranch Main_menu}
AA27: 'Thanks
AB27: 'Quit
AA28: 'Thanks for volunteering
AB28: 'Return to Main Menu
AA29: '{Thankvol}
AB29: '{MenuBranch Main_menu}
AA31: 'Add
AB31: 'Delete
AC31: 'Update
AD31: 'Send
AE31: 'Match
```

```
AF31: 'Quit
AA32: 'Add a new student
AB32: 'Delete a student
AC32: 'Update student data
AD32: 'Send student letters
AE32: 'Match student with volunteers
AF32: 'Return to Main Menu
AA33: '{AddStu}
AB33: '{DelStu}
AC33: '{UpStu}
AD33: '{MenuCall Slet_Menu}
AE33: '{MatchSV}
AF33: '{MenuBranch Main_menu}
AA35: 'Initial
AB35: 'Quit
AA36: 'Welcome to the program
AB36: 'Return to Main Menu
AA37: '{Sinitial}
AB37: '{MenuBranch Main_menu}
AA39: 'Students
AB39: 'Volunteers
AC39: 'Donors
AD39: 'Quit
AA40: 'Master List of Students
AB40: 'Master List of Volunteers
AC40: 'Master List of Donors
AD40: 'Return to Main Menu
AA41: '{StuServ}
AB41: '{VolMaslst}
AC41: '{DonList}
AD41: '{MenuBranch Main_menu}
AA45: '\c
AB45: '{blank a1..a1}{blank a318..w318}
AB46: '{blank a565..w565}{blank a811..w811}
AB47: '{S}wuMAIN~
AB48: '{MenuBranch Main_Menu}
AA50: 'AddDon
AB50: '{S}wuDONOR~{m}ci
AA52: 'DelDon
AB52: '{S}wuDONOR~{m}ce{?}~{Insert}{ESC}u{delete}{?}~{esc}
AB53: '{blank a318..w318}
AB54: '{S}wuMAIN~{Home}{MenuBranch Main_Menu}
AA56: 'UpDon
AB56: '{GetLabel "Do you want to update a group of donors? (y or
      n) ",a1}~
AB57: '{if a1="y"#OR#a1="Y"}{branch updgr}
AB58: '{S}wuDONOR~{m}ce{?}~{Insert}{esc}u{?}~{insert}{esc}
AB59: '{blank a318..w318}{blank a1}
AB60: '{S}wuMAIN~{Home}{MenuBranch Main_Menu}
AA62: 'Updgr
AB62: '{S}wuDONOR~{m}ce{?}~{Insert}{esc}u{?}~{insert}
AA64: 'Dinitial
AB64: '{S}wuDONOR~{m}ce{tab 17}IN~{insert}{esc}u{esc}
AB65: '{S}pasnuDONINTL~qgpq
AB66: '{blank a318..w318}
AB67: '{S}wuMAIN~{Home}{MenuBranch Main_Menu}
AA69: 'Thankdonor
```

```
AB69:  '{S}wuDONOR~{m}ce{tab 19}TD~{insert}{esc}u{esc}
AB70:  '{S}pasnuDONTHX~qgpq
AB71:  '{blank a318..w318}
AB72:  '{S}wuMAIN~{Home}{MenuBranch Main_Menu}
AA74:  'AddVol
AB74:  '{S}wuVOLUNTEER~{m}ci
AA76:  'DelVol
AB76:  '{S}wuVOLUNTEER~{m}ce{?}~{Insert}{ESC}u{delete}{?}~{esc}
AB77:  '{blank a565..w565}
AB78:  '{S}wuMAIN~{Home}{MenuBranch Main_Menu}
AA80:  'UpVol
AB80:  '{GetLabel "Do you want to update a group of volunteers? (y
       or n) ",a1}~
AB81:  '{if a1="y"#OR#a1="Y"}{branch upvgr}
AB82:  '{S}wuVOLUNTEER~{m}ce{?}~{Insert}{esc}u{?}~{insert}{esc}
AB83:  '{blank a565..w565}{blank a1}
AB84:  '{S}wuMAIN~{Home}{MenuBranch Main_Menu}
AA86:  'Upvgr
AB86:  '{S}wuVOLUNTEER~{m}ce{?}~{Insert}{esc}u{?}~{insert}
AA88:  'Thankvol
AB88:  '{S}wuVOLUNTEER~{m}ce{tab 17}T1~{insert}{esc}u{esc}
AB89:  '{S}pasnuVOLT1~qgpq
AB90:  '{blank a565..w565}{blank a1}
AB91:  '{S}wuMAIN~{Home}{MenuBranch Main_Menu}
AA93:  'MatchVS
AB93:  '{S}wuVOLUNTEER~{m}ci
AB94:  '{m}ce{?}~{Insert}{esc}u
AB95:  '{type}s{m}rv0562..Q562~N811~
AB96:  '{type}f{S}wuSTUDENT~{m}ce{?}~{insert}{esc}u
AB97:  '{onerror reset}
AB98:  '{type}s{m}qeq
AB99:  '{S}pasnuMAV2S~qgpq
AB100:  '{blank a811..w811}{blank a565..w565}
AB101:  '{type}f{m}ci~
AB102:  '{S}wuMAIN~{Home}{MenuBranch Vol_Menu}
AA104:  'AddStu
AB104:  '{S}wuSTUDENT~{m}ci
AA106:  'DelStu
AB106:  '{S}wuSTUDENT~{m}ce{?}~{Insert}{ESC}u{delete}{?}~{esc}
AB107:  '{blank a811..w811}
AB108:  '{S}wuMAIN~{Home}{MenuBranch Main_Menu}
AA110:  'UpStu
AB110:  '{GetLabel "Do you want to update a group of students? (y
        or n) ",a1}~
AB111:  '{if a1="y"#OR#a1="Y"}{branch upsgr}
AB112:  '{S}wuSTUDENT~{m}ce{?}~{Insert}{esc}u{?}~{insert}{esc}
AB113:  '{blank a811..w811}{blank a1}
AB114:  '{S}wuMAIN~{Home}{MenuBranch Main_Menu}
AA116:  'Upsgr
AB116:  '{S}wuSTUDENT~{m}ce{?}~{Insert}{esc}u{?}~{insert}
AA118:  'Sinitial
AB118:  '{S}wuSTUDENT~{m}ce{tab 16}S1~{insert}{esc}u{esc}
AB119:  '{S}pasnuSTULT1~qgpq
AB120:  '{blank a811..w811}{blank a1}
AB121:  '{S}wuMAIN~{Home}{MenuBranch Main_Menu}
AA123:  'reset
AB123:  '{esc}{m}ce{?}~
```

```
AB124:  '{return}
AA126:  'MatchSV
AB126:  '{S}wuSTUDENT~{m}ci
AB127:  '{m}ce{?}~{Insert}{esc}u
AB128:  '{type}s{m}rvN808..P808~0565~
AB129:  '{type}f{S}wuVOLUNTEER~{m}ce{?}~{insert}{esc}u
AB130:  '{onerror reset}
AB131:  '{type}s{m}qeq
AB132:  '{S}pasnuMAS2V~qgpq
AB133:  '{blank a811..w811}{blank a565..w565}
AB134:  '{type}f{m}ci~
AB135:  '{S}wuMAIN~{Home}{MenuBranch Stu_Menu}
AA137:  'StuServ
AB137:  '{S}wuSTUDENT~{m}ci
AB138:  '{S}pasnuSTUMAS~qgpq
AB139:  '{S}wuMAIN~{Home}{MenuBranch Main_Menu}
AA141:  'VolMaslst
AB141:  '{S}wuVOLUNTEER~{m}ci
AB142:  '{S}pasnuVOLMAS~qgpq
AB143:  '{S}wuMAIN~{Home}{MenuBranch Main_Menu}
AA145:  'DonList
AB145:  '{S}wuDONOR~{m}ci
AB146:  '{S}pasnuDONMAS~qgpq
AB147:  '{S}wuMAIN~{Home}{MenuBranch Main_Menu}
```

NONPROFIT ORGANIZATION NAMED RANGES

```
# OF REFS      W323
#OFREFS        W323
$'S TO DATE    O323
$'STODATE      O323
ADDDON         AB50
ADDRESS        C323
ADDSTU         AB104
ADDVOL         AB74
C              AB45..AB48
CITY           D323
CO ADDRESS     J323
CO CITY        K323
CO PHONE       N323
CO STATE       L323
CO ZIP         M323
COADDRESS      J323
COCITY         K323
COMPANY        I323
COPHONE        N323
COSTATE        L323
COZIP          M323
DELDON         AB52
DELSTU         AB106
DELVOL         AB76
DINITIAL       AB64
DLETT_MENU     AA19..AC21
DON SOURCE     V323
DONATION DATE  Q323
DONATIONDATE   Q323
```

```
DONLIST         AB145
DONOR_AB        A314..W314
DONOR_CR        A317..W318
DONOR_DB        A322..W327
DONOR_DF        A290..H312
DONOR_EN        A275..A287
DONOR_MA        A315..W315
DONSOURCE       V323
DON_MENU        AA15..AE17
DSTODATE        O323
EXIT            IV8192
FIRST NAME      A323
FIRSTNAME       A323
GRADE           L816
HOME PHONE      G323
HOMEPHONE       G323
LAST $ AMT      P323
LAST NAME       B323
LAST$AMT        P323
LASTNAME        B323
MAIN_MENU       AA11..AE13
MATCHSV         AB126
MATCHVS         AB93
NOPRO           AB7..AB8
OCCUPATION      H323
REPORT_MENU     AA39..AD41
RESET           AB123
RPFNAME         H816
RPLNAME         I816
RPPHONE         J816
SADDRESS        C816
SCHOOL          K816
SCITY           D816
SDAY            O816
SFNAME          A816
SHOUR           P816
SINITIAL        AB118
SLETR           Q816
SLET_MENU       AA35..AB37
SLNAME          B816
SOLIC DATE      S323
SOLIC TYPE      R323
SOLICDATE       S323
SOLICTYPE       R323
SPHONE          G816
SSTATE          E816
SSUBJECT        N816
STATE           E323
STUDENT_AB      A807..Q807
STUDENT_CR      A810..Q811
STUDENT_DB      A815..Q819
STUDENT_DF      A789..H805
STUDENT_EN      A770..A786
STUDENT_MA      A808..Q808
STUSERV         AB137
STU_MENU        AA31..AF33
SV              A900..W950
```

```
SZIP            F816
TEACHER         M816
THANK TYPE      T323
THANKDON        AB69
THANKDONOR      AB69
THANKTYPE       T323
THANKVOL        AB88
THX SENT        U323
THXSENT         U323
UPDGR           AB62
UPDON           AB56
UPSGR           AB116
UPSTU           AB110
UPVGR           AB86
UPVOL           AB80
VADDRESS        C570
VCITY           D570
VCOADDRESS      J570
VCOCITY         K570
VCOMPANY        I570
VCOPHONE        N570
VCOSTATE        L570
VCOZIP          M570
VDAYS           P570
VFNAME          A570
VHOURS          Q570
VHPHONE         G570
VLET_MENU       AA27..AB29
VLNAME          B570
VOCCUPATION     H570
VOLMASLST       AB141
VOLUNTEER_AB    A561..U561
VOLUNTEER_CR    A564..U565
VOLUNTEER_DB    A569..U573
VOLUNTEER_DF    A539..H559
VOLUNTEER_EN    A524..A536
VOLUNTEER_MA    A562..U562
VOL_MENU        AA23..AF25
VREF#           U570
VS              A600..W650
VSOURCE         T570
VSTATE          E570
VSUBJECTS       O570
VTHKTYPE        R570
VTHXSENT        S570
VZIP            F570
ZIPCODE         F323
\C              AB45
```

GOVERNMENT DELIVERY ORDER

This set of listings provides the listings for the GOVERNMENT DELIVERY ORDER, the master data entry and report areas, the graph printing instructions text, and the named ranges. The data entry and report listing should be saved as a master file to work with the macro.

GOVERNMENT DELIVERY ORDER MACRO

```
AA1: 'A job or delivery order project tracking and management
     system,
AA2: 'suitable for use in monitoring cost plus fee contracts.
AA3: '(C) 1985, The Waite Group
AA4: 'Macro by Mary Johnson
Z6: 'TRACK
AA6: '{MenuCall Main_Menu}
AA7: '{esc}{esc}{esc}{S}
AA9: 'Update
AB9: 'Print
AC9: 'Graphs
AD9: 'Quit
AA10: 'Update delivery order data
AB10: 'Print reports
AC10: 'Print out graphic reports
AD10: 'Return to Symphony
AA11: '{MenuCall DO_Menu}
AB11: '{MenuCall Pri_Menu}
AC11: '{MenuCall Grap_Menu}
AD11: '{S}
Z13: '\s
AA13: '{S}fxf{?}~WOOSH~
AA14: '{right}~{m}eWOOSH~
AA15: '{S}wuMAIN~
AA16: '{MenuBranch Main_Menu}
Z18: 'DO_Menu
AA18: 'Start
AB18: 'Update
AC18: 'Quit
AA19: 'Start a new delivery order file
AB19: 'Update each delivery order
AC19: 'Return to Main Menu
AA20: '{StNew}
AB20: '{DelOrd}
AC20: '{MenuBranch Main_Menu}
Z22: 'StNew
AA22: '{home}
AA23: '{S}fccnWOOSH~
AA24: 'rfMAS~
Z26: 'DelOrd
AA26: '{home}
AA27: '{S}fccnWOOSH~
AA28: 'rf{?}~
Z31: 'Pri_Menu
AA31: 'Task
AB31: 'Group
```

```
AC31: 'Quit
AA32: 'Print a report for one delivery order only
AB32: 'Print the group of delivery order reports
AC32: 'Return to Main Menu
AA33: '{PriTsk}
AB33: '{PriGrp}
AC33: '{MenuBranch Main_Menu}
Z35: 'PriTsk
AA35: '{home}
AA36: '{S}fccnWOOSH~
AA37: 'rf{?}~
AA38: '{S}pasnuTSKSUM~qgp
AA39: 'snuMANHR~qgll
AA40: 'snuOBLIG~qgpq
AA41: '{m}eWOOSH~
AA42: '{S}wuMAIN~
AA43: '{MenuBranch Main_Menu}
Z46: 'PriGrp
AA46: '{home}
Z47: 'loop
AA47: '{S}fccnWOOSH~
AA48: 'rf{?}~
AA49: '{S}pasnuTSKSUM~qgp
AA50: 'snuMANHR~qgll
AA51: 'snuOBLIG~qgpq
AA52: '{m}eWOOSH~
AA53: '{GetLabel "Are there more tasks to be printed out? (y or
      n) ",a1}~
AA54: '{If a1="Y"#OR#a1="y"}{Branch aa47}
AA55: '{Blank a1}
AA56: '{S}wuMAIN~
AA57: '{MenuBranch Main_Menu}
Z60: 'Grap_Menu
AA60: 'Update
AB60: 'Print
AC60: 'Quit
AA61: 'Update data for a project's graph
AB61: 'Read instructions for printing out graphs
AC61: 'Return to Main Menu
AA62: '{UpGraph}
AB62: '{PriInst}
AC62: '{MenuBranch Main_Menu}
Z64: 'UpGraph
AA64: '{home}
AA65: '{S}fccnWOOSH~
AA66: 'rf{?}~{right 6}
AA67: '{S}wuGRAFVU~{esc}
Z69: '\a
AA69: '{m}m.{right 8}{down}~
AA70: '{down}~
Z72: '\c
AA72: '{m}c{right 8}~{down}~
AA73: '{down}{m}e~
AA74: '{right 3}{m}e~
AA75: '{right 4}{m}e~
AA76: '{left 7}
Z78: '\d
```

```
AA78: '{home}{S}wuMain~{home}
AA79: '{m}g1nuDOLLARS~qp{?}~
Z81: '\h
AA81: '{home}{S}wuMain~{home}
AA82: '{m}g1nuHOURS~qp{?}~
Z84: 'PriInst
AA84: '{S}wuINST~{?}~
AA85: '{S}wuMAIN~
```

GOVERNMENT DELIVERY ORDER MASTER

```
A1: 'Delivery Order
I1: 'DELIVERY ORDER NO.:
J1: +B3
N1: "As of:
O1: (D1) +$B$2
A2: "as-of DATE:
B2: (D1) @DATE(85,10,1)
C2: 'WEEKS EXP:
D2: (F0) @INT(B2-B4)/7
E2: "Fee
I2: "Start:
J2: (D1) +$B$4
K2: "End:
L2: (D1) +$B$5
M2: "End/fund:
N2: (D1) +$B$6
A3: 'DELIVERY ORDER NO:
B3: (D1) 'MDJ-xxx
C3: '85% letter
E3: " per hour:
F3: (C2) 1.25
A4: "START DATE:
B4: (D1) @DATE(85,10,1)
C4: "sent:
D4: (D1) @DATE(0,0,0)
J4: "WEEKS
K4: "HOURS
L4: "LABOR $
M4: "ODC $
N4: "FEE $
O4: "TOTAL $
A5: "END DATE:
B5: (D1) @DATE(86,9,30)
E5: "G&A
I5: "AUTH/ALLOC:
J5: (F0) +$B$9
K5: (F0) +$C$9
L5: (F0) +$D$9
M5: (F0) +$E$9
N5: (F0) +$F$9
O5: (F0) +$G$9
A6: "est END OF FUNDS:
B6: (D1) @DATE(86,9,30)
C6: 'WEEKS REM:
D6: (F0) @INT(B6-B2)/7
```

```
E6: "    per $:
F6: (C2) 0.05
I7: "FUNDED:
J7: (F0) +$B$11
K7: (F0) +$C$11
L7: (F0) +$D$11
M7: (F0) +$E$11
N7: (F0) +$F$11
O7: (F0) +$G$11
B8: "WEEKS
C8: "HOURS
D8: "LABOR $
E8: "ODC $
F8: "FEE $
G8: "TOTAL $
A9: "AUTH/ALLOC:
B9: (F0) @INT((B5-B4)/7)
F9: (F0) +C9*$F$3
I9: "EXPENDED:
J9: (F0) +$D$2
K9: (F0) +$C$13
L9: (F0) +$D$13
M9: (F0) +$E$13
N9: (F0) +$F$13
O9: (F0) +$G$13
A11: "FUNDED:
B11: (F0) @INT((B6-B4)/7)
F11: (F0) +C11*$F$3
I11: "OBLIG(total):
J11: (F0) +$J$9
K11: (F0) +K9+B61
L11: (F0) +L9
M11: (F0) +M9+C61
N11: (F0) +N9+D61
O11: (F0) +O9+E61
A13: "EXPENDED:
B13: (F0) +$D$2
F13: (F0) +C13*$F$3
I13: "REMAINING:
J13: (F0) +J7-J11
K13: (F0) +K7-K11
L13: (F0) +L7-L11
M13: (F0) +M7-M11
N13: (F0) +N7-N11
O13: (F0) +O7-O11
I15: "OBLIG/AUTH:
J15: (%0) +J11/J5
K15: (%0) +K11/K5
L15: (%0) +L11/L5
M15: (%0) +M11/M5
N15: (%0) +N11/N5
O15: (%0) +O11/O5
I17: "OBLIG/FUNDED:
J17: (%0) +J11/J7
K17: (%0) +K11/K7
L17: (%0) +L11/L7
M17: (%0) +M11/M7
```

```
N17: (%0) +N11/N7
017: (%0) +011/07
L19: 'HOURS
N19: 'DOLLARS
A21: "LABOR CAT     HOURS:
B21: "AUTH
C21: "ALLOC
D21: "EXPEND
E21: "REM
F21: "PER WEEK
I21: '100% of funded at cu
J21: 'rrent rate
L21: (D1) 7*(+K7*J11/K11)+J2
N21: (D1) 7*(07*J11/011)+J2
A23: '400 PROJECT MGR
E23: (F0) +C23-D23
F23: (F0) +E23/$D$6
I23: ' 85% of funded at cu
J23: 'rrent rate
L23: (D1) 0.85*(7*(K7*J11/K11))+J2
N23: (D1) 0.85*(7*(07*J11/011))+J2
A24: '401 ADMIN SPEC
E24: (F0) +C24-D24
F24: (F0) +E24/$D$6
A25: '402 MGT SYS SPEC
E25: (F0) +C25-D25
F25: (F0) +E25/$D$6
I25: ' 85% of funded at pl
J25: 'anned rate
L25: (D1) 0.85*(7*(K7*J5/K5))+J2
N25: (D1) 0.85*(7*(07*J5/05))+J2
A26: '403 SECRETARY
E26: (F0) +C26-D26
F26: (F0) +E26/$D$6
L26: (D1) '----------
N26: (D1) '----------
A27: '404 SR ENGR
E27: (F0) +C27-D27
F27: (F0) +E27/$D$6
I27: '               85%
J27: 'letter
K27: "due:
L27: (D1) @MIN(J30..K30)
M27: (D1) "sent:
N27: (D1) +D4
A28: '405 ENGR
E28: (F0) +C28-D28
F28: (F0) +E28/$D$6
A29: '406 SYS ENGR SPEC
E29: (F0) +C29-D29
F29: (F0) +E29/$D$6
J29: '=========
K29: '=========
L29: '=========
M29: '=========
A30: '407 TECH WRITER
E30: (F0) +C30-D30
```

```
F30: (F0) +E30/$D$6
J30: @MIN(L21..N25)-30
K30: +N2-30
A31: '408 TECH DATA ENGR
E31: (F0) +C31-D31
F31: (F0) +E31/$D$6
A32: '409 DRAFTER
E32: (F0) +C32-D32
F32: (F0) +E32/$D$6
A33: '410 SR ANALYST
E33: (F0) +C33-D33
F33: (F0) +E33/$D$6
A34: '411 COMP SYS ANAL
E34: (F0) +C34-D34
F34: (F0) +E34/$D$6
A35: '412 COMP PROGR
E35: (F0) +C35-D35
F35: (F0) +E35/$D$6
A36: '413 COMP S/W SPEC
E36: (F0) +C36-D36
F36: (F0) +E36/$D$6
A37: '414 SYS MGT SPEC
E37: (F0) +C37-D37
F37: (F0) +E37/$D$6
A38: '415 SYS REQ ENGR
E38: (F0) +C38-D38
F38: (F0) +E38/$D$6
A39: '416 COMP OPER
E39: (F0) +C39-D39
F39: (F0) +E39/$D$6
A40: '417 SR COMP OPER
E40: (F0) +C40-D40
F40: (F0) +E40/$D$6
A41: '897 SUBCON/CONSULT
E41: (F0) +C41-D41
F41: (F0) +E41/$D$6
I41: 'GRAPH AREA
K41: +$B$3&" Delivery Order Status"
A42: '898 CONTRACT TYPIST
E42: (F0) +C42-D42
F42: (F0) +E42/$D$6
K42: 'DOLLARS
O42: 'HOURS
A43: '899 INTER-DIVISION
E43: (F0) +C43-D43
F43: (F0) +E43/$D$6
I43: "WEEKS
J43: "ALLOC
K43: "FUNDED
L43: "OBLIG
M43: "85%
N43: "ALLOC
O43: "FUNDED
P43: "OBLIG
Q43: "85%
B44: "-------
C44: "-------
```

```
D44: "-------
E44: (F0) "-------
F44: (F0) "-------
I44: (F0) 0
J44: (F0) 0
K44: (F0) +$G$11
L44: (F0) 0
M44: (F0) +$G$11*0.85
N44: (F0) 0
O44: (F0) +$C$11
P44: (F0) 0
Q44: (F0) +$C$11*0.85
B45: (F0) @SUM(B23..B43)
C45: (F0) @SUM(C23..C43)
D45: (F0) @SUM(D23..D43)
E45: (F0) @SUM(E23..E43)
F45: (F0) @SUM(F23..F43)
I45: (F0) 0
J45: (F0) ($G$11/$B$11)*I45
K45: (F0) +$G$11
M45: (F0) +$G$11*0.85
N45: (F0) ($C$11/$B$11)*I45
O45: (F0) +$C$11
Q45: (F0) +$C$11*0.85
I46: (F0) +$B$11
J46: (F0) +$G$11
K46: (F0) +$G$11
M46: (F0) +$G$11*0.85
N46: (F0) +$C$11
O46: (F0) +$C$11
Q46: (F0) +$C$11*0.85
I47: (F0) +$B$9
J47: (F0) +$G$9
K47: (F0) +$G$11
M47: (F0) +$G$11*0.85
N47: (F0) +$C$9
O47: (F0) +$C$11
Q47: (F0) +$C$11*0.85
Q48: (F0) +$C$11*0.85
A61: 'OBLIGATIONS:  totals
B61: @SUM(B63..B72)
C61: @SUM(C63..C72)
D61: @SUM(D63..D72)
E61: +C61*(1+F6)
B62: "hours
C62: "ODC $
D62: "FEE $
E62: "TOT $w/G&A
A63: '1
D63: +B63*$F$3
A64: '2
D64: +B64*$F$3
A65: '3
D65: +B65*$F$3
A66: '4
D66: +B66*$F$3
A67: '5
```

```
D67: +B67*$F$3
A68: '6
D68: +B68*$F$3
A69: '7
D69: +B69*$F$3
A70: '8
D70: +B70*$F$3
A71: '9
D71: +B71*$F$3
A72: '10
D72: +B72*$F$3
A75: +"Delivery Order "&$B$3&" Manhour and Obligations Report"
```

GOVERNMENT DELIVERY ORDER GRAPH PRINTING INSTRUCTIONS

```
AA200: 'To print out the graphs that this program creates
       requires the PrintGraph
AA201: 'diskette.
AA203: '1.  Follow the instructions on the PrintGraph disk.  Run
       the PrintGraph
AA204: 'program after you have finished updating all of your
       project files.
AA206: '2.  Make very sure that you have saved all of your work
       before proceeding
AA207: 'with the printing of the graphs.
AA209: '3.  After pressing the return key when you are ready to
       continue, wait
AA210: 'for the screen menu to appear.  When it does, press "E"
       for exit.  If
AA211: 'you have saved your work, and you are ready to continue,
       press "Y", and
AA212: 'then choose the "PrintGraph" option.  Follow the
       instructions from there.
```

GOVERNMENT DELIVERY ORDER NAMED RANGES

```
C               A1
DELORD          AA26
DO_MENU         AA18
FEERATE         F403
GALLOC          J44..J96
GATEF           M44..M96
GFUND           K44..K96
GHALL           N44..N96
GHATEF          Q44..Q96
GHFUND          O44..O96
GHOBL           P44..P96
GNARATE         F405
GOBLIG          L44..L96
GRAP_MENU       AA60
GRAR            I41
GWEEKS          I44..I96
LOOP            AA47
LTRS            D404
MAIN_MENU       AA9..AD11
```

PRGRU	B101..H103
PRIGRP	AA46
PRIINST	AA84
PRITSK	AA35
PRI_MENU	AA31
STNEW	AA22
TRACK	AA6
TRANSIT	I41..Q47
UPGRAPH	AA64
WOOSH	A1..Q104
\A	AA69
\C	AA72
\D	AA78
\H	AA81
\R	A81..A84
\S	AA13

CODA C

Symphony, Release 1.1

In its desire to remain the leading force in integrated software products, Lotus Development Corporation released a new version of Symphony, designated Symphony, Release 1.1 in the late summer of 1985. The purpose of this Coda is to present those parts of this release that can affect the way you orchestrate your applications. The material that we have presented in *Orchestrating Symphony* has been designed to be used by the widest possible audience of Symphony users. Coda C continues this design.

What Release 1.1 gives you, if you have upgraded from the earlier release of Symphony, or if that is the version you are using, is the ability to address up to 4 megabytes of expanded memory if your hardware system is so configured. If you have a system with up to the standard 640K of memory, Release 1.1 has an improved memory management system. Other hardware-related enhancements include the ability to use the 8087 or 80287 mathematics coprocessor chips. For those of you who use Symphony in an environment with 1-2-3 users, Release 1.1 now allows you to translate files from Symphony 1.1 to 1-2-3 release 1A spreadsheet files. Additional enhancements include an easier-to-use installation program, revised documentation, help screens, and tutorials. The most significant change, and one which we will explore in Coda C, is an add-in application, the Macro Library Manager.

How to Use Coda C

What we have tried to do in Coda C is give you the information that you need about Release 1.1 to make more effective use of the macro techniques that we have shown you in the rest of the book. Coda C is structured in three parts. The first part addresses the new features that Release 1.1 introduces. The second part describes each of the new commands, and is structured similarly to the Second Movement. The third part presents the details of the Macro Library Manager and gives you some ideas to think about when developing applications.

With this in mind, let's move on to the Symphony encore, Release 1.1.

New Features

We are going to give you a quick summary of the new features that Release 1.1 provides. For more detailed descriptions of how to install Symphony, or the add-in applications, memory expansion, or how to use the tutorial, refer to the How-To Manual or Reference Manual that Lotus supplied with Symphony.

Macro Library Manager and DOS Add-In Applications

The Macro Library Manager, the add-in application which allows you to develop very sophisticated and complex macros for use in a variety of worksheets, is perhaps the most significant change in Symphony. It overcomes the problem of copying a macro from one worksheet into another using the file extract techniques that we showed you in the Fourth Movement. It also gives you the ability to set up data files that remain in memory and can be used by a series of worksheets without having to save the data with each worksheet. It allows you to consolidate formulas, data, and useful macros into an environment that is separate from individual worksheets, and that can be accessed over and over again. We show you how to make use of this powerful add-in in the third part of this Coda.

The DOS add-in application gives you the ability to leave a Symphony work session, perform operating system (DOS) or DOS-related program commands, and return to your Symphony work session. This can be useful if you need to suspend what you are doing to run another program that operates in the DOS environment. There are a couple of precautions to be observed however:

> **If you are in a Symphony work session, and you want to use the DOS add-in, save your work before going to DOS.**
>
> **Do not use the DOS print command. You may write over part of Symphony in your memory. Some other DOS application programs may do this as well, so always save your work before going to DOS.**

As time goes on, you may want to add additional add-in applications available to enhance Symphony, such as Spelling Checker, Text Outliner, or Link available from Lotus or others that will come from non-Lotus vendors. By getting comfortable with the Macro Library Manager and the DOS add-ins, you will be able to incorporate other add-in applications with little difficulty.

Additional Commands

The feature of the Symphony Command Language that makes it so powerful has been its programlike command structure. Release 1.1 adds twelve additional commands to the more than 30 commands that made up the original SCL. These new commands, in addition to making the development of powerful worksheet macros possible, allow access to library macros and data files resident in libraries. They make control of files and libraries and manipulation of file contents much easier. We will describe each of these commands in greater detail in the New Commands section of this coda.

Memory Expansion and Efficiency

By redesigning the way that Symphony allocates memory, the room that you have to design your worksheets has been greatly expanded. This has been done in two ways: Expanded Memory Access and Enhanced Memory Management.

Expanded Memory Access

Symphony, Release 1.1 has been designed to support the Lotus/Intel Expanded Memory specification. What this means is that if you have an expanded memory card installed in your system, you can make use of the memory greater than the usual 640K limit. When you run your system with Release 1.1, you can check to see how much of the extended memory you have by looking at the Services settings worksheet. You will see some new entries. If you have the 8087 or 80287 math coprocessor installed (more on this later) you'll see it indicated. The amount of Conventional Memory is indicated as the number of bytes of conventional random access memory (RAM) currently available out of the total conventional (to 640K) RAM available in your system. The percentage of conventional RAM currently available is also shown. The Expanded Memory indicator works the same way. The amount of expanded memory currently available out of the total expanded memory you have in your system is shown in both bytes and as a percentage.

Symphony, Release 1.1 uses the two types of memory differently. The expanded memory is used to store only cell contents. The cell contents that can be stored in extended memory can include formulas, labels, and floating point (decimal) numbers. Blanks and integers aren't stored in extended memory. It's also not used to store worksheets, settings sheets, or add-ins. This means that it is possible to have plenty of memory available in expanded memory and still run out and get a "Memory Full" message when conventional memory is full. This problem of memory management has been also dealt with in Release 1.1 as we will see next.

Enhanced Memory Management

One of the difficulties experienced by many spreadsheet users in the past had to do with the way that information was stored in the computer. Early versions of spreadsheet products including Symphony would store the entire worksheet, blanks and all, in memory. This typically accounted for a lot of wasted space. With Release 1.1, this problem has been solved. While an entire worksheet is stored in the conventional memory (or main memory if you don't have extended memory capacity), its arrangement has been optimized.

The revised Reference Manual gives you additional tips on managing your memory as well. Many of these are quite useful and you should refer to the Reference Manual for the details. In summary, these include:

Eliminate unnecessary data in the worksheet.

Detach add-ins when you no longer need them.

When using the Macro Library Manager, delete any libraries you are no longer using (more on this in the last section of this Coda).

When you no longer need a formula, just the value that it calculated, convert it to a value.

Delete windows and range names you are no longer using; they are stored in conventional memory and take up space.

Save files on disk with File Save and retrieve with File Retrieve.

Delete named settings sheets (Print, or GRAPH, FORM, or COMM environments) when you no longer need them.

While most of these are just common sense, they can foster good housekeeping and memory management. They also highlight the wisdom in drawing up a map of your worksheet before you begin designing an application, and for updating the map as you work through your design.

Math Processing Support

If your hardware system is equipped with the 8087 or 80287 (if you have the IBM PC AT system) math coprocessor chip, Symphony now supports this plug-in enhancement. When you initially install Symphony for your system you need to select the appropriate driver. If you aren't sure about this, check your Getting Started documentation that came with Symphony.

Once you have installed the driver for the coprocessor chip, or if you install both drivers in your driver set, Symphony automatically checks to see if you have the chip installed. If it is, the coprocessor is used for all floating-point arithmetic operations. We aren't going to get into the details of what this means here. What is important if you do have this hardware enhancement is that your larger mathematical computations will be speeded up by as much as four to five times. If you have very large computation needs, you may want to look into adding a math coprocessor chip to your hardware. The chips are easy to install in your hardware, and with the new Symphony installation routines.

1-2-3 Compatibility

For those of you that work in a mixed, Symphony/1-2-3 environment Release 1.1 will allow you to exchange spreadsheet files between Symphony 1.1 and 1-2-3 Release 1A. In the past this was a one-way exchange in that you could bring 1-2-3 spreadsheet files into Symphony, but you couldn't transfer Symphony spreadsheets back to 1-2-3. Now you can, and Release 1.1 has been designed to have total spreadsheet compatibility with 1-2-3 Release 2.

New Command Power

With the introduction of Release 1.1, you now have a dozen new commands to power up your applications. Most of them are used in conjunction with files and subroutines. This part of Coda C will give you a capsule description of the command, the arguments that it needs, and a short example. We will follow the same conventions that we used in the Second Movement and in Coda A.

File Related Commands

You can now directly access files with a series of commands that Release 1.1 provides. These include {CLOSE}, {FILESIZE}, {GETPOS}, {OPEN}, {READ}, {READLN}, {SETPOS}, {WRITE}, and {WRITELN}. These commands let you set up additional ways to manipulate data. By using various files, you can save information in a string format that can be used by other macros, or by other programs. The entire range of programming is now available as files of information can be saved as other than worksheet, print, graph, or library files. If you don't need or want to get involved in advanced programming with SCL, you probably won't make much use of these commands. They are here if you need them.

Closing a File: {CLOSE}

When you are finished with a file, you need to end access to it. This is done by issuing a {CLOSE} command. This will end read/write access to the file that was opened with an {OPEN} command. This command needs no argument. In our example here, assume that you have opened a file named "snakes" for write access (see Opening a File: {OPEN} for more information), that you have written some information, and that you now are going to close the file. Your macro would look like this:

```
{OPEN "snakes","W"}
{WRITE "gophcr"}
{CLOSE}
```

The {CLOSE} command has no effect if there is no open file. Symphony continues processing the macro with the next statement, just as if there was no {CLOSE} statement.

Keeping Track of Sizes: {FILESIZE}

Frequently, when you are programming something, it is useful to know the size of the file that you are working with. SCL provides a command to answer just this question. If you don't have a file open, Symphony ignores the command and continues processing. If you do have an open file, Symphony will determine the size of the open file, and store the value, in bytes, in the location that you have provided as the argument. The format for the {FILESIZE} command looks like this:

```
{FILESIZE location}
```

The location you give as an argument can be a cell location or a range name. As an example, let's open our "snakes" file, find out how many bytes it contains, and store that figure in cell A125. The macro would look like this:

```
{OPEN "snakes","M"}
{FILESIZE A125}
```

After the size of the file was stored in cell A125, the macro would continue with the next command.

Finding Out Where You Are in a File: {GETPOS}

Sometimes you need to know where you are in a file. The way that Symphony handles this is with a byte pointer. This is just another name for a marker that indicates where the next operation to be done on the file will occur. In the scheme of things, the first position in a file is assigned a value of 0, not 1, so if you are performing file operations that depend on where you are in the file, keep this numbering scheme in mind. The general format for this command is:

```
{GETPOS location}
```

Symphony will check the location of the pointer in the file that is open (if no file is open, processing of the macro continues in the current cell), and will store the number that corresponds to this pointer location in the worksheet location you have spelled out in the command. This worksheet location can be a cell or a range name. An example of this command in a macro looks like this:

```
{OPEN "snakes", "M"}
{WRITE "garter"}
{GETPOS endofline}
```

In this example, we open our "snakes" file for modification (reading or writing) and write the string "garter". Then we look for the pointer location in the file, and write this value to the range named *endofline* in our worksheet.

Opening a File: {OPEN}

In order to do anything with a file, a file needs to exist, and it must be opened. Creating a file can be done with an {OPEN} command. There are certain things to keep in mind in the discussion that follows. When files are saved on a disk, they are saved to a certain disk drive, and frequently are saved in a particular directory, and sometimes a subdirectory. If any of these terms are unfamiliar to you, you need to refer to the disk operating system documentation, or to the Getting Started manual. If you do understand these terms, we can continue.

Opening a file lets you perform actions on the information in the file, you can {READ} the information, you can {WRITE} new information, or you can modify (read or write) existing information in the file. The format for the {OPEN} command looks like this:

```
'OPEN filename, access-mode^
```

The filename tells the {OPEN} command which file you want to open. It is a string of no more than 64 characters, and can either be expressed as a string in the command, or can refer to a location within the worksheet where a string with the filename is stored. If the file isn't in the current directory, or isn't on the disk in the default drive, you need to include the drive location and the path through the directories to the file. For example, if you had our file "snakes" stored on the disk in the B drive in your system, and it was stored in the subdirectory *reptiles* in the directory *bones*, and you wanted to modify the information in the file, you would enter this command:

```
{OPEN "B:\bones\reptiles\snakes",M}
```

If you had made a mistake, and didn't have the "bones" disk in drive B, the {OPEN} command would fail, and your macro would continue processing in the same cell. This can be a problem, but Symphony does give you a solution. You just enter a command that sends you to a location to continue processing, or you can enter a command that sends you to a backup (Lotus calls this a fall-back) subroutine. In our example, if we want processing to go to a subroutine named "wrongdisk", our macro line would read:

```
{OPEN "B:\bones\reptiles\snakes",M}{WRONGDISK}
```

When we saw that processing had gone to the "wrongdisk" subroutine, we would know that we needed to do something about putting the right disk in the drive.

The other argument that the {OPEN} command needs is the access-mode. This is a single character string, either an R, a W, or an M. The R stands for the Read access-mode. This opens an existing file with the name you entered in filename, and allows you to use the {READ} and {READLN} commands. If you have opened a file with the R access-mode, you cannot write to it.

The W stands for the Write access-mode. This opens a new file, gives it the name you entered as the filename (including any drive, directory, or subdirectory information you may have specified), and lets you access the file with the {WRITE} and {WRITELN} commands. Be careful with this access-mode. If you specify a filename that you already have on the disk, it will be **erased** and replaced by the new file.

The M stands for the Modify access-mode. This lets you open an existing file and lets you use both the read ({READ} and {READLN}) commands and the write ({WRITE} and {WRITELN}) commands.

In using the {OPEN} command, it is a good idea to use a fall-back subroutine on the same command line. The only access-mode that doesn't need a fall-back subroutine is W as it always opens a new file. There is one other precaution that you should be aware of as well. If you have a range name in your worksheet with the same name as the filename you specify in your {OPEN} command, Symphony will go to the range and use the **contents** of the named range as the filename. To avoid this problem, put quotation marks around the filename in your command.

Using the Contents of a File: {READ}

The {READ} command is used to move a certain number of characters from an open file into some location on the worksheet. To do this, Symphony goes to the file, and starts at the current position of the byte pointer (see our earlier discussion of the {GETPOS} command), and copies the number of bytes that you specify (in the arguments for the command) into the location in the worksheet. The format for the {READ} command looks like this:

```
{READ bytecount,location}
```

The argument, bytecount, must be a number, or an expression that evaluates to a number, between 0 and 240. If it is a negative, it becomes 240. The location argument can be either a cell address or a range name. If it is a range name, it is the same as specifying the upper left corner of the range.

To give you an example, let's suppose that our "snakes" file has the following entries:

```
garter gopher king coral asp cobra
```

If the byte pointer was at 15, and our {READ} command was this:

```
{READ 5,A128}
```

then the label *'king* would be created in cell location A128, and the byte pointer would be moved 5 characters to the beginning of the word *coral*.

If there is no open file, processing continues in the same cell. If there is an open file, the {READ} command is executed, and processing continues in the **next** cell in the macro.

Reading a Line at a Time: {READLN}

The {READLN} command works in a similar way to the {READ} command. In this case, it reads an entire line from a file, rather than a specified number of characters. The format for the {READLN} command looks like this:

```
{READLN location}
```

where the location is the same sort of argument as used for the {READ} command: the cell location or range name where you want the information stored on the worksheet.

{READLN} reads the information in from a file, starting at the location of the byte pointer (See {GETPOS}) and ending with the character that indicates a carriage return-line feed. After reading the information into the worksheet, the byte pointer is advanced to the beginning of the next line. Everything else about the command is the same as {READ}.

To show you an example of how {READLN} works, let's assume that the information in our "snakes" file is saved this way:

```
garter
gopher
king
coral
 ...
```

If we use the command line:

```
{READLN A128}
```

and the byte pointer was at the beginning of the second line, we would find that label 'gopher was entered in cell location A128. Our next {READLN} command would enter the label *'king* in the next location specified if we didn't change files or byte pointer locations.

Changing Positions: {SETPOS}

Symphony lets you find out what the current byte pointer position is for an open file with the {GETPOS} command. The {SETPOS} command lets you move the byte pointer in a file that you have open. The format that the command takes is:

```
{SETPOS file-position}
```

In this command, the argument, file-position, is a number, or an expression that evaluates to a number that is the location you want to place the byte pointer (see GETPOS) in the file. Remember that the character locations in a file start at 0.

This command can be handy in locating information in a file, but it is tricky, too. Symphony will let you place the byte pointer beyond the end of the file. Use the {FILESIZE} command to determine the location number of the last character in your file.

As an example of how this command might be used, let's assume that our "snakes" file really looks like this now:

```
snakes garter gopher king coral
```

If our file was open, we could set the byte pointer to the beginning of the list of snake varieties with the command:

```
{SETPOS 7}
```

As with so many of these file-related commands, if no file is open, the command is ignored, and processing continues on the same line. If the file is open, processing contiues on the next line of the macro after the command is executed.

Putting Information into a File: {WRITE}

The {WRITE} command lets you put information into a file. This command takes the information that you want in the file from the worksheet, and writes it to the current position in the file. {WRITE} works only with string information. This information may be an actual string, a range name which defines a single cell, or an expression that is string-valued. The format that the command uses is:

```
{WRITE string}
```

where string stands for the information you want to go into the file from your worksheet.

Let's say you have opened a new file, *poisnsnk*, and you want to put some information in the file. The following commands would enter the information:

```
{WRITE "rattler"}
{WRITE "cobra"}
{WRITE "asp"}
```

If you looked at the file, it would read:

```
rattlercobraasp
```

Not too easy to read. If you wanted spaces, you would have to leave a space in your arguments such as "cobra ".

What Symphony does when you issue a {WRITE} command is to convert each character in the argument string to an ASCII character which can be read by the disk operating system, and sends it to the open file. As with so many of these file-related commands, if no file is open, the command is ignored, and processing continues on the same line. If the file is open, processing continues on the next line of the macro after the command is executed.

Writing a Line at a Time: {WRITELN}

As might be suspected, the {WRITELN} command works similarly to the {WRITE} command. The major difference is that {WRITELN} adds a carriage return-line feed character sequence at the end of every string that is written to the open file. The format for {WRITELN} is:

```
{WRITELN string}
```

For our example this time, we will use the following:

```
{WRITELN "rattler"}
{WRITELN "cobra"}
```

which would look like this:

```
rattler
cobra
```

Not too bad looking.

If you want to add some blank lines in a file, you can do this by using the {WRITELN} command with an empty string. The command would look like this:

```
{WRITELN ""}
```

{WRITELN} is like the other file-related commands. If no file is open, the command is ignored, and processing continues on the same line. If the file is open, processing continues on the next line of the macro after the command is executed.

Non-File Related Commands

There are three non-file related commands that Release 1.1 includes. These are {DISPATCH}, {FORBREAK}, and {RESTART}.

Routing Processing: {DISPATCH}

This command is similar to the {BRANCH} command, and is indeed equivalent if the location you specify is a multiple-cell range. Its format looks like this:

```
{DISPATCH location}
```

and it is very useful for using a variable location cell to send a macro process depending on certain conditions in a worksheet. For example, if we wanted to send a letter to a client if his bill was overdue, we could set up the following macro commands.

```
{IF A125>30}{LET action,letter}
{IF A125<30}{LET action,flowers}
 . . .
{DISPATCH action}
```

If the client was over 30 days late, we want to send the letter, if he was less than 30 days, we want the macro to go to the location *flowers*. If we were really clever, we would program the macro to automatically wire the flowers.

Changing Processes in a FOR Loop: {FORBREAK}

This command should only be used in a subroutine called by a FOR statement. It is used to immediately end a subroutine called by a FOR statement, and returns the processing to the command following the FOR statement. Its format is:

```
{FORBREAK}
```

Starting Again: {RESTART}

{RESTART} is used to continue the processing of a macro at the next character or cell as if it were a new macro. Its most common use is in subroutines. If it is at the end of a macro, followed by a blank line, macro processing stops. If it is followed by a subroutine call, processing continues at the called location. If it is followed by the rest of a macro, the macro is processed to the end, but if it reaches a RETURN, or a blank line, processing stops rather than returning to the original calling macro.

Macro Library Manager

The Macro Library Manager, as we mentioned in our discussion of new features, is an add-in application that lets you develop much more complex and sophisticated macro applications than you could formerly create. In this part of Coda C we are going to look at why you should use the Macro Library Manager, how you can make use of it, how its menu works, what you need to be careful about, and how to use it in an application. When you finish, we hope that you will go back to the applications in the Fourth Movement and look for ways to make the Macro Library Manager work for you.

Why Use It?

A very good question, why should you use a macro library, a macro, or a library for that matter? The answer is quite simple: it helps you to save resources. Just as a book library saves you storage space, not to mention the cost of the books, so a macro library will save you time (which usually translates into money). Once you have developed a good macro, you can use it again and again. In much the way that we took some of the file extract techniques in the Professional Billing application in the Fourth

Movement, and used them again in the Non-Profit Organization application, so we could have (had Release 1.1 been available) saved some time by saving the macros to a library, and then calling them as we needed them.

As applications grow in size and complexity, it may be useful to load a library into memory, use the macros, and then move it out of memory until it is needed again. This frees up conventional memory which is still limited to 640K.

So there are savings in time (and money) and space to be realized by using the Macro Library Manager. Those seem to be pretty good reasons to learn how to use it.

How to Become a Macro-Librarian

Before you can become a macro-librarian, you must attach the Macro Library Manager add-in. You can do this by following the instructions in the Getting Started and Reference Manual that came with Symphony. Once you have attached the application, you will see that the Services menu that you have been used to has changed. You now are presented with Macros as a choice. If you select M from the Services menu, or highlight Macros, you will move into the Macro Library Manager menu (more on this in a bit). Other changes you will notice are when you select such things as File List, File Table, or File Erase.

To become a librarian, you also need something to store away in the library. The something that you store in the library can be any type of data. It can include labels, numbers, formulas, strings, named ranges, or macros. The only limitations are that a library can contain no more than 16,376 cells, or a range that is 8188 rows by 2 columns; and you can have no more than 10 libraries open at a time. Because libraries are stored in Conventional Memory, you may find that the area available for your worksheet is limited if you have a lot of library space used. To deal with this, only load in those libraries that you are going to use, and remove them when you are finished with them.

Some of the other interesting things about Symphony's libraries are that just as you need a library card in some libraries, you can password-protect libraries if you want to. This way, other users can load your library to memory, use it, but they can't change it. You also can, after loading a library to memory, use the Services New and File Retrieve commands, and not wipe out the data in your library. This is particularly useful if you wish to have data that will be used in a number of worksheets.

Once you have saved a macro in a library, you can invoke it from a worksheet in the usual ways. When you specify a range name to start a macro, or in an SCL statement, Symphony will first search the worksheet for the range name, then it will search your loaded libraries in order. We warn you about some of the things to be careful about in naming ranges a little later, after we show you how to use the Macro Library Manager menu.

The Macro Library Manager Menu

One of the beauties of Symphony is that once you understand how the menus work, you can move through each one smoothly. The Macro Library Manager Menu is no exception. It has six commands: Save, Remove, Load, Edit, Name-List, and Quit. We will briefly describe how you use each of them in working with your libraries. For the rest of this discussion, we will refer to the Macro Library Manager Menu as the Macro Menu. And for reference, you bring up the Macro Menu by pressing [F9] Services and selecting Macros.

Save

Save is where it all begins. After you have entered information into your worksheet, you bring up the Macro Menu and select Save. You will be asked for the name of the library you wish to save. The file extension .MLB will automatically be added. If you are going to overwrite an old library, you will be given a chance to change your mind. When you have entered the name you want, you will be asked to select the range in the worksheet which contains the data you wish to save to the library. You will also be asked if you want to password-protect your library. If you do, you will be asked for the password.

Once you have done all these things, the range you have specified is saved to the library. This means that the cell contents are no longer in the worksheet. The range names that were associated with the cells in the range now refer to the locations in the library. At the same time that the information is saved to the library location, it is also saved to a disk file with the name that you gave the file, and the .MLB extension.

Remove

It may be all well and good that you have saved your information into a library in memory, but let's say you are finished with it, and you want to free up the space it is occupying for other projects. This is where the

Remove command is used. Bring up the Macro Menu, and select Remove. You select the library you want to remove from memory, and out it goes. The library file, with its .MLB is still on the disk. If you want the library back in memory, you must use the Load command.

Load

When you want to bring a library that you have saved into memory, you will use the Load command from the Macro Menu. You will be prompted for the name of the .MLB file that you want to load. If there is a library with the same name already in memory, you will be given a chance to change your mind. If you don't want to overwrite the library in memory, you will be returned to the Macro Menu. If you do, your selection will be loaded, and it will be the only library in memory with that name. A copy of the library will be resident on the disk that you loaded from.

You can now make use of the library in memory, accessing it, or making changes with the Edit command.

Edit

If you wish to make some changes to a library, you can load it **into** the current worksheet using the Edit command. After selecting the Edit command from the Macro Menu, a copy of the library is loaded into the worksheet. If you have password-protected the library, you will have to provide the password before it can be loaded. You will also be given the option to Ignore or Overwrite the worksheet range names that are the same as those in your library. The last thing you are asked for is the location in the worksheet in which you want the library loaded. Be careful, the Macro Library Manager will **write over worksheet cells if the range specified is not large enough to hold the entire library**.

Once you have made changes to your library, you can save it. The Macro Library Manager will act as if the library was loaded into memory for the first time. Its name will be moved to the end of the library list, and it will be searched last for range names.

Name-List

The Name-List command on the Macro Menu is handy for showing you what named ranges are contained in a particular library. As with the Range Name-List command, you will need to have a space clear in your worksheet before you begin, unless you don't mind overwriting some material.

After selecting the Name-List command from the Macro Menu, you will be asked for the library in which you are interested. After selecting the one-column range to display the list of range names, you find Symphony displaying the list in the worksheet. This list can be handled just as the Range Name Lists are.

Quit

As usual, there isn't too much that can be said about Quit. In this case, what happens is that the Macro Menu disappears. The application is still attached, and all the libraries currently loaded or saved are available. In order to bring the Macro Menu back, you select it from the [F9] Services menu.

Watch Out

The major problems that you can run into using libraries are associated with ranges, range names, and cell arguments. These include:

In a library, a named range or a cell can be referenced only to begin a macro, or in an SCL statement.

Library range names cannot be used as locations with menu commands like Copy.

Don't use the same range name in more than one library. The first occurrence will be the one that Symphony uses.

Applications with the Macro Library Manager

In this Coda, we have given you some more tools and techniques to add to your repertoire. In a few instances, we have referred to places where you might use a library. If you think about some of the applications that we developed in the Fourth Movement, you can see where libraries can be very useful. Those applications which made heavy use of the File Combine Copy Named-Range sequence are prime candidates. The rate area for the Professional Billing application is another.

Space considerations prevent us from developing a full application making use of a library, but you might refer to the First Movement and design yourself a Glossary library. Instead of limiting yourself to single keystroke macros, you could save keywords, maybe three or four letters long that would stand for salutations, closes, return addresses, and commonly used phrases in your correspondence. By saving them to a Glossary library, and then loading the library when you sit down to write, you find yourself saving a lot of keystrokes.

Index

About the Authors

DAN SHAFER is an independent product consultant and freelance writer who has been employed for eight years in various phases of high technology in California's Silicon Valley. A former journalist and public relations consultant, he lists writing as his first love, even though he is also keenly interested in programming, chess, stamp collecting, law, and religion. Dan recently published *Games and Utilities for the Macintosh*, (New York: Plume/Waite, New American Library, 1985), and dozens of his product reviews and feature articles have appeared in computer magazines during the past five years. Dan lives in Redwood City, California, with his wife, Carolyn, and their four daughters.

MARY JOHNSON, a managing editor for The Waite Group, has been involved with computers for more than 23 years. She built her first microcomputer, an IMSAI, in 1977. While working as a support contractor to the Department of the Navy, she managed the development and operation of business information systems for mainframes, minis, and micros. She lives on a houseboat in Sausalito with her son and daughter, and holds a Master's degree in Management from the Naval Postgraduate School, Monterey.